CALIFORNIA STATE UNIVERSITY SACRAMENTO

This book is due on the last date s

Failure to return books on the date

ment of prescribed fines.

JAN 9 1974
DEC 19 1973

THESIS

D1108199

Planning and Managing the Economy of the City

Joseph Oberman
with a contribution by
Robert Bingham

The Praeger Special Studies program—
utilizing the most modern and efficient book
production techniques and a selective
worldwide distribution network—makes
available to the academic, government, and
business communities significant, timely
research in U.S. and international economic, social, and political development.

Planning and Managing the Economy of the City
Policy Guidelines for the Metropolitan Mayor

Praeger Publishers   New York   Washington   London

PRAEGER SPECIAL STUDIES IN U.S. ECONOMIC AND SOCIAL DEVELOPMENT

PRAEGER PUBLISHERS
111 Fourth Avenue, New York, N.Y. 10003, U.S.A.
5, Cromwell Place, London S.W.7, England

Published in the United States of America in 1972
by Praeger Publishers, Inc.

All rights reserved

© 1972 by Praeger Publishers, Inc.

Library of Congress Catalog Card Number: 72-79544

Printed in the United States of America

To my wife, Peg,

and my son, Paul

This book is as much about management problems in the complex systems of city governments as it is about achieving economies (least-cost solutions to city operating problems) along with healthy growth and development. Originally the work was undertaken for the benefit of the Mayor of Philadelphia, to indicate how the tools of economics and systems analysis can clarify critical issues in program and policy formulation.

The message can be stated simply: Cities must survive, but they cannot survive unless they have a healthy economy within their limits. We have managed the national economy for more than two decades; now we must consider to what extent we can and should manage the local economies and to what extent we can do so within the limits of our resources.

There is hardly a city, large or small, that is not caught in the vise between hard costs and a softness in its economic viability. Few suburban jurisdictions, despite their growth, are generating an economic base that matches the rising demands for services. Thus, strengthening the local economic base and making maximum and efficient use of local resources is becoming a sheer matter of survival.

There are only three ways in which the fiscal gap can be closed: First, rates on already existing taxes can be raised on already overburdened real estate, and on the salaried worker base, or an infinite number of new taxes of the nuisance variety can be imposed; second, greater subventions from state and federal governments can be sought; third, clearly, a growing economic base and more efficient use of resources can reduce local government costs. A fourth possibility is a no-choice alternative; namely, cut services and lower standards of local government performance.

Many concepts of economic development appear in the literature covering the subject. The focus of economists studying the problems of underdeveloped countries has been and continues to be on maximizing the rate of growth of per capita income. In contrast, development economists for the United States as a whole concentrate their attention on the grand designs of gross national product, income accounts, the impact of federal income on private investments, and so forth. Nowhere in the literature produced by leading economists and planners who are addressing themselves to the problems of urban society do we find a determined effort to confront the problem directly and define economic development for a city. (Notable exceptions are Wilbur Thompson's A Preface to Urban Economics [Baltimore: The Johns Hopkins Press, 1965] and Jane Jacob's The Economy of Cities [New York: Random House, 1969].)

Since this book will deal with economic development as a necessary concern of local government we believe the reader will get a better idea of how the separate issues are related from the author's definition of the subject. Economic development as a concern of local government involves the allocation of limited resources--land, labor, capital, and entrepreneurship--in such a way as to induce desired public and private actions that have a positive effect on the level of business activity, employment and income, distribution patterns, and fiscal solvency.

By systematic planning and policy, based on sound data and evaluation, those strategic possibilities are identified from which additional development can and will flow; or, in the case of nondevelopment, intelligent adjustment will be made. Economic development considerations cannot be divorced from capital and operating budget planning and programming, tax policies, zoning, land-development policies, reconstruction of the central business district, industrial and commercial business development, neighborhood or community development, and tax programs.

This does not imply an approach that leaves out of account that accomplishing economic development

goals is both conditioned by, and conditions, a
broader set of social, political, and demographic aspects of human experience. Gunner Myrdal, among
others, has effectively pointed out that in many ways
economic development can succeed in bringing about
necessary changes in social attitudes and financial
and political institutions.

Such is our hope when we think of urban economic
development as a catalyst. Regrettably, the possibilities for this approach to economic development as
we understand it today within the context of city
governments are severely constrained by attitudes of
politicians, the business and financial institutions
that should be involved, the existing bureaucracy,
and the present prejudices and predilections of
planners.

The writing of this book, based principally on
the work of the Philadelphia Economic Development
Unit between 1966 and 1969, was undertaken in the
hope that the aforementioned constraints would be
loosened if the many ways the economist can apply his
skills could be clarified and the potentials could
be identified.

Despite limitations of time and resources as
well as demand for the Unit's services at a frequency
and magnitude never anticipated--not mentioned or
included in any of the Unit's reports of the consul-
tative and advisory analyses carried out for various
agencies, boards, departments, and private businesses
throughout the City--this work was undertaken with
the expectation that it would have substantial utility
for the Mayor and his advisers in their day-to-day
policy- and decision-making efforts and for other
city governments throughout the nation.

The findings and experience detailed in this
volume indicate that more urgently than ever there
is a need for community leaders and decision makers
at all levels collectively to give increasingly concentrated and systematic attention to the problems
of metropolitan economic development.

September 1971

ACKNOWLEDGMENTS

To all those whose abilities and energies made this book possible I wish to express my deepest gratitude. My greatest thanks go to the officials of the Office of Technical Assistance of the Economic Development Administration, John Nixon, Arnold Liebowitz, and Andrew Bennett, who believed in the value of this undertaking. And to Prentice-Hall and the American Assembly of Columbia University for permission to reprint material originally appearing as a paper "Where Does the Money Come From?" by Peter F. McNeish in the book <u>Black Economic Development</u> published in 1969. And to David S. Arnold, Editor of <u>Public Management</u>, published by the International City Management Association, Washington, D.C., for permission to reprint the article "Economic Development: Cities Fight Back," in the June 1971 issue. And to Paul N. Zimmerer, Executive Director, Mayor's Committee for Economic and Cultural Development, City of Chicago, for permission to draw on his report "Partnership for Action: Mid-Chicago Economic Development Project." And to the Philadelphia Economic Development Unit staff, James Crummett, David Carlin, Robert Lembke, Henry Stewart III, Virginia Kesterson, and C. Wilford Grover, for their excellent research and analytic efforts and prelimanary reports.

Also to Shellie Burns, Sarah B. Edeiken, and Anita M. Kline for their dedicated assistance on the final manuscript.

Last, but not least, to my beloved wife, whose encouragement persuaded me that the effort was worthwhile.

CONTENTS

Chapter   Page

xvii

LIST OF TABLES

LIST OF CHARTS

1

INTRODUCTION:
THE BEGINNINGS
OF URBAN
ECONOMIC DEVELOPMENT
IN PHILADELPHIA

When the history of city economic development is written, it will perforce identify the origins of the concept in a one-man operation organized by Kirk Petshek in 1954, first as Assistant Director of Commerce and later in the office of its Mayor in the City government of Philadelphia, for Philadelphia up to that time did not differ substantially from other large, old cities in its approach to dealing with the many facets of the problem. Functions coming under the heading of economic development were performed by at least a dozen agencies, commissions, boards, and offices. Among the more important areas covered were central business district development; industrial development; zoning and other business service problems; assistance in small business; port and airport development; development of tourism, trade, and conventions; zoning and location assistance to business; manpower development and training; and a land bank operation.

Petshek and John Culp, his successor, in their zeal and almost Herculean efforts, within a period of about eight years managed to move principles of economic analysis and concepts of development from the realm of the unknown into a position front and center on a broad array of problems; that is, setting priorities in capital programming, industrial development and renewal, central business district devel-

opment, small business development, and manpower.
These efforts culminated in the writing of the first
overall economic development program in the nation
in 1964 by Culp.

A change in the City administration produced a
hiatus, which was ended when the author of this book
assumed the duties of City Economist in 1966 and, on
the recommendation of the Philadelphia Community Renewal Program, proposed that an office for economic
development planning be established within Philadelphia's City government. Its mission was defined as
providing a full range of informational, educational,
technical, and coordinative services. Its real product was to come in the form of reports and analyses
identifying priorities for capital investments, formulations of fiscal policy, evaluation of manpower
and business development problems, and, it was hoped,
a coordinative mechanism for operations that would
be recognized by the separate public, quasi-public,
and private organizations concerned with the development of the City.

A proposal was made to the Economic Development
Administration of the U.S. Department of Commerce
requesting funds for a demonstration project directed
to the objective of establishing such an office--
and the proposal was accepted.

In his proposal, the City Economist reasoned that
economic development should be viewed as a process,
not as a series of disjointed efforts. He argued
that if the functional elements in this process could
be structured as a system, several things might be
accomplished:

1. Gaps, as well as overlapping and duplication, in the City's economic development efforts
might be identified.

2. Development agencies--both inside and outside government--might see themselves more clearly
in relation to each other and to the system as a
whole.

3. An instrument for coordination and improved delivery of business retention and development activity might emerge.

The process that the office would put into motion was visualized as shown in the following flow diagram depicting general functional components, within which scheme any specific agency can be appropriately filled with ease.

Data Input →	Economic Structure of City and Region →	

Formulation of Goals and Objectives; Revisions of Policy	→ Economic Development Planning →	Implementation and Delivery (New and Existing Machinery) →

→ Construction- Performance and Function →	Growth and Change Measurement	

Operations at the level and on the scale proposed to the Economic Development Administration date from the autumn of 1966, at which time the staff, consisting of a director and five economists with varied backgrounds, began grappling with basic problems of urban economic development. The project produced substantial and useful results in the development of data and information systems setting forth economic objectives for the City and in development planning.

As for the implementation of new machineries for development, the Economic Development Unit was immediately affected by the 1967-69 surge of federal legislation that was so momentously involved in the urban development problem. No sooner had the Unit begun its work than it found itself assigned the task force for qualification in the HUD Model Cities program and the Labor Department's Concentrated Employment program. Simultaneously the Office of

Economic Opportunity's Title III-d proffering direct
assistance to black enterprise development called
forth the staff's energies in relation to elaborate
proposals for ghetto economic development.

Ironically, though the most powerful and effective tools for economic development that the federal
establishment was able to convey reposed with the
Economic Development Administration, these were de-
nied to Philadelphia on the basis of unemployment
level qualification rules. Throughout the years
1966-70 the official unemployment level in the City
was less than 6 percent even though depressed inner
city areas suffered a jobless rate of 30 percent.
As a consequence, much of the new Unit's potential
for innovation was dissipated in struggles to achieve
a change in priorities with entrenched agencies,
such as the Planning Commission, the Redevelopment
Authority, and the City's Department of Commerce.
Economic Development on an imaginative and dynamic
scale just was not to be expected at such a time,
when agency heads' and planners' responses to crises
were largely reactive and adaptive rather than generative.

The difficulties mentioned above called for a
decision, which had not been made at the outset, as
to whether the City Economist should have solely informational and analytic functions or engage in operational functions as well. A decision favoring the
latter alternative would have involved, of course,
the conveyance of appropriate power to him. This
was never done. An additional question emerged--
whether the City Economist should have direct access
to the Mayor as a special adviser or should channel
his recommendations through one of the members of the
Mayor's inner circle of advisers. (The former had
been the status of City Economist Petshek, who had
been organizationally placed in the Mayor's office.)

It also seemed desirable that the Economist
himself should have recourse to an advisory council
made up of economists on the faculties of institutions of higher learning and executives of major
businesses and institutions outside government, who

could be called upon to assist him in formulating
and reviewing his own work program and to address
themselves to formulating short and long range goals
and policies and to raising specific issues requiring
the attention of the City administration. (Such a
body, the Mayor's Economic Advisory Council, had also
operated earlier under Petchek's chairmanship.) The
institution of such a body, it was reasoned, should
supply the Mayor with high level support on matters
of fiscal policy, manpower development, priorities
in capital programs, and so forth.

Over the course of two years such a group did
meet and render valuable comment and guidance on the
separate studies that constitute the chapters of this
book. The goal established by the author of locking
planning, policy formulations, and operations together cannot in a real sense be said to have been
realized. What success has been achieved in this direction is for the reader to judge in the chapter on
Program Planning Budgeting, and on the Economic Development Program for the Model Cities Area.

Although not originally intended as a scholarly
and educational work, the body of this text contains
a series of analyses of major policy issues that confront every American city today. It presents, it is
hoped, a fresh approach to thinking about problems of
metropolitan economic development as well as fresh
approaches to their solution. The methodology employed, together with empirical measurement and more
precise analysis, can produce sounder solutions to
problems even though data may be inadequate.

Chapter 1 describes the actual and conceptual
inception of the Philadelphia Economic Development
Unit, whose work is the source of the empirical data,
organizational formulations, and practical recommendations in the following chapters.

In an effort to meet the challenge of providing
adequate statistical data, instruments for measurement and analysis, and information retrieval to support planning and policy decisions, Chapter 2 sets
forth (1) a blueprint for the construction of a

sophisticated data bank; (2) a comparative cost analysis showing how Philadelphia compares with other
cities in key overhead, production, and consumer costs
that affect business location decisions; and (3) an
unemployment index as a predictive indicator of the
timing and extent of external economic changes and
their impact on the city's economy.

Chapter 3, co-authored with Philadelphia City
Planner Robert Bingham, confronts us with the stark
facts that emerge from an analysis and forecast of
the city's fiscal conditions. Expenditures and revenues analyzed by both the Economic Development Unit
staff and the staff of the Philadelphia Federal Reserve Bank indicate that expenditures would considerably surpass revenues—and the inexorable dilemma
of increasing taxes or cutting services is posed.
Careful review and analyses are made of alternatives,
including an evaluation of city taxes in terms of
equity and yield, the inequities of the state subsidy
formula, and the promise of federal revenue sharing.
If nothing else, the problem is shown to be clearly
managerial, not political.

Chapter 4 reviews the promise that rests in the
concept of Program Planning Budgeting (PPB) as more
rational than traditional approaches to planning public expenditures—and one that may indeed substantially reduce costs.

At present there are—to the author's knowledge
—no systematic and reliable measures of economic
change for the metropolis through time. Further, although local government levies taxes, licenses enterprise, controls land use, and builds and maintains
transportation networks, none of these activities is
viewed as an overt instrument of economic policy.
Chapter 5 deals with this subject matter.

Chapter 6 presents an analysis of pressing and
urgent issues related to resources, their development,
their full employment (the construction industry is
singled out for special attention), and the supply
of entrepreneurs and managers for enterprise. The
last item is given specific attention because expe-

rience seems to suggest that the cost and supply of
management and entrepreneurial talent is a locational
variant that may offset other cost difference.

Implementation means capital formation, which
is the generative force for the rest of the system.
Chapter 7 demonstrates that the banking system can
respond in imaginative and productive ways to the
problem of rechanneling investment capital to the
inner city, where it is so desperately needed.

The latter part of Chapter 7 sets forth a blueprint for the creation of systems for delivery of
enterprise and "job places," the substance required
for the black entrepreneurship movement, and ways of
getting a piece of the action under the Model Cities
program.

Chapter 8 outlines what cities throughout the
nation are doing; and, finally, Chapter 9 offers a
brief sketch of a course for the future.

The findings and experience detailed in this
volume indicate that, more urgently than ever, there
is a need for community leaders and decision makers
at all levels collectively to give increasingly concentrated and systematic attention to the problems
of metropolitan economic development. As was stated
in the original project proposal to the Economic Development Administration, economic development will
not "just happen." Without unremitting self-appraisal,
well-conceived and proven programs, experimentation,
and salesmanship--all of which form the basis for
new growth--the negative forces of dispersing markets
and the disincentives to investment will not be
reversed.

2

DATA BANKS
AND MEASUREMENTS

CREATING A DATA BANK AND
INFORMATION RETRIEVAL SYSTEMS

The common complaint of many planning and development officials is that an inadequate and disorga-
nized data base prevents them from executing sophisticated analyses appropriate to the problems they
are trying to solve. It is the author's contention
that this is not the case--that most planners feel
that the system design and data gathering that follows
is somehow invalid if they have not generated it.
Long experience both in the United States and in underdeveloped countries has convinced the author that
their doing so is costly and unnecessary. Most planners are just unwilling to make a thorough search or
to explore the obvious possibilities and multiple
sources that could be made the foundation for an
analytic and data retrieval system of high utility.

The foundation of the Philadelphia Economic Development Unit's analytic resources rests largely on
the records of the City's operational systems relating
to tax billing and collection (to be discussed), licenses and permits for construction, births and
deaths, housing and commercial building inspections,
school registration, and so forth.

In addition, a data bank was created storing
time series information on such economic indicators

as retail sales, wholesale trade volume, bank debits,
building construction volume, unemployment claims,
consumer credit, electric power consumption, and
truck and freight-car loadings.

More general series were processed into machine-
readable format because of their general usefulness
to the analytic work of the Unit's staff. These include periodic census population and manufacturing
reports, reports for the state and the nation, and
price indexes to be used as deflators.

In all, the system contains about two hundred
individual data decks organized into two subsets:
(1) an intensive collection of economic indicators
for the Philadelphia economy and (2) those special
series that are most frequently demanded by staff
analysts.

These decks are integrated into a system that
allows convenient storage, retrieval, and identification of the source or origin of the data they contain.

To analyze these collections of data the staff
operations research specialist developed or adapted
over forty different programs for processing data on
the IBM 1130 computer. Some of these programs have
general utility for either simple data manipulation
or more sophisticated statistical analyses, such as
multiple-correlation or analysis-of-variance routines.
Others were developed for project-specific computations, such as the data comparison program to evaluate
the completeness of employment information from a
source described in Chapter 6, an evaluation that
could not have been performed by hand because of the
thousands of data points involved.

Thus, the Unit developed a firm analytic and
data base that facilitates undertaking significant
new projects, such as the establishment of a business-
monitoring system, the determination of prospective
employment opportunities for semiskilled male workers displaced from manufacturing employment, and,
perhaps of greatest import, the simulation modeling
of the local economy on a sector-by-sector basis.

Development of Internal
City Data

One of the major emphases in the original work of the Economic Development Unit was making maximum use of tax payment records that had been formerly internal operational material only. Previously the costs of access to and manipulation and aggregation of these materials had been so high that their use for economic analysis had been precluded, despite the valuable information they contained. Recently, however, the City's data-processing operations had been automated, placing most of the data files in machine-readable form. This change opened the way for their application to economic analysis at reasonable cost. And it was found that routine data-processing operations offer possibilities for the continuous production of valuable data for little additional expense, other than modest one-time modification costs for minor changes in the original instruction coding in normal City record-processing routines. The work of the Unit in converting these series into usable form for economic analysis is detailed below.

Wage Tax Data

Wage tax data are received in two forms. All employers withholding an excess of $50 per month of wage taxes (at 3 percent) are required to file monthly returns. These returns are due by the thirtieth of the month following the month in which the tax is withheld. There were approximately 13,000 employers required to file monthly, who, together, accounted for approximately 90 percent of total employment. All employers not required to file monthly report their withholding quarterly. There were approximately 30,000 such employers, accounting for approximately 10 percent of total employment.

Formerly the returns of these employers had contained the following data: three-digit Standard Industrial Classification (SIC) code, gross wages paid, and taxable wages paid. But the Unit persuaded the Department of Finance to add number of employees to this data field. On the basis of this information a

quarterly "Statistical Report on the Self-Assessed
Wage Taxes" is now being produced by the Department
of Collections. This report details employment and
wage rates in the City on a three-digit SIC basis.
To counteract the failure of some firms to report
number of employees, a special interpolation routine
based on wage rates was developed. The report as
now received constitutes a valuable resource for determining employment fluctuation in the City. Further
experience with the data source, however, will be necessary to determine the seasonality affecting the
employment totals.

For the future, plans were made to obtain a
similar monthly wage tax report, since the largest
employers, who employed 90 percent of covered employees, must report on a monthly basis. Such a monthly
report would fill a major data gap since, although
total unemployment can be estimated quite accurately
from secondary sources, no such corresponding sources
are available from which to derive monthly Philadelphia unemployment statistics.

General Business Tax Data

To complement the information contained in the
wage tax records the Unit obtained the assistance of
the Department of Collections in securing semiannual
reports by SIC code of general business tax collections. Since this is a tax on gross receipts, excepting receipts to points other than Philadelphia,
it was expected that data from this tax source would
provide a good approximation to a time series on retail and service sales. Also, the difference between
general business taxable sales by manufacturing establishments and total value of production, as shown
by annual surveys of manufacturers conducted by the
Department of Internal Affairs, was seen as providing
an excellent means for estimating exports in a regional accounting system.

Unfortunately the School Board's general business
tax was replaced by the recently enacted corporate
net income tax, and this information was lost. But
a mechanism whereby the Unit would receive returns

by SIC code of the corporate net income tax was established. Although it was no longer possible to structure estimates of regional exports, it was expected that retail and service sales from this new tax source could be estimated by applying annual Dun and Bradstreet net income/sales ratios to the net income figures reported from the corporate net income tax collections.

Net Profits Tax Data

The net profits tax is a 3 percent tax on the profits of all unincorporated businesses in Philadelphia. It is essentially part of the "income tax" package in Philadelphia, taxing primarily nonwage-earners on their net income. The greatest portion of the taxable base comes from the net profits taxable income on professionals--and there were approximately 60,000 net profits taxpayers, constituting a large part of the higher income workers in the City.

The Unit arranged to receive semiannual reports by SIC code on the number of accounts and total net profits taxes paid. Although the number of accounts is not strictly comparable to the number of individuals because of the large number of partnerships involved, the data on both account numbers and tax paid are being utilized as a valuable resource in detecting trends in one of the City's most vital sectors--highly paid professional employment.

Utilization of Internally
Generated Data

Although developmental work still continues on mining the City's internal data system, a number of significant applications of these data were developed or formulated during the project, as enumerated below.

The Master Billing File

The Economic Development Unit arranged to have the Department of Finance's master billing file on taxpayers sorted by ZIP code, printed in multiple copies, and also partially punched onto Hollerith

cards for further manipulation. The printouts are
sorted within the ZIP code by SIC code and also incorporate certain account number totals, which facilitates their use for analytic purposes. This inex-
pensive manipulation of the City's data provides a
valuable listing of virtually every economic activity
within the City of Philadelphia, a data source that
would be infeasible to obtain in any other manner.
The sorted master billing file is also stored on
tape to provide a useful means of access to other
City data through the simple device of a constant
number associated with each account.

The major use of this data source is in the identification of commercial patterns within the City--
and during the project the data were used to prepare
a master list of firms in the Model Cities area of
North Philadelphia for use by the City's Department
of Health in implementing a new federally sponsored
industrial health project.

Economic Structure Mapping

A basic by-product of the wage tax file and master billing file data system was the Economic Development Unit's participation with the City Planning
Commission and the City Data Processing Bureau in
designing an economic mapping of the City. Specifically, a commercial study sponsored by the Planning
Commission in cooperation with the Bureau and the
Unit was designed to provide detailed economic data
on a firm-by-firm, block-by-block, area-by-area basis, to put to use mapping programs so that information including growth rates, employee numbers, and
industry mix could be mapped back to the land itself.
The program was designed to produce 110 detailed maps
of the City, a six-digit information field being assigned to each block within the City.

Identification of Major City Employers

Based on the wage tax information on file a
computer search was initiated to identify the 750
largest noninstitutional taxpayers within the City,
which accounted for approximately 66 percent of all

private noninstitutional employment within the City
and, as such, held the key to the future growth or
decline of the City's business base. Periodic readings are taken on these firms by SIC code to identify
trends among the City's major employers. Additionally,
these data were used to establish a mailing list for
the recently completed management demand survey conducted by the Unit.

Coordinated Manpower
Planning System

In addition to carrying out the data collection
efforts already described, the Economic Development
Unit was continuously involved in developing the
data resources necessary to provide a comprehensive
manpower planning program for the Philadelphia area.
The first effort in this direction was the preparation of labor demand statistics for the year 1965 as
part of the Coordinated Area Manpower Planning System
(CAMPS) study. As a participant in this study the
Unit developed detailed data on the demand for labor
by sixteen occupational classifications for industrial
groupings at the two-digit SIC level, whether covered
or not covered for unemployment insurance. This information was developed for each of the eight counties
in the Philadelphia SMSA.

The computer programs written at that time and
the data generated formed the nucleus around which
the development of a comprehensive manpower planning
system could be structured. Subsequently detailed
employment statistics for the remaining years 1962-67
for each of the SMSA counties was added to the system.

Once these historical data resources were collected, it was possible to begin significant manpower
planning studies. Using the historical data, the
Unit completed labor demand projections to 1975 by
occupational classes for both Philadelphia County and
the Philadelphia SMSA.

On the basis of these established employment
data projections it is possible to proceed with relative ease (1) to evaluate the sex distribution of the

predicted labor demand, (2) to establish the number
of potential job openings from manufacturing employment expected to be available for semiskilled males
being displaced, and (3) to project the wage structure that should evolve for Philadelphia through the
1970s.

Analytical and Manipulative Routines

During the period of the Unit's operation, the
staff of the Economic Development Unit evolved over
40 computer programs for the preparation and analysis
of the economic data bank it established. Many of
these programs are simple data manipulation routines,
which although unsophisticated in nature, are general
in application and save analysts considerable time
in converting data to usable formats. Examples of
these programs are routines for the deflation of economic time series on either a monthly or a yearly
basis, first-differencing of data to remove autocor-
relation, logarithmic data transformation, and simple
linear trending techniques.

More sophisticated programs with wide general
application were developed through the conversion of
existing programs to language suitable for the IBM
1130 computer. The most frequently used of these
programs is the regression analysis package, a program designed to allow the analyst maximum flexibility.
The program is capable of simple linear regression,
stepwise regression, and multiple regression analysis.
These subprograms are often used with data reduced
to first differences or transformed to logarithms by
a subprogram routine. Additionally, the regression
package produces an analysis-of-variance table for
each run so as to provide for maximum statistical
analysis of the regression results.

A correlation analysis program adapted to the
1130 computer by the staff is a frequently used complement to the regression package. The program is
capable of producing up to a 22-by-22 correlation
matrix. This program is primarily used either for
eliminating highly intercorrelated variables before

regression analysis or for independent analysis of
variable interrelationships.

Based on the correlation program a simplified
lead-lag analysis routine was developed with the use
of a computer dial. In this method the original
data are stored on the computer disk, and, by manipulation of the data fields, a complete multivariate
correlation analysis from a 12-month lag to a 12-month
lead is obtained in one computer run.

Furthermore, because many of the economic time
series require deseasonalization before they are
amenable to further analysis, an arrangement was effected whereby the Unit's data series could be de-
seasonalized by use of the Philadelphia Federal Reserve Bank's Census X-9 seasonal adjustment program.

In addition to these more general programs a
number of routines were developed by the Operations
Research Specialist to handle project-specific computational problems. Perhaps the most interesting
of these were the data-comparison programs. When the
staff was confronted with two sources of employment
information, each containing thousands of data points,
a program was developed whereby the consistency and
inconclusiveness of the two series could be evaluated
to determine which was the superior data source.
Because of the enormous number of data points involved,
this determination could never have been made by hand.

Future Applications of
Present Analytical Resources

Though the analytical systems outlined above
soon began to yield impressive results, the potential
uses of the system were by no means fully exploited
within the life span of the project; several additional uses of the system were contemplated. Specifically, one of the greatest problems confronting the
Philadelphia economy is the widespread exodus of
business firms seeking room for expansion. Often
the City is informed of a decision to relocate outside the City only after the relocation is nearly
effectuated. With the data available from the wage

tax records, a business monitoring system was envisioned as an answer to this problem. The monitoring system would alert the City to business firms expanding employment at such a rate as to be ripe for relocation. Having an early warning, the City would be able to obtain and propose a relocation site for the firm before it had made a definite decision to move outside the City.

Furthermore, the data developed in the labor demand study provided a basis for the analysis of the future of the City's semiskilled male labor force. It is well known that semiskilled manufacturing employment is subject to a continued decline, largely compensated by a corresponding increase in service industry employment, particularly of a clerical nature. By applying sex distribution and wage rate information to the already compiled labor demand data, it is possible to determine historical changes in the relative status of semiskilled male employees, predict their future situation, and gain the information required to propose relevant training programs for these people.

Additionally, as previously indicated, the development of the leading economic index for the Philadelphia economy provided a basis for proceeding with sector-by-secotr modeling of the local economy utilizing data series contained in the economic indicator data file.

MEASURING COMPARATIVE ADVANTAGE
OF THE CITY'S ECONOMY

Philadelphians have long been aware of the benefits afforded by the lower living costs enjoyed in Philadelphia as compared with the other major Northeastern metropolitan areas. Area businessmen are equally cognizant of the economic advantages that accrue as a result of these lower costs. And now for the first time--to the author's knowledge--a uniform body of data can be presented to document some of the comparative cost advantages afforded the business community in the metropolitan area.

The relative advantages will be documented in
six areas: living costs, wage rates, labor turnover,
work stoppages, construction costs, and business
taxes. This type of analysis is particularly pertinent if businesses and individuals are to make accurate decisions about where their least-cost location
may be. It is also an indication to high-cost cities
that measures must be taken to stabilize and equalize
cost structures within their sphere of influence.

The results of the Economic Development Unit's
study showed that in living costs Philadelphia compared favorably with the most populous areas, ranking
eleventh or twelfth highest for four different income
classes. Only Detroit, of the nine largest SMSAs,
ranked lower in cost of living. The costs of "moderate" living for a city worker's family of four, as
defined by the U.S. Bureau of Statistics in 1967, required an income of $9,193, $900 less than was needed
in New York and $700 more than in Houston, respec-
tively the highest and lowest among 20 metropolitan
areas. Similarly, housing costs were low for Philadelphia, ranking fourteenth among the 20 metropolitan
areas studied.

In wage rates the Philadelphia employer had an
advantage over his competitors in other metropolitan
areas. Of seventeen occupations studied, only in
three--truckdriver, draftsman, and carpenter--did
Philadelphia rank relatively high. Philadelphia's
low ranking in secretarial and clerical wage rates
is of particular importance to the rapidly prolifer-
ating service-based industries that are increasingly
supplanting manufacturing industries in major metropolitan areas.

The rate of labor turnover for Philadelphia is
lower than that of practically every other metropolitan area studied. And labor turnover is one indication of the degree of utilization of labor forces, a
high rate indicating a high rate of use and, consequently, a relatively low availability of workers.
Philadelphia's relatively stable employment pattern
indicates a decided advantage in labor availability.

Philadelphia ranked sixteenth among the 22 metropolitan areas studied in work stoppages and the
resulting ratio of total man-days idle for the region.
In addition, Philadelphia had experienced a continuing
decline in work stoppages since 1964, indicating a
generally improving climate of labor relations.

Construction costs in the Philadelphia area compared favorably with costs in other large metropolitan areas. For all types of buildings Philadelphia
ranked twelfth of the 20 metropolitan areas included.
In 1968 building costs in Philadelphia were 16 percent lower than in New York City, and no metropolitan
area in the Northeast enjoyed an index value lower
than that for Philadelphia. In factory and commercial construction Philadelphia ranked twelfth lowest
among the 17 metropolitan areas studied. However,
as Chapter 5 indicates, this condition was not expected to prevail much longer, since inflation in
construction worker wages was moving up at 90 percent
a year without any measurable increase in productivity.

Finally, Pennsylvania ranked very low in tax
burden on industry--and Philadelphia was no exception
to the rule. In a report to the Federal Reserve
Bank of Boston, Erie, Pennsylvania, ranked tenth of
the 11 cities studied. The 8 percent differential
in taxes between Erie and Philadelphia would not have
altered this ranking as the next highest area showed
total taxes 60 percent higher than Erie. One of the
major advantages to manufacturing in Philadelphia is
that tangible personal property is exempt from local
property taxation.

Such findings, coming during a time when industry
is finding location in the populous market centers
of the industrial Northeast increasingly expensive,
should provide a powerful incentive in attracting important new industry.

Cost of Living

National Industrial Conference Board Study for 1963

Living costs of suburban Philadelphians in 1963
were slightly below the median for the four income

levels studied by the National Industrial Conference
Board (NICB). (See Table 1.) It cost more to live
in San Francisco than in any other of the 20 areas
for which data were produced, and it cost least to
live in Houston.

Philadelphia compared favorably with the most
populous areas, including the major centers of the
North, Midwest, and Far West, ranking eleventh and
twelfth highest over the four income classes. Of
the nine largest SMSAs, only Detroit had lower living
costs than Philadelphia.

Indexes of equivalent pretax incomes showed
Philadelphia in the same relative position as straight
cost-of-living indexes, although Philadelphia lost
ground slightly in the higher income classes.

The data on which these conclusions were based
apply to homeowning suburban residents. NICB utilized BLX budget studies and the Housing Census of
1960 to arrive at the indexes that appear in Table 1.

Changes after 1963

Changes in the Consumer Price Index (CPI) between
1963 and 1966 (Table 2) give an indication of the
cost-of-living situation. The CPI, of course, cannot
be directly related to NICB findings; it does, however, give a good picture of trends in the various
areas.

Among the 20 regions studied Philadelphia ranked
eleventh in 1964-66 increases in the CPI. This indicates that Philadelphia probably maintained its 1963
ranking with respect to other areas. Of the five
SMSAs with the largest increases in the CPI over the
three-year period (Kansas City, Portland, Detroit,
Scranton, and St. Louis), four were among those with
the lowest cost of living in 1963. As a result, these
areas experienced a worsening in their relative positions.

TABLE 1

Cost-of-Living Indexes, 1963, Four-Person Suburban Families
(Washington, D.C. = 100)

Metropolitan Area	$6,000/Year Family Income	$12,000/Year Family Income	$18,000/Year Family Income	$24,000/Year Family Income
San Francisco	108.1	108.3	108.4	108.5
Seattle	104.1	104.7	104.6	104.3
New York	106.1	103.8	102.6	101.7
Boston	106.0	103.7	102.4	101.4
Los Angeles	102.7	102.6	102.5	102.4
Chicago	102.7	102.3	101.6	100.8
Cleveland	103.2	101.0	99.8	99.1
PITTSBURGH	99.4	100.2	100.3	100.0
Portland, Ore.	98.2	100.2	100.7	100.5
Washington, D.C.	100.0	100.0	100.0	100.0
PHILADELPHIA	97.7	98.4	98.5	98.3
Minneapolis	98.3	98.2	98.0	97.6
Cincinnati	97.5	97.8	97.9	97.8
Baltimore	96.5	97.1	97.1	96.7
SCRANTON	94.3	96.9	97.7	97.7
St. Louis	95.0	96.5	96.9	97.0
Kansas City (Kans. and Mo.)	95.4	96.2	96.4	96.2
Detroit	95.9	95.2	94.4	93.6
Atlanta	92.1	94.0	94.7	94.8
Houston	87.9	90.6	91.2	90.8

Source: National Industrial Conference Board, Technical Paper Number Fourteen, 1964.

24

TABLE 2

Changes in Consumer Price Indexes, 1963-66

Metropolitan Area	Consumer Price Index 1963	Consumer Price Index 1966	1966 Index as Percentage of 1963
Kansas City (Kans. and Mo.)	107.2	116.3	108.5
Portland, Ore.	106.6	115.3	108.2
Detroit	103.2	111.1	107.7
SCRANTON	107.3	114.9	107.1
St. Louis	106.2	113.5	106.9
Boston	109.5	117.0	106.8
New York	108.7	116.0	106.7
Washington, D.C.	106.4	113.3	106.5
San Francisco	108.9	115.6	106.2
Baltimore	106.8	113.4	106.2
PHILADELPHIA	107.2	113.7	106.1
Atlanta	105.1	111.5	106.1
Los Angeles	108.2	114.7	106.0
Houston	105.6	111.5	105.6
PITTSBURGH	107.1	113.0	105.5
Seattle	108.2	114.1	105.5
Cincinnati	104.7	110.3	105.3
Minneapolis-St. Paul	107.0	112.2	104.9
Cleveland	104.7	109.7	104.8
Chicago	105.7	110.7	104.7

Source: Bureau of Labor Statistics, U.S. Department of Labor, Handbook of Labor Statistics 1967 (Washington, D.C.: Government Printing Office, 1967).

25

Bureau of Labor Statistics Study for Spring 1967

The U.S. Bureau of Labor Statistics (BLS) makes estimates of the family budget required to support an urban working class family of four at a standard of living considered to be "moderate."* As of the spring of 1967, such a family living in the Philadelphia area would require an annual income of $9,193. This figure was arrived at by computing a weighted average of living costs both for families that rent and for families that own their own homes. It was about $900 less than the amount needed by the same family living in New York and about $700 more than would be needed in Houston, these cities being ranked the highest and lowest among the 20 metropolitan areas studied. Thus, Philadelphia appeared to have maintained its relatively favorable position over the 1963-67 period, ranking thirteenth in the BLS study (Table 3).

It was also found that families paying rent in the Philadelphia area averaged lower outlays for housing than did families in any other among the nation's 20 largest metropolitan areas (Table 4). Homeownership costs were also very low, so that the area's overall rank in family housing costs was fourteenth among the 20 areas and thirteenth for homeowner families separately.

Wage Rates

The Philadelphia area employer had an advantage over his counterpart in many other metropolitan areas with respect to wages. Of the seventeen occupations

---

*The city worker's family, as defined by BLS, consists of an employed husband aged thirty-eight, a wife not employed outside the home, a girl aged eight, and a boy aged thirteen. The "moderate" standard is essentially what the BLS investigators found "reflects the collective judgment of families as to what is necessary and desirable to meet the conventional and social as well as the physical needs of families . . . ."

TABLE 3

Moderate Living Standard Annual Family Budget Costs, Spring 1967 (in dollars)

Metropolitan Area	Total	Renter Families	Home-owner Families
New York-Northeast New Jersey	9,977	8,911	10,333
Boston	9,973	8,925	10,322
San Francisco	9,774	9,391	9,902
Buffalo	9,624	8,842	9,885
Seattle	9,550	9,195	9,669
Milwaukee	9,544	8,650	9,842
Minneapolis-St. Paul	9,399	8,772	9,608
Chicago	9,334	8,636	9,567
Los Angeles	9,326	8,960	9,449
Washington, D.C.	9,273	8,683	9,470
Cleveland	9,262	8,311	9,580
St. Louis	9,140	8,542	9,340
PHILADELPHIA	9,079	8,353	9,321
Detroit	8,981	8,374	9,183
Cincinnati	8,826	8,152	9,051
PITTSBURGH	8,764	8,273	8,928
Baltimore	8,685	8,512	8,743
Dallas	8,345	8,130	8,417
Atlanta	8,328	8,053	8,420
Houston	8,301	7,979	8,408

Note: The total is a weighted average of costs for renter families (25 percent) and owner families (75 percent).

Source: Bureau of Labor Statistics, U.S. Department of Labor, Three Standards of Living for an Urban Family of Four Persons, Bulletin No. 1570-5 (Washington, D.C.: Government Printing Office, 1967).

TABLE 4

Moderate Living Standard Annual Family Housing Costs,
Spring 1967
(in dollars)

Metropolitan Area	Total	Renter Families	Home-owner Families
Boston	2,728	1,890	3,007
New York-Northeast New Jersey	2,637	1,800	2,916
Chicago	2,555	1,978	2,748
Cleveland	2,529	1,745	2,791
Milwaukee	2,463	1,779	2,691
San Francisco	2,411	2,105	2,513
Buffalo	2,382	1,769	2,587
Seattle	2,332	2,038	2,431
Minneapolis-St. Paul	2,323	1,845	2,482
Washington, D.C.	2,316	1,852	2,471
St. Louis	2,247	1,763	2,409
Cincinnati	2,190	1,642	2,373
Los Angeles	2,189	1,896	2,287
PHILADELPHIA	2,140	1,548	2,337
Detroit	2,120	1,627	2,284
Baltimore	2,003	1,870	2,048
PITTSBURGH	1,963	1,562	2,097
Dallas	1,923	1,745	1,983
Atlanta	1,851	1,630	1,925
Houston	1,844	1,577	1,932

Note: The total is a weighted average of costs for renter families (25 percent) and owner families (75 percent).

Source: Bureau of Labor Statistics, U.S. Department of Labor, Three Standards of Living for an Urban Family of Four Persons, Bulletin No. 1570-5 (Washington, D.C.: Government Printing Office, 1967).

surveyed, Philadelphia wage rates were comparatively
high in only three: draftsman, carpenter, and truck-
driver. (Tables 5-11 present earnings data for a
selected seven of the seventeen occupations studied.)

Wage rates for truckdrivers saw the greatest
change in ranking over the period studied, moving
from a rank of fifteenth to ninth. Draftsman and
carpenter, the other comparatively high wage rate occupations, maintained median positions over the five-
year period; Philadelphia ranked twelfth in both
occupations as of the last survey. In all other occupations, except shipping clerk (thirteenth), Philadelphia ranked sixteenth or lower out of 22 metropolitan areas, and rankings were fairly consistent
over the period studied.

Detroit, Los Angeles, and San Francisco shared
the distinction of having the highest wage levels
for given occupations; Dallas was most often among
the lowest. Philadelphia compared favorably with
other northern manufacturing centers, such as New
York, Chicago, and Detroit, and with the far western
metropolitan areas of San Francisco, Los Angeles,
and Seattle. Boston is the only area that was consistently below Philadelphia's low wage rate position
in the Northeast.

Comparisons with southern and southwestern metropolitan areas were not so favorable to Philadelphia;
however, Dallas was the only area to have consistently
lower wage rates than Philadelphia.

Wage rates in several areas, including Baltimore,
Washington, D.C., and Atlanta, were higher than those
in Philadelphia about as often as they were lower.
Washington, D.C., and Atlanta generally had higher
wage rates in office occupations and lower wage rates
in blue-collar occupations, while Baltimore showed a
mixed pattern.

In using this information, it must be remembered
that data are collected over all industries, negating
intraindustry differentials. That is, the data are
useful indicators of relative differences among the

TABLE 5

Average Weekly Earnings for Female Secretaries in All Industries, July 1962–June 1967
(in dollars)

Metropolitan Area	July 1962 June 1963	July 1963 June 1964	July 1964 June 1965	July 1965 June 1966	July 1966 June 1967
Detroit	110.00	113.00	117.00	122.50	128.00
Los Angeles	105.00	108.50	112.50	117.00	122.00
New York	101.00	104.50	108.50	114.00	118.00
San Francisco	102.50	106.00	109.00	112.50	117.00
Seattle	100.50	103.50	106.50	112.00	117.00
Chicago	101.50	104.00	107.00	108.50	113.00
Houston	98.50	100.50	103.00	110.50	113.00
Newark and Jersey City	98.50	102.00	104.50	109.50	112.50
Cleveland	101.00	103.50	105.00	107.50	111.50
Milwaukee	96.50	100.50	104.00	106.00	111.50
PITTSBURGH	99.00	100.00	103.50	107.00	111.00
Washington, D.C.	94.50	97.50	102.50	107.00	111.00
Cincinnati	98.00	100.50	102.50	105.00	110.00
Buffalo	98.00	99.50	102.00	104.50	109.00
Paterson-Clifton-Passaic	97.50	101.00	103.00	105.00	108.50
Atlanta	93.50	96.00	100.00	102.00	108.00
PHILADELPHIA	94.00	96.50	100.00	105.50	107.50
Baltimore	91.00	95.50	98.00	101.50	104.50
St. Louis	93.50	95.50	98.00	100.50	104.00
Boston	89.00	92.00	95.00	99.00	103.50
Dallas	90.50	92.50	96.00	98.50	101.00
Minneapolis-St. Paul	89.50	91.00	93.00	95.00	99.50

Note: Data prior to July 1965 are not strictly comparable with those for subsequent years because of change in job description.

Sources: Data for July 1962–June 1965 are from U.S. Department of Labor Statistics BLS Bulletin Numbers 1430-83 (Part I), 1345-83 (Part I). For July 1965–June 1967 see individual BLS, Metropolitan Area Bulletins.

TABLE 6

Average Hourly Earnings for Truckdrivers in All Industries, July 1962-June 1967
(in dollars)

Metropolitan Area	July 1962	July 1963	July 1964	July 1965	July 1966
San Francisco	3.21	3.33	3.41	3.52	3.65
Seattle	2.94	3.09	3.26	3.46	3.63
Milwaukee	2.89	2.99	3.07	3.20	3.43
Newark and Jersey City	3.07	3.17	3.25	3.30	3.42
Chicago	3.04	3.14	3.24	3.37	3.41
Los Angeles	2.90	3.02	3.16	3.28	3.41
New York	3.02	3.12	3.24	3.35	3.40
Detroit	2.93	3.01	3.10	3.18	3.32
PHILADELPHIA	2.75	2.97	3.12	3.21	3.31
Paterson-Clifton-Passaic	2.84	2.91	3.06	3.19	3.28
PITTSBURGH	2.95	3.03	3.10	3.17	3.27
St. Louis	2.87	2.97	3.07	3.18	3.27
Cincinnati	2.85	2.95	3.03	3.18	3.23
Cleveland	2.86	2.95	3.06	3.13	3.22
Minneapolis-St. Paul	2.82	2.93	3.03	3.12	3.22
Buffalo	2.74	2.83	2.95	3.04	3.11
Boston	2.56	2.66	2.80	2.91	3.02
Baltimore	2.49	2.60	2.70	2.77	2.86
Washington, D.C.	2.30	2.39	2.49	2.60	2.76
Atlanta	2.40	2.46	2.55	2.52	2.71
Dallas	2.30	2.34	2.39	2.41	2.53
Houston	2.18	2.20	2.30	2.41	2.53

Sources: Data for July 1962-June 1965 are from U.S. Department of Labor Statistics BLS Bulletin Numbers 1430-83 (Part I), 1345-83 (Part I). For July 1965-June 1967 see individual BLS, Metropolitan Area Bulletins.

TABLE 7

Average Weekly Earnings for Male Class B Draftsmen in All Industries, July 1962-June 1967
(in dollars)

Metropolitan Area	July 1962 June 1963	July 1963 June 1964	July 1964 June 1965	July 1965 June 1966	July 1966 June 1967
Detroit	164.50	170.00	168.50	159.00	163.50
Newark and Jersey City	129.00	132.00	n.a.	143.00	148.50
New York	132.50	137.00	138.50	141.00	148.00
Houston	123.50	125.00	n.a.	136.00	144.00
Los Angeles	132.50	139.00	137.50	143.50	144.00
Paterson-Clifton-Passaic	132.50	132.00	n.a.	137.00	144.00
PITTSBURGH	141.50	142.50	139.50	145.00	144.00
Buffalo	134.50	139.00	133.50	139.00	143.00
San Francisco	127.00	132.50	134.50	137.00	142.50
Cleveland	134.50	138.00	134.00	136.50	141.50
Baltimore	126.00	129.00	133.50	135.50	141.00
PHILADELPHIA	131.00	134.00	131.00	136.00	141.00
Seattle	118.00	124.00	n.a.	135.00	139.50
St. Louis	128.00	135.00	137.00	133.00	139.50
Boston	129.00	131.00	135.00	135.50	139.00
Chicago	134.50	135.00	133.00	132.50	138.00
Washington, D.C.	122.50	127.00	128.00	134.00	135.50
Milwaukee	129.50	134.50	125.50	128.00	134.00
Cincinnati	133.00	132.50	n.a.	139.50	133.50
Atlanta	126.50	125.00	n.a.	117.50	130.50
Minneapolist-St. Paul	119.00	123.50	119.00	123.00	128.00
Dallas	108.00	112.00	114.50	115.50	116.00

Note: Data prior to July 1964 are for Senior Draftsmen and are not strictly comparable with those for subsequent surveys.

Sources: Data for July 1962-June 1965 are from U.S. Department of Labor Statistics BLS Bulletin Numbers 1430-83 (Part I), 1345-83 (Part I). For July 1965-June 1967 see individual BLS, Metropolitan Area Bulletins.

TABLE 8

Average Hourly Earnings for Maintenance Electricians in All Industries, July 1962–June 1967
(in dollars)

Metropolitan Area	July 1962 June 1963	July 1963 June 1964	July 1964 June 1965	July 1965 June 1966	July 1966 June 1967
Detroit	3.45	3.54	3.60	3.73	3.95
Milwaukee	3.38	3.48	3.56	3.70	3.95
San Francisco	3.47	3.63	3.65	3.84	3.95
Minneapolis–St. Paul	3.28	3.42	3.56	3.69	3.87
Los Angeles	3.37	3.48	3.60	3.68	3.83
Chicago	3.38	3.47	3.57	3.67	3.79
St. Louis	3.26	3.39	3.50	3.63	3.78
Houston	3.27	3.33	3.38	3.69	3.76
Seattle	n.a.	n.a.	n.a.	n.a.	3.69
Atlanta	3.08	3.20	3.35	3.46	3.68
Newark and Jersey City	3.19	3.34	3.43	3.52	3.65
Buffalo	3.19	3.24	3.35	3.49	3.64
Cleveland	3.22	3.30	3.34	3.46	3.61
New York	3.18	3.29	3.38	3.46	3.58
Paterson-Clifton-Passaic	3.11	3.22	3.28	3.41	3.56
PITTSBURGH	3.18	3.25	3.27	3.45	3.52
Cincinnati	3.09	3.19	3.26	3.35	3.51
PHILADELPHIA	3.05	3.12	3.21	3.33	3.47
Baltimore	2.92	2.99	3.11	3.23	3.41
Boston	2.95	3.05	3.12	3.24	3.40
Washington, D.C.	2.93	2.96	3.09	3.30	3.33
Dallas	2.85	2.94	3.03	3.18	3.22

Sources: Data for July 1962–June 1965 are from U.S. Department of Labor Statistics BLS Bulletin Numbers 1430–83 (Part I), 1345–83 (Part I). For July 1965–June 1967 see individual BLS, Metropolitan Area Bulletins.

TABLE 9

Average Hourly Earnings for Tool and Die Makers in All Industries, July 1962-June 1967
(in dollars)

Metropolitan Area	July 1962 June 1963	July 1963 June 1964	July 1964 June 1965	July 1965 June 1966	July 1966 June 1967
San Francisco	3.74	3.90	3.98	4.16	4.29
Detroit	3.60	3.71	3.76	3.90	4.11
Milwaukee	3.65	3.75	3.82	3.93	4.10
Chicago	3.50	3.61	3.71	3.84	4.01
St. Louis	3.48	3.58	3.69	3.82	3.91
Los Angeles	3.36	3.44	3.48	3.62	3.90
Buffalo	3.37	3.48	3.53	3.64	3.88
Seattle	3.16	3.41	3.53	3.63	3.88
Cleveland	3.44	3.56	3.59	3.66	3.84
Atlanta	3.29	3.38	3.54	3.60	3.83
Cincinnati	3.31	3.38	3.44	3.57	3.78
Minneapolis-St. Paul	3.36	3.47	3.55	3.64	3.76
PITTSBURGH	3.32	3.37	3.42	3.58	3.71
Paterson-Clifton-Passaic	3.34	3.43	3.51	3.58	3.68
Newark and Jersey City	3.22	3.35	3.43	3.59	3.66
Baltimore	3.21	3.31	3.41	3.55	3.65
PHILADELPHIA	3.25	3.32	3.39	3.49	3.65
New York	3.25	3.29	3.37	3.51	3.62
Boston	3.14	3.23	3.28	3.40	3.60
Houston	3.19	3.23	3.34	3.39	3.55
Dallas	3.00	3.09	3.17	3.29	3.53
Washington, D.C.	n.a.	n.a.	n.a.	n.a.	n.a.

Sources: Data for July 1962-June 1965 are from U.S. Department of Labor Statistics BLS Bulletin Numbers 1430-83 (Part I), 1345-83 (Part I). For July 1965-June 1967 see individual BLS, Metropolitan Area Bulletins.

34

TABLE 10

Average Hourly Earnings for Maintenance Carpenters in All Industries, July 1962-June 1967
(in dollars)

Metropolitan Area	July 1962 June 1963	July 1963 June 1964	July 1964 June 1965	July 1965 June 1966	July 1966 June 1967
Chicago	3.33	3.52	3.62	3.66	3.89
San Francisco	3.58	3.63	3.63	3.63	3.78
Detroit	3.24	3.32	3.37	3.51	3.70
Houston	3.22	3.27	3.33	3.61	3.65
Seattle	2.94	3.08	3.22	3.40	3.59
Milwaukee	3.04	3.10	3.26	3.40	3.58
Los Angeles	3.13	3.20	3.30	3.39	3.57
Paterson-Clifton-Passaic	3.00	3.07	3.22	3.40	3.55
Cleveland	3.07	3.18	3.22	3.36	3.53
New York	3.00	3.10	3.22	3.35	3.51
PHILADELPHIA	3.03	3.13	3.27	3.38	3.50
Newark and Jersey City	3.05	3.13	3.24	3.38	3.47
St. Louis	3.12	3.24	3.32	3.34	3.44
Minneapolis-St. Paul	3.02	3.10	3.18	3.24	3.43
PITTSBURGH	3.13	3.11	3.15	3.34	3.42
Cincinnati	2.94	3.04	3.13	3.26	3.41
Buffalo	2.96	2.96	3.10	3.17	3.40
Boston	2.89	2.96	2.97	3.13	3.30
Washington, D.C.	2.86	2.91	3.00	3.19	3.21
Baltimore	2.80	2.91	3.00	3.11	3.22
Atlanta	2.59	2.68	2.84	2.97	3.14
Dallas	2.69	2.79	2.93	2.95	3.08

Sources: Data for July 1962-June 1965 are from U.S. Department of Labor Statistics BLS Bulletin Numbers 1430-83 (Part I), 1345-83 (Part I). For July 1965-June 1967 see individual BLS, Metropolitan Area Bulletins.

TABLE 11

Average Hourly Earnings for Maintenance Sheet-Metal Workers in All Industries, July 1962-June 1967
(in dollars)

Metropolitan Area	July 1962 June 1963	July 1963 June 1964	July 1964 June 1965	July 1965 June 1966	July 1966 June 1967
Houston	3.49	3.54	3.57	3.76	3.93
Detroit	3.38	3.46	3.54	3.66	3.89
Minneapolis-St. Paul	n.a.	n.a.	3.23	3.32	3.87
San Francisco	3.32	3.67	3.82	3.63	3.77
Los Angeles	3.13	3.31	3.50	3.56	3.72
Milwaukee	3.32	3.36	3.46	3.56	3.71
Buffalo	3.18	3.23	3.36	3.51	3.69
Cleveland	3.18	3.30	3.31	3.47	3.68
Chicago	3.25	3.33	3.41	3.52	3.67
Cincinnati	3.19	3.28	3.37	3.56	3.67
St. Louis	3.31	3.39	3.47	3.58	3.66
New York	3.10	3.22	3.27	3.55	3.52
Newark and Jersey City	3.18	3.28	3.27	3.40	3.52
Paterson-Clifton-Passaic	3.06	3.17	3.26	3.36	3.47
PITTSBURGH	3.15	3.24	3.28	3.44	3.45
Baltimore	3.00	3.02	3.19	3.31	3.38
PHILADELPHIA	2.97	3.06	3.16	3.28	3.37
Boston	2.90	3.02	3.08	3.18	3.33
Atlanta	n.a.	n.a.	n.a.	n.a.	n.a.
Dallas	n.a.	n.a.	n.a.	n.a.	n.a.
Seattle	n.a.	n.a.	n.a.	n.a.	n.a.
Washington, D.C.	n.a.	n.a.	n.a.	n.a.	n.a.

Sources: Data for July 1962-June 1965 are from U.S. Department of Labor Statistics BLS Bulletin Numbers 1430-83 (Part I), 1345-83 (Part I). For July 1965-June 1967 see individual BLS, Metropolitan Area Bulletins.

given metropolitan areas, but they will not tell a corporate official exactly what he will have to pay a secretary in Philadelphia as against New York. Furthermore, one should emphasize in promotional arguments that one can often better the average by matching a particular firm's site and labor needs so as to meet its site requirements at lowest wage costs.

Labor Turnover

Accessions per 100 workers employed during a period, in conjunction with job separations per 100 workers, are used to compute labor turnover rates. These rates are used to reflect the degree of utilization of the labor force in an area. If the market for labor experiences intense competition, wage rates are bid up, opportunities arise for worker advancement, and there is considerable job-hopping. As a result of tight labor market conditions, turnover rates are high; conversely, when business is slack, job-hopping becomes both difficult and risky, and labor turnover rates decline.*

The same considerations apply when regions are compared in terms of labor turnover rates. In areas under the pressure of rapid regional economic growth, the turnover rate is consistently higher during both recession and recovery than it is in area economies experiencing less intense utilization of the local labor force. Atlanta and Los Angeles, for example,

---

*For the period 1961-67 this statement applies without exception to both accession and separation rates. Separation rates rise during periods of labor scarcity because increases in quits overwhelm the effect of decreases in layoffs. Accession rates rise because more and more new employees are hired.

In deep recessions separation rates may rise rather than fall, as happened in 1957-58, because increases in layoffs are greater than decreases in quits. But it takes a recession to effect this situation. During the so-called economic "pauses" of 1962 and 1967, separation rates decreased along with accession rates.

during the mid-1960s had turnover rates more than 33
percent higher than rates in Buffalo and Pittsburgh.

Because competitive conditions in the labor
market are reflected in labor turnover rates, and because they can be used to make interregional comparisons, labor turnover rates are useful overall indicators of the availability of workers with a region.

Philadelphia's Position

Charts 1-3 clearly show that, by this measure,
the Philadelphia area maintained a decided advantage
in labor availability. During the period from 1963
to 1968, when the national economy was moving toward
full employment, labor turnover was increasing. But
Philadelphia retained its relative position when compared with other metropolitan areas, having a turnover lower than that in all but two of the other
large metropolitan areas surveyed.

While this condition made Philadelphia attractive
for new industry location, it did have a negative aspect: it confirmed other indications of economic
slack in the Philadelphia area and pointed to the
need for a larger effort to develop the local economy.

Promotional Uses

The Philadelphia area's low labor turnover was
a fact having considerable potential promotional
value. It provided a clear body of evidence that
the region contained a stable work force and thus
presented relatively few personnel problems for management and relatively few of the costs that accompany
high turnover. Furthermore, the turnover data provided objective evidence of labor availability, a
consideration that was becoming more and more crucial
in locational decisions as the labor force became
more and more fully utilized. There is no point in
expanding investment where people are not available
to man the new plant.

The Philadelphia area's unemployment rate used
to be high, indicating availability of labor. In

CHART 1

Labor Turnover Rates in Large Metropolitan Areas

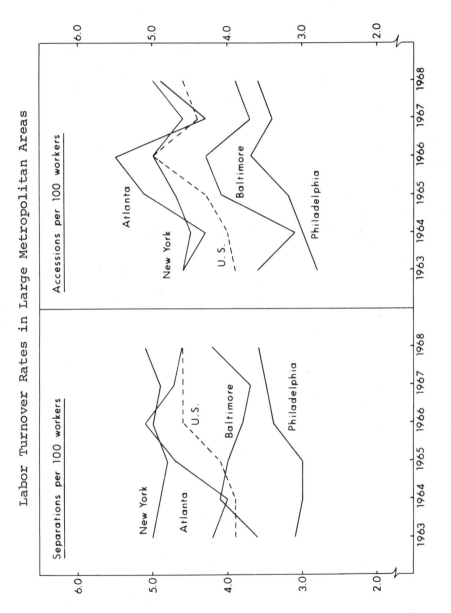

39

CHART 2

Labor Turnover Rates in Manufacturing
Industries Metropolitan Areas

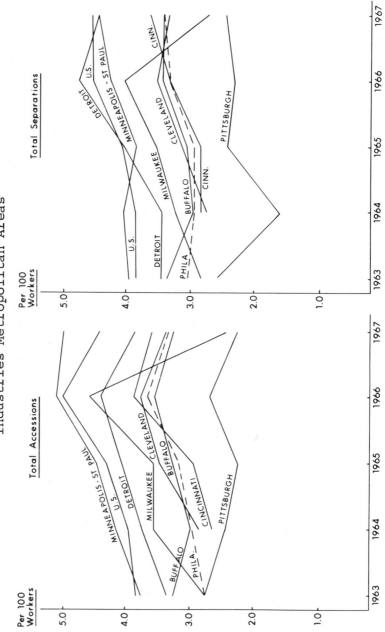

Total Accessions

Total Separations

CHART 3

Labor Turnover Rates in Manufacturing
Industries Metropolitan Areas

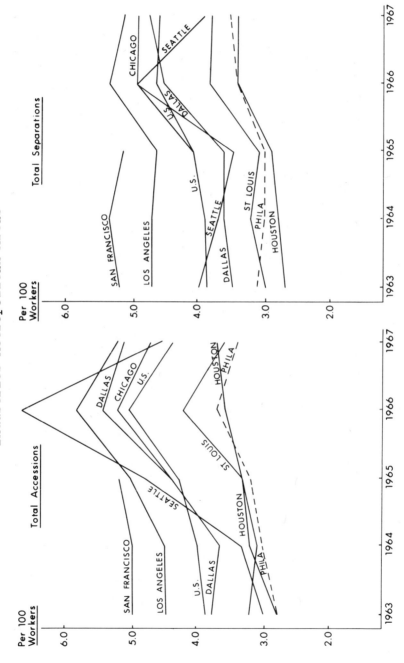

41

1968 it was below the national rate, but Philadelphia's relatively advantageous position with respect to labor turnover continued.

Arguments based on the low local labor turnover should be composed with some care. Certain local industries--fabricated metals and food processing in particular--have not usually had low turnover rates, despite the low overall turnover experienced in the region. An examination of data for all industries should be made before low labor turnover is advanced as an argument for a particular industry to locate in Philadelphia.

Work Stoppages

Philadelphia's record of time lost because of work stoppages was somewhat poor in the early 1960s: indeed, in 1963 Philadelphia ranked third highest among 22 areas surveyed in terms of man-days lost due to work stoppages per private nonfarm worker. Between 1964 and 1968, however, the work stoppage picture in Philadelphia steadily improved (Chart 4). By 1968 Philadelphia work stoppages were considerably below the national average, and the city ranked sixteenth among 22 areas in percentage of days lost to strikes.*

----

*Data on work stoppages are based on figures published by the U.S. Bureau of Labor Statistics. BLS collects information on existence of stoppages from many sources, including newspapers, state employment security agencies, other state and federal agencies, employers and employer associations, and international unions and their publications. The Bureau then mails questionnaires to parties involved in stoppages, requesting information on establishments and unions involved, dates the stoppage was in force, number of workers involved, and several other items. Data are collected for each strike lasting one full day or shift or longer and involving six or more workers.
For metropolitan areas the following data are published: number of stoppages beginning in a given year, number of workers involved in these stoppages,

CHART 4

Man–Days Idle per Private Nonfarm Worker
Due to Work Stoppages

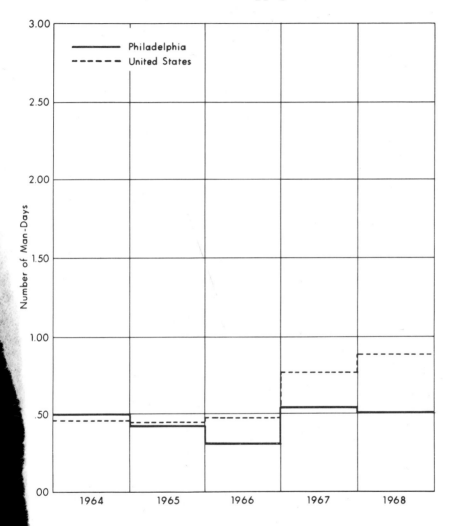

Construction Costs

According to two different measures construction costs in Philadelphia compared favorably with costs in other large metropolitan areas. The first source was the Dow Building Cost Calculator, published by F. W. Dodge Company, which gives a total cost-to-build index covering all types of buildings. The other source was the Boeckh Division of the American Appraisal Company, which lists cost indexes according to type of building.

The Dow indexes (based on New York City = 100) showed Philadelphia in 1968 twelfth in rank among 20 metropolitan areas (Table 12). In 1962 the Philadelphia index was 89 and in 1968 it was 84, 11 percent lower than for New York in 1962 and 16 percent lower in 1968. Of the metropolitan areas considered, New York was always highest over the period 1962-68, with construction costs at least 5 percent higher than in any other area. Cleveland, Pittsburgh, Buffalo, and St. Louis were generally highest after New York. Areas with costs higher than Philadelphia were located, generally, in the Northeast and North Central regions of the United States. No metropolitan area in the Northeast, except Boston, showed an index value lower than that for Philadelphia.

Areas in the South, Southwest, and Far West had lower construction costs than Philadelphia over the period 1962-68. Atlanta and Dallas were consistently lowest, with construction costs running from 21 percent to 27 percent less than those for New York.

For both steel and concrete-brick buildings, Philadelphia ranked about twelfth of 17 metropolita

---

and man-days idle due to all stoppages in effect the year. To obtain a measure of strike activity that admits of interarea comparison, a ratio of total man days idle for a given region to employment in that region was constructed by the Philadelphia Economic Development Unit. For this purpose employment in private nonfarm industries was taken as the relevant basis of comparison.

TABLE 12

Indexes of Building Costs
(New York City = 100)

Metropolitan Area	1962	1963	1964	1965	1966	1967	1968
New York	100	100	100	100	100	100	100
Cleveland	94	93	93	92	93	88	90
St. Louis	90	90	91	91	92	87	87
PITTSBURGH	92	92	92	91	91	88	87
Newark	91	91	92	91	91	94	92
Buffalo	93	91	91	91	91	90	90
Chicago	88	88	88	89	89	87	86
Detroit	95	89	90	89	89	91	91
Milwaukee	89	88	88	88	89	88	89
Cincinnati	90	89	89	88	88	82	82
erson	90	87	88	88	88	n.a.	n.a.
neapolis	90	89	88	88	87	84	83
ADELPHIA	89	87	88	87	87	85	84
Francisco	85	85	86	85	86	87	90
on	86	84	85	85	85	87	87
tle	86	85	85	84	85	83	83
Angeles	86	84	84	83	83	87	85
more	82	80	80	79	80	80	71
on	81	80	80	79	79	75	75
s	78	79	78	77	77	73	73
ta	72	72	72	72	72	78	79

Sources: Data for 1962-66, Dow Building Cost Calculator
Dodge Co.); data for 1967 and 1968, Robert Snow Means.

45

areas, according to the indexes published by the
Boeckh Division of the American Appraisal Company
(Table 13).

Philadelphia's building cost index for brick
and concrete structures, based on the U.S. average
1926-29 = 100, was 365 in 1964 and increased to 441
in 1968; comparable figures for steel structures were
313 and 386. As with the overall Dow index the indexes for these particular types of buildings indicate that New York had the highest construction costs
of major metropolitan areas. San Francisco, Cleveland, and Detroit showed the highest costs after New
York for both types of construction materials, and
once again the southern areas, Atlanta and Dallas,
exhibited the lowest costs.

Taxes

Pennsylvania ranked very low in tax burden on
industry, according to analyses by two different and
independent institutions, the Federal Reserve Bank of
Boston and the Pennsylvania Economy League. (The advantage to manufacturing firms in Pennsylvania lies
primarily in the fact that tangible personal property
is exempt from local property taxation.) The Federal
Reserve report showed that two areas in Pennsylvania
and two in New York had the lowest total state and
local taxes of 83 locations studied. Looking at the
largest urban center studied in each state, Pennsylvania was again in a very favorable position; Erie,
Pennsylvania, ranked tenth in total taxes; only Utica,
New York, had a lower tax burden (Table 14).

Although Philadelphia itself was not studied,
its tax burden was only 8 percent higher than that
of Erie, as indicated in the note to Table 14. The
Philadelphia suburb Upper Merion Township had a tax
burden on industry about equal to that in Erie.
Philadelphia area locations therefore offered significant tax savings to manufacturing firms.

Both the Federal Reserve study and the Pennsylvania Economy League study utilized the concept of
hypothetical corporations, representing certain major

TABLE 13

Indexes of Building Costs for Commercial and Factory Buildings
(U.S. average 1926-29 = 100)

Metropolitan Area	Steel			Brick and Concrete		
	1964	1966	1968	1964	1966	1968
New York	383.3	420.5	460.1	479.4	535.1	577.5
Cleveland	324.8	356.1	436.1	386.5	428.2	522.4
San Francisco	345.8	377.7	428.1	409.9	455.4	518.7
Detroit	325.1	355.5	420.0	387.0	423.4	496.5
St. Louis	322.5	352.2	409.3	387.0	426.4	484.3
Chicago	322.8	346.2	403.9	389.9	420.8	471.1
PITTSBURGH	323.5	347.2	402.2	385.8	412.9	468.2
Seattle	338.5	361.5	401.8	378.6	407.9	467.8
Los Angeles	350.0	373.2	400.4	385.9	416.7	458.2
Boston	327.9	347.6	394.9	380.2	408.0	453.2
Cincinnati	314.1	332.7	393.3	362.7	384.1	448.6
U.S. average	318.5	341.7	389.4	365.4	395.3	445.6
PHILADELPHIA	313.3	336.4	386.1	365.4	395.2	441.0
Minneapolis	314.6	336.8	384.8	366.1	386.8	438.0
Washington, D.C.	317.3	334.5	368.5	348.9	370.8	403.5
Baltimore	300.7	319.5	353.0	327.7	348.4	384.6
Atlanta	281.3	299.1	344.5	311.5	332.2	367.8
Dallas	284.7	298.0	338.2	299.6	321.4	355.5

Source: Milwaukee, Wis.: Boeckh Division, American Appraisal Co.

TABLE 14

Total State and Local Taxes of a Firm Having $4 Million
Total Assets, by Major Industry Group, 1967
(in dollars)

Urban Center	Chemicals	Nonelectrical Machinery	Textile Mill Products
Utica, N.Y.	34,273 (11)	36,111 (11)	33,751 (11)
ERIE, PENNSYLVANIA	42,376 (10)	42,145 (10)	40,439 (10)
Worcester, Mass.	65,121 (9)	67,372 (9)	66,886 (9)
Manchester, N.H.	67,472 (8)	69,152 (8)	78,866 (7)
Burlington, Vt.	68,749 (7)	69,791 (7)	69,068 (8)
Paterson, N.J.	76,867 (6)	79,620 (6)	88,285 (4)
Charleston, W. Va.	78,781 (5)	80,192 (5)	86,678 (5)
Portland, Me.	83,964 (4)	86,024 (3)	95,879 (2)
Hagerstown, Md.	84,425 (3)	81,648 (4)	82,449 (6)
Providence, R.I.	96,570 (2)	91,847 (2)	94,877 (3)
Hartford, Conn.	101,634 (1)	99,817 (1)	103,576 (1)

Note: Numbers in parentheses are ranks.

Computed on a comparable basis, taxes for the three
hypothetical firms were about 8 percent higher in the City of
Philadelphia than in Erie. The increase was mainly because of
higher real estate taxes in Philadelphia and only to a minor extent because of the general business and mercantile taxes levied
by the City. In suburban Upper Merion Township, the total taxes
on the three firms were about the same as in Erie. Had Philadelphia been substituted for Erie in the original study, the ranking
would not have changed, because the next higher area, Worcester,
Mass, showed total taxes 60 percent higher than Erie.

Source: James W. Wightman, The Impact of State and Local
Fiscal Policies on Redevelopment Areas in the Northeast, Research
Report to the Federal Reserve Bank of Boston, No. 40.

industries, to determine tax burdens in given areas
on a comparable basis.

The study by the Pennsylvania Economy League,
which utilized state "averages" rather than specific
locations within states, corroborated the findings
of the Federal Reserve report. Total taxes paid by
firms in Pennsylvania were generally lower than in
other states, Pennsylvania ranking ninth or tenth in
five industry groups, eighth in another, and sixth
in the remaining industry (Table 15). Delaware was
the only state to maintain a consistently lower tax
position than Pennsylvania, having the smallest tax
burden for all industries, and New York again showed
a relative tax advantage. In line with the Federal
Reserve report, Pennsylvania's tax advantage was at
the local level. In local tax dollars paid Pennsylvania firms ranked tenth across all industries, while
in state taxes paid they ranked from second to sixth.

Two qualifications must be made to statements
on comparative tax costs to industry. First, the
subject of unemployment compensation cost has been
ignored; it is a complex subject better to be taken
up separately and was not included in the tax cost
calculations in either study. Second, state and local
services provided industry in various locations were
not taken into consideration.

Summary and Conclusions

1. Of the 20 metropolitan areas recently surveyed by the Bureau of Labor Statistics, Philadelphia
ranked thirteenth lowest in terms of general cost of
living.

2. With few exceptions, Philadelphia ranked below most metropolitan areas of the industrial Northeast in relative wage rates. Philadelphia's low
ranking in secretarial and clerical wage rates has
been of particular importance because service industries are increasingly supplanting manufacturing industries in major metropolitan centers.

3. High labor turnover usually means high costs
for employers. Philadelphia, however, has been shown

TABLE 15

Total State and Local Taxes of a Firm Having $10 Million
Total Assets, by Major Industry Group, 1967
(in dollars)

State	Primary Metals	Food	Apparel
Delaware	80,454 (11)	79,174 (11)	64,751 (11)
PENNSYLVANIA	111,238 (10)	94,648 (10)	77,302 (9)
New York	112,745 (9)	99,515 (9)	68,963 (10)
Ohio	134,820 (8)	125,048 (8)	111,906 (6)
New Jersey	147,671 (7)	135,657 (7)	102,954 (8)
Massachusetts	161,666 (6)	147,507 (6)	109,615 (7)
Illinois	173,045 (5)	152,730 (5)	123,141 (5)
West Virginia	179,219 (4)	216,271 (3)	214,368 (3)
Indiana	192,286 (3)	245,568 (1)	237,093 (1)
Maryland	194,133 (2)	184,210 (4)	165,014 (4)
Michigan	206,711 (1)	241,540 (2)	228,095 (2)

State	Chemicals	Fabricated Metals	Electrical Machinery	Instruments
Delaware	101,083 (11)	86,252 (11)	84,703 (11)	120,370 (11)
PENNSYLVANIA	132,910 (8)	115,266 (9)	108,384 (9)	157,445 (6)
New York	127,899 (10)	105,868 (10)	102,428 (10)	149,896 (7)
Ohio	129,570 (9)	130,841 (8)	118,767 (8)	125,212 (10)
New Jersey	142,393 (7)	133,940 (7)	122,565 (7)	143,216 (9)
Massachusetts	179,563 (4)	155,233 (6)	148,305 (5)	202,854 (2)
Illinois	165,197 (6)	158,444 (5)	137,981 (6)	145,382 (8)
West Virginia	176,184 (5)	195,583 (4)	179,803 (4)	173,811 (5)
Indiana	189,340 (3)	216,315 (2)	196,264 (2)	188,615 (4)
Maryland	218,048 (1)	200,108 (3)	185,835 (3)	236,715 (1)
Michigan	202,301 (2)	223,328 (1)	201,530 (1)	201,798 (3)

Note: Numbers in parentheses are ranks.

Source: Pennsylvania Economy League, Taxes Paid by Industry (Harrisburg, December 1967).

to have one of the lowest labor turnover rates of
the nation's major metropolitan areas.

4.   Philadelphia showed a continuous decline in
rank among metropolitan areas in terms of idle days
caused by work stoppages, ranking sixteenth among 22
metropolitan areas in terms of the relative level of
days lost due to strikes.

5.   Philadelphia was in a position to compete
very favorably in construction costs. For all building types, Philadelphia consistently ranked twelfth
lowest of 20 metropolitan areas surveyed. In commercial and factory construction costs, Philadelphia
ranked twelfth lowest among 17 areas studied. More
important, in all the construction types surveyed,
Philadelphia had the lowest construction costs of
any metropolitan area in the industrial Northeast.

6.   Two studies showed that Philadelphia had
almost the lowest business tax burden of all metropolitan areas in the industrial Northeast.

In living costs, wage rates, labor turnover,
work stoppages, construction costs, and business
taxes, Philadelphia was shown to have a decided comparative advantage in competition with comparable
metropolitan areas.

MEASURING UPTURNS AND DOWNTURNS

Establishing a Coincident Indicator

It appeared that the Philadelphia Economic Development Unit had at hand the appropriate technology
and an adequate data base that would permit the construction of an index that could accurately forecast
accelerations and retardations in the City's economy.
Such a barometer promised to be of inestimable value
to businessmen in making investment and production
decisions, to retailers, and to the City government
in predicting revenue fluctuations. Of even greater
value, if the lead time was six months or more, advance notice could help the City in timing its pur-

chases and in creating employment programs in public
works and special services to reduce the unemployment
level resulting from cyclical forces.

The data file of heterogeneous indicators that
had been maintained on a current basis by the City
Economist and his predecessors was the point of departure.

Since these indicators had been presented formerly as a heterogeneous collection of data, often
conflicting, considerably lacking in representative-
ness, and altogether lacking in reckoning of the time-
sequencing of the series—leading, lagging, or coincident—unifying them into a single index of like-
timed series, and discarding those that were
unrepresentative, became the first objective. Next,
to construct a predictive economic index for Philadelphia, it was clear that it would be necessary to
have a current measure of the economy against which
the various historical data series collected by the
Unit could be tested to determine relative timing in
the business cycle, that is, leading, lagging, or
coincident.

The National Series of Coincident Indicators

Nationally, a current measure of the state of
the economy is readily available in the form of the
GNP in constant dollars and other broad indicators,
such as the industrial production index and the indexes of personal income. Using these broad indexes
of the current state of the economy the National Bureau of Economic Research has determined the timing
of business cycle peaks and troughs in the national
economy. Against this timing of peaks and troughs
the National Bureau has determined the relative cyclical timing of a wide variety of U.S. economic indicators.

One effort had been made in the early 1960s to
establish a broad current index of the Philadelphia
economy. This was the index of Basic Private Demand
prepared for the Community Renewal Program by National
Analysts.[1] Although the index is conceptually sound,

and while it did represent 90 percent of the components corresponding to the GNP, it did not meet
the need felt for intelligent readings. The index
was sufficient for the purpose for which it was designed, namely, the comparing of the long-term economic growth rates of Philadelphia with those of the
Philadelphia SMSA and the nation as a whole. However,
for purposes of cyclical identification the index has
several deficiencies: (1) It makes no estimate of
inventory changes, the most volatile cyclical component of the GNP; (2) it lacks regional sensitivity to
changes in retail trade; and (3) it cannot account
for variations in extraregional trade. Additionally,
the index is formulated on an annual basis, whereas
a monthly series was needed. And the fact that a
number of the index components are only reported an-
nually--valuation of building permits, local government expenditures, and expenditures on plant and
equipment, for example--rendered it impossible to
convert the index to a monthly basis for the project
period.

Unemployment as an Alternative Current Indicator for Philadelphia

In the absence of a broad-based indicator comparable to that of the GNP, it was decided that the
unemployment rate was the most acceptable alternative.
The unemployment rate was chosen because it (1) represents a broad-based measure of the local business
cycle and (2) has been identified by the National
Bureau as a coincident indicator. Although the unemployment series possesses the desired attributes of
a current indicator, no such index for Philadelphia
was being prepared on a current basis. It was necessary, therefore, to construct such an index for Philadelphia based on the Pennsylvania Bureau of Employment Security's unemployment rate statistics for the
SMSA and certain subsidiary indicators available for
Philadelphia. In obtaining an unemployment index for
Philadelphia it was necessary to estimate unemployment as a percentage of the available labor force
(resident labor force plus in-commuters) rather than
as a percentage of the resident labor force alone.
The index thus constructed, while not being a precise

measure of the absolute unemployment rate in the
City alone, constituted a valid indicator of cyclical
movements in the Philadelphia economy.

Basically the unemployment series was constructed
as follows: On the basis of New Jersey statistics,
unemployment for the three New Jersey counties contained in the Philadelphia SMSA--Burlington, Camden,
and Gloucester--was subtracted from the SMSA totals.
The remaining unemployment total was allocated to
Philadelphia on the basis of Philadelphia's percentage
of the five SMSA Pennsylvania counties' total of unemployment claims filed with the Pennsylvania Bureau
of Employment Security. Total employment for Philadelphia was separated from that of the other counties
in the SMSA by using data prepared by the Pennsylvania
Department of Internal Affairs on the work force
covered by unemployment insurance, historical estimates from the Development Coordinator's Office, and
bench-mark data prepared by Warren Lutz of the Pennsylvania Bureau of Employment Security. A complete
description of methodology and sources of data are
given in Appendix A.

The Philadelphia Unemployment Rate

Monthly data on estimates made of the Philadelphia unemployment rate as a percentage of the available labor force are presented graphically in Chart
5 (monthly values being given in Table A.1). For the
period estimated, 1956-68, three distinct business
cycles are identified: 1957-58, 1960-61, and 1967.*

Foreshadowing the 1957-58 recession the unemployment rate reached a peak of 6.03 in September
1956, followed by somewhat lower peaks of 6.10 in

---

*Although 1967 has not been identified by the
National Bureau of Economic Research as a recession
year, it is so identified here as the adjustment of
that year appears to have affected the Philadelphia
economy much more strongly than it did the national
economy.

CHART 5

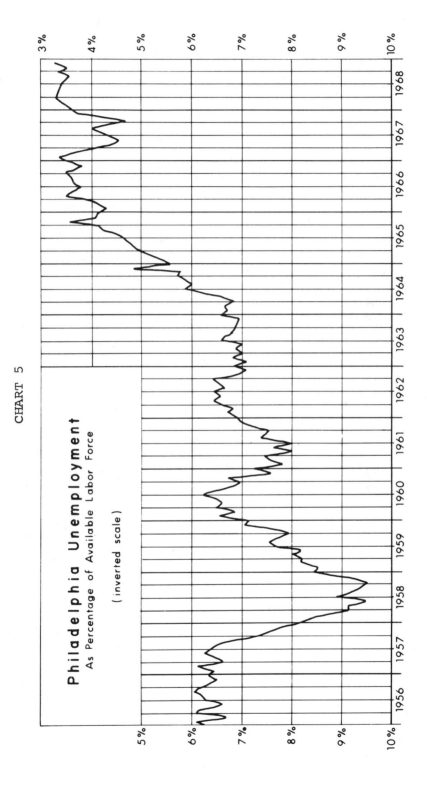

Philadelphia Unemployment
As Percentage of Available Labor Force

(inverted scale)

March 1957 and 6.21 in June 1957.* Subsequently,
in 1958, a double bottom was formed at 9.48 in June
and 9.49 in October. In the 1960-61 recession the
unemployment rate had a clear peak of 6.17 in July
1960 and troughed at 8.02 in May 1961. In 1967 the
unemployment rate reached a peak of 3.32 in February
and troughed at 4.67 in October.

In a comparison of this series with the national
unemployment series, few differences emerge. In
general the two unemployment series are coincident
except that the national series peaked in March 1957,
whereas the local series peaked in September 1956;
and in 1960 the national unemployment rate peaked in
February, whereas the local peak occurred in July.

Constructing a Leading Index
for Philadelphia

Once a suitably broad current cyclical indicator
had been obtained in the form of the unemployment
rate, a set of economic data series potentially constituting a leading index was formulated. In the
formation of this set all indicators classified as
lagging indicators for the national economy were excluded. Furthermore, because of the extreme paucity
of indicators for Philadelphia alone--particularly
indicators that should be very important a priori in
constructing the index--it was found necessary to
include a number of data series for which information
was only available on an SMSA basis.

The indicators thus chosen for potential inclusion in the leading index, with area of coverage indicated, were:

---

*Because the unemployment rate moves inversely
to the rate of economic growth, it is convenient here
to refer to the lowest unemployment rate as the peak
rate and the highest unemployment rate as the trough
rate, to be consistent with the characterization of
peaks and troughs in the local economy.

Accession rate in manufacturing, SMSA

Average workweek in manufacturing, SMSA

Average weekly earnings in manufacturing, SMSA

Bank debits, SMSA

Business failures, Philadelphia

Consumer credit outstanding, Third Federal Reserve District

Help wanted advertising index, SMSA

Initial unemployment claims, Philadelphia

Large commercial and industrial electric power consumption, Philadelphia

Layoff rate in manufacturing, SMSA

Postal receipts, Philadelphia

Small commercial and industrial electric power consumption, Philadelphia.

Testing Potential Leading Series

Statistical adjustment was necessary before these series could be tested for inclusion in the index:

1. Most of the series exhibited various patterns of seasonality. For example, electric power consumption increases sharply in the summer as a result of air-conditioning, whereas the unemployment rate typically rises in July with an influx of students into the labor market and again in January with post-Christmas layoffs. For this reason it was necessary to have each of the series seasonally adjusted before testing for its relative timing in the business cycle. This seasonal adjustment was performed on each series by the Philadelphia Federal Reserve Bank using the Census X-9 seasonal adjustment program.

2. A number of the data series were in current
dollars and thus required deflation to constant dollars. Average weekly earnings in manufacturing, consumer credit extended, and consumer credit outstanding were deflated by the Department of Labor's monthly
consumer price index for Philadelphia. Bank debits
were deflated by the U.S. wholesale price index.

The series thus adjusted were tested against the
unemployment rate to determine their relative cyclical timing. Correlation analysis was used for this
determination, each series being tested from a six-
month lag to a twelve-month lead. A total, then, of
nineteen correlations was obtained for each series
tested.*

A series was classified as a leading indicator
if its highest correlation occurred at more than a
two-month lead from the unemployment index. The following series were thus classified as leading indicators:

Average workweek in manufacturing

Average weekly earnings in manufacturing

Bank debits

Consumer credit extended

Initial unemployment claims

Large commercial and industrial electric power
consumption

Small commercial and industrial electric power
consumption.

---

*With the assistance of Robert Wenzinger of the
Department of Water's Computer Center these correlations were obtained in one computer run by entering
the original data onto a computer disk and manipula-
ting the disk files of the dependent and independent
variables.

Two series--monthly business failures and the index of help wanted advertising--were classified as coincident indicators. Three series were not classified. Data on the accession and layoff rates in manufacturing were available only for the period 1963-68, but it was felt that these series might be used to form a modified index for this shorter period; probably because of the very short time period the series did not exhibit the expected leading characteristics, and the idea of constructing a modified index with these series included was dropped. The postal receipt series was eliminated because of an inability to adjust for change in postal rates.

Additionally, the series on large commercial and industrial electric power consumption was dropped because it seemed largely to duplicate the information contained in the small commercial and industrial electric power consumption series, which had a slightly longer lead time.

Formulation of the Leading Index

The six leading indicators chosen could not be used immediately to form an index because of the considerably different cyclical amplitudes exhibited by the various series. The most notable illustration is the extremely narrow range of variation exhibited by the average workweek series as opposed to the amplitude of the other five series. Consequently, an amplitude adjusted index was formed following National Bureau methodology.[2] The amplitude adjusted series was formed as follows:

1. The month-to-month percentage change in each indicator was computed.

2. These percentage changes were standardized for each series so that the average, without regard to sign, for each indicator over the period 1956-68 was equal to 1.0 percent per month.

3. After the sign on the initial unemployment claim series was reversed, the standardized percentage changes for the six indicators were summed.

4.   The sum of the standardized percentage changes for each month was standardized such that the average change over the six indicators for each month was equal to 1 percent.

5.   Starting with January 1956 = 100, a cumulative index was constructed on the basis of the standardized average percent change from (4).

The leading index thus constructed is shown in conjunction with the inverted unemployment rate in Chart 6 (monthly values of the index being given in Table A.2).

The Leading Index and the Philadelphia Unemployment Rate

The test of the validity of the leading index is, of course, how consistently it has peaked before the unemployment series and turned up in advance of the unemployment rate. In general the index has performed well historically, performing somewhat better in identifying cyclical recoveries than in pinpointing cyclical downturns.

The index's performance in forecasting the 1957-58 recession was not as clear-cut as would have been desired. To be sure the index hit a peak of 103.35 in April 1956, which led by six months the peak or lowest unemployment level of 6.03 percent in September 1956, but both the index and the unemployment series fluctuated around their highs for nearly a year. The performance of the index is not, however, unlike that of the national series of leading indicators, which has a tendency to plateau rather than decline sharply before recessions. Thus, the national index peaked slightly at 154.4 in November 1956 but remained at that level for the next eight months, not declining noticeably until after the July 1957 index of 153.4, which coincided with the identified cyclical peak. Nevertheless, the index cannot be faulted in its prediction of the late 1958 upturn. The index troughed in March of 1958 at 93.57 and began a clear-cut uptrend thereafter, whereas the unemployment rate formed a double bottom in June and

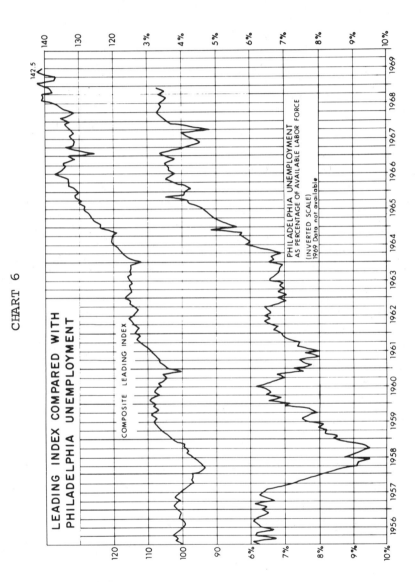

CHART 6

LEADING INDEX COMPARED WITH
PHILADELPHIA UNEMPLOYMENT

COMPOSITE LEADING INDEX

PHILADELPHIA UNEMPLOYMENT
AS PERCENTAGE OF AVAILABLE LABOR FORCE

(INVERTED SCALE)
1969 Data not available

October of 1958--the low point occurring in October
with the unemployment rate at 9.49 percent.

In the 1960-61 recession the index peaked in
February 1960 at 109.70 and began a slow downtrend
thereafter, whereas the unemployment rate reached
its low of 6.17 percent in July and increased somewhat precipitously thereafter. The index reached
bottom in December 1960 and increased steadily thereafter, while the unemployment rate did not reach its
nadir till May 1961 at 8.02 percent--and then hit
another low at 7.95 percent in July 1961 before turning steadily upward.

In the 1967 recession the index reached a peak
of 137.25 in July of 1966, which was followed by a
peak of 3.32 percent in the unemployment rate in
February 1967. Similarly, the index reached a nadir
of 125.51 in February 1967 and turned up thereafter,
whereas a trough in the unemployment rate did not
occur until October 1967.

Although there was no clearly identified recession, the economy was somewhat sluggish in 1963 before
the beginning of a very strong, sustained upthrust
in mid-1964. The strong 1964 revival was well her-
alded as the index bottomed in January 1964 at 112.17
and rose sharply thereafter, whereas the unemployment
rate did not begin to decline until July.

Overall, then, the index had a creditable record
in its identification of cyclical turning points,
tending to foreshadow changes in the local economy by
an average of from five to six months. Its most
striking characteristic was doubtless its ability to
forecast dramatically resurgences in the economy well
in advance of the turn in the unemployment rate.

The ultimate test of the usefulness of any series
based on historical data is, of course, its ability
to function with continued accuracy in predicting
future cyclical movements. Only the experience of
time can serve for this evaluation. Computed through
July 1969 the index appears to have plateaued with
peaks of 142.47 in February and 142.49 in June. The

formation of such a plateau in the index in the past
often foreshadowed a business downturn--and thus
showed the index again performed quite well.

Indicated Uses for the
Leading Index

The index is immediately useful for making pre-
dictions at the aggregate level, that is, for forecasting trends in such comprehensive coincident
series as retail sales, overall unemployment, and
the level of City revenues. It is still not possible
to predict either the strength of upturns and down-
trends or their duration in time, and, unfortunately,
it appears unlikely that it will be possible to make
such forecasts on the basis of the leading index
constructed by the Unit or any other composite economic series.

Further work toward making disaggregated predic-
tions on the basis of the leading index should, however, result in a substantial increase in its usefulness. Namely, for the index to be of most value to
the individual businessman it must be possible to
define the relative timing and sensitivity of individual business sectors.

From experience at the national level it is evident that individual components of a given business
sector are subject to substantially different cyclical timing. Thus, in the retail sector sales of
durable goods decline earlier and more sharply than
nondurable sales; in the manufacturing sector orders
for producers' durable equipment are generally the
last to decline. Similarly, bank loans to businesses,
the interest rate, and consumer prices all tend to
lag behind declines in retail sales and employment.
Additional experience with the leading index for
Philadelphia should then make it possible to predict
when softness in the various sectors of the economy
will appear, thereby considerably assisting businessmen in their planning. Furthermore, the extent of
the decline in those sectors earliest affected should
make it possible to estimate the expected level of
decline for the lagging sectors.

SUMMING UP

The procedures involved in constructing the lead index for the Philadelphia economy are as follows:

1. A set of thirteen economic indicators of the Philadelphia economy was formed. This set consisted only of economic series that, on the basis of national data, could be construed as either coincident or leading indicators.

2. Unemployment in Philadelphia was chosen as the only feasible broad-based current economic indicator that could be obtained for the Philadelphia economy. The Philadelphia unemployment rate as a percentage of the available labor force was estimated on the basis of Bureau of Employment Security data for the Philadelphia SMSA and other subsidiary indicators for the Philadelphia economy.

3. On the basis of correlation analysis results, six of the indicators considered were identified as leading indicators suitable for inclusion in the index.

4. Following the National Bureau of Economic Research's amplitude adjustment procedure these six economic series were combined into an overall leading index in such a way that each indicator was equally weighted in influencing the index, despite the considerable differences in relative variation of the individual series.

5. The leading index was tested against the Philadelphia unemployment series to determine its validity as a forecaster of business downturns and revivals.

Results show that in the period covered, 1954-68, three distinct business cycles were identified: 1957-58, 1960-61, and 1967. After careful study it was concluded that the leading index had performed remarkably well in foreshadowing economic downturns and predicting cyclical revivals.

3

FINANCING
THE METROPOLIS

In this chapter a substantive analysis will be presented of Philadelphia's fiscal plight as revealed in several studies prepared by the Economic Development Unit. On the whole the material presented in this chapter is much the same in effect as the documents circulated inside the City government and used, in some measure, as a basis for City policy in 1968/69 and 1969/70*--though the text of the Unit's reports has been amended in the light of subsequent studies, and some arguments and statistical technicalities and methodological niceties have been modified.

Although the reports were not released to the public, copies were available to the Federal Reserve Board staff members who prepared the 1971 report "The Financial Future of City and School Government in Philadelphia," which covered exactly the same ground, using slightly different projection methods, and came to even gloomier conclusions.**

---

*Beginning July 1, 1968, the City Department of Finance shifted its budget programming from a calendar year to a fiscal year.

**A portion of the Federal Reserve Bank report is included in the appendix to this chapter and its methodology is commented on there.

PHILADELPHIA'S FINANCIAL OUTLOOK
FOR FISCAL 1975/76

Economic Development Unit
Revenue Forecasts

In preparing revenue estimating equations for
Philadelphia, it was decided to correlate, where
possible, the major revenue series against independently projectable economic variables. Thus, the
three Philadelphia income taxes as well as the mercantile license and personal property taxes were regressed against local and national economic variables.
Other revenue sources, such as licenses and fines and
income from other governmental units, having no fundamental relationship to regular economic variables,
were projected by trend extrapolation.

In the trend of each of the revenue series two
components of growth were recognized: (1) that part
of revenue growth caused by increases in the cost of
living and (2) that residual component of revenue
growth that represents a gain in "real" dollar revenues. In forecasting dollar series, greatest accuracy
is obtained when the two components of growth are
estimated separately. Each of the revenue series
was, therefore, expressed in 1968 dollars before being projected.* The projected yield in 1968 dollars
was then increased by an estimate of the extent of
inflation.

Projection of the rate of inflation was based on
the well-known inverse relationship between inflation
and the rate of unemployment. The following inflation equation was derived:

$$Y = 594.50 - 81.77X_1$$

where

---

*Deflation was based on averaging the four quar-
terly Philadelphia Consumer Price Indexes as reported
by the Pennsylvania Bureau of Employment Security.

Y = average annual percent inflation

X_1 = the unemployment rate*

Based on the assumption of an average annual rate of
unemployment of 4 percent to 1957/76 this equation
yields an average annual inflation rate of 2.67 percent, implying a 23.5 percent increase in prices
through fiscal 1975/76.**

The City's major tax sources are the three Philadelphia income taxes and the mercantile license,
personal property, and real estate taxes. Two adjustments were necessary to the historical yield of
these series. First, the historical yields exhibited
extreme variability because of variations in the rate
at which the taxes were imposed. To correct for this
all revenue collections were adjusted to reflect 1967
tax rates so that projections would reflect estimated
revenue at current tax levels.*** Second, each
series contained a regular component--current tax
collections--and an irregular component--collections
on delinquent accounts. Whereas current collections

---

*U.S. data were used in this relationship because
of the availability of better national unemployment'
data. The correlation between the U.S. and Philadelphia Consumer Price Index is so high that little er-
ror is likely from the use of U.S. data.

**This inflation estimate agrees very closely with
the National Planning Association estimate of 2.7
percent. Should current federal attempts to cool inflation fail, it would doubtless be an underestimate.
It must be remembered, however, that, historically,
declines in the rate of inflation have lagged considerably behind downturns in the business cycle.

***The last tax year considered was 1967, as data
on many of the local economic series were not available for 1968. The 50 percent increase in the Philadelphia income taxes in 1968 was recognized by increasing the revenue estimates for these taxes by 50
percent.

fluctuate regularly with respect to economic conditions, collections on delinquent accounts reflect,
primarily, the vigor and level of staffing of collection agencies. Fluctuations in the irregular component are sufficient to obscure the basic relationship of the revenue series to economic conditions.
Because of this effect forecasting equations were
based on current collections alone, these forecasts
being subsequently increased by the 1968 ratio of
total to current revenue collections. (This correction factor is given with each equation below.)

The Philadelphia Income Tax

The Philadelphia income tax is a tax on wages,
salaries, and unincorporated business profits. For
collection purposes it is divided into three categories. The wage and salary portion is collected on
the wages and salaries of all workers employed in
the City, regardless of residence. The earnings tax
applies to wages and salaries paid residents employed
outside the City and employees of government agencies
in Philadelphia that do not withhold the tax. The
net profits tax is collected on the earnings of all
unincorporated businesses located in Philadelphia.

Wage and Salary Tax. The derived equation for forecasting wage and salary revenues was

$$Y = -1,341.162 + 232.75X_1' \quad R^2 = 0.91$$

where

Y = current wage and salary tax collections (thousands of 1968 dollars)

X_1 = total U.S. wages and salaries (millions of 1968 dollars)

Correction factor for collection of delinquent accounts = 1.008*

─────────────────────

*The prime (') notation indicates that the varia-
ble was regressed in first-difference form, that is,
as the deviation from its average value.

Although an exhaustive list of economic variables was considered, only one variable was significant in explaining variations in the yield of this tax. It is notable that a national rather than a local income variable provided the best explanation, cogently indicating the deficiency of local income statistics.

Based on projections of the National Planning Association, U.S. wages and salaries were projected to increase at an average annual rate of $21.3 billion per year in 1968 dollars.[1] Using this value in the above equation and multiplying the result by 1.5 to reflect the 50 percent increase in that tax rate yields an estimated annual increase in the tax of $5.349 million, implying that current collections from this tax will reach $207.414 million in 1968 dollars by fiscal 1975/76. Adjusting for the expected 23.5 percent inflation gives an estimated current tax yield of $256.156 million by fiscal 1975/76, which is further adjusted to $258,205 million total tax yield.

Earnings Tax. For forecasting the earnings tax, no data were available on the most important variable-- the average annual number of Philadelphia residents employed outside the City. To compensate for this defect the equation was formulated in standard, rather than first-difference, form with a linear time trend introduced to reflect the obviously increasing number of Philadelphia residents employed outside the City. The derived forecasting equation was

$$Y = 2,145.739 + 9.080X_1 + 188.318X_2 2$$

$$R^2 = .98$$

where

Y = current earnings tax collections (thousands of 1968 dollars)

X_1 = U.S. wages and salaries (millions of 1968 dollars)

X_2 = linear time trend

Correction factor for collection of delinquent accounts = 1.373

Using the aforementioned estimate of U.S. wages
and salaries in this equation and multiplying the
result by 1.5 to reflect the 50 percent increase in
the tax rate yields an estimated annual increase in
the tax of $509.000, implying current collections
from this tax to reach $18.370 million in 1968 dol-
lars by 1975/76. Adjusting for the expected 23.5
percent inflation gives an estimated current tax
yield of $22.687 million by fiscal 1975/76, which is
further adjusted to a total tax yield of $31,148,000.

Net Profits Tax. In forecasting the net profits tax
it was necessary to recognize that the tax collected
in a given year is based on income from the preceding
year. In predicting the tax it was necessary to recognize this factor by lagging the dependent variables,
that is, by regressing the current year's collections
against economic variables for the year preceding.
The derived forecasting equation was

$$Y' = -221.252 + 3.233\,(X_1')_{-1} + .115\,(X_2')_{-1} + .135\,(X_3')_{-1}$$

$$R^2 = .75$$

where

Y = current net profits collection (thousands of 1968 dollars)

X_1 = U.S. personal income per capita (1968
dollars)

X_2 = small account commercial and industrial power consumption (thousands of kilowatt hours)

X_3 = number of Philadelphia businesses reported by Dun and Bradstreet

Correction factor for collection of delinquent accounts = 1.098

It is notable in this instance that both local and
national economic trends are represented in the equation. Although the level of net profits collections
is primarily dependent on the major national trend
as reflected by personal income per capita, it is
also influenced by differential movements in the local
economy as expressed by commercial electric power
consumption and the number of local businesses. The
failure of local economic variables to appear in the
preceding two equations doubtless reflects more the
deficiency of local income data than it does their
lack of importance.

On the basis of National Planning Association
estimates, personal income per capita was projected
as increasing by $77 annually in 1968 dollars. By
linear extrapolation small account commercial and
electric power consumption should increase by 1,918
thousand kilowatt hours and the number of Philadelphia
businesses decrease by 540 annually. These statistics
imply an annual increase in 1968 dollars of $259,700
per year in current net profits collections, after
adjusting for the 50 percent increase in the tax
rate. By 1975/76 current net profits revenues should
reach $22,978,000 after allowing for the estimated
23.5 percent inflation.

Mercantile License Tax

The mercantile license tax is a business gross
receipts tax. At the time of this study the tax was
applied to Philadelphia businesses at the rate of 3
mills on receipts resulting from deliveries inside
the City. Receipts from deliveries outside Philadelphia were not taxable. The tax was due May 15 for
the entire year, computed in advance on the basis of
the previous year's activities. The fact that the
current year's collections were dependent on the preceding year's activity was recognized by lagging the
independent variables by one year. The derived forecasting equation for the mercantile license tax was

$$Y' = -22.434 + 0.0306X_1' + 0.758(X_2')_{-1} + 0.111(X_3')_{-1} + 0.179(X_4')_{-1}$$

$$R^2 = .80$$

where

Y = current mercantile tax collections (thousands of 1968 dollars)

X_1 = U.S. industrial profits (millions of 1968 dollars)

X_2 = Federal Reserve Board industrial production index

X_3 = small account commercial and industrial electric power consumption (thousands of kilowatt hours)

X_4 = number of Philadelphia businesses reported by Dun and Bradstreet

Correction factor for collection of delinquent taxes = 1.088

Here again, although national economic variables--total industrial profits and the index of industrial production--are of primary importance in determining the level of collections, variations in the local economy are also important as reflected by two variables--commercial electric power consumption and the number of local businesses.

National Planning Association figures indicated a 7.74 point annual increase in the industrial production index and a $4,703 million annual increase in constant dollar industrial profits. As before, it was expected that small commercial power consumption would increase by 1,918 thousand kilowatts and businesses decrease by 540 annually. These figures yielded a constant dollar increase of $400,000 annually at the new tax rate. Allowing for inflation, it was projected that current mercantile license tax collection should reach $29,762,000 by fiscal 1975/76.

Personal Property Tax

The personal property tax was a 4 mill tax on the financial assets of Philadelphia residents,

excepting, primarily, savings accounts and obliga-
tions of the federal and local governments.* The
tax collected in a given year is based on the valua-
tion of financial assets at the close of the preceding year. For this reason the dependent variables
are lagged by a year.

Again, as was the case with the earnings tax,
data were lacking on the most important variable--
asset holdings of Philadelphia residents. To overcome this deficiency the forecasting equation was
formulated in standard, rather than first-difference,
form, with a linear time trend introduced to reflect
the level of assets of Philadelphia residents. The
derived forecasting equation was

$$Y = 2,240.338 - 94.955(X_1) + 35.600(X_2)_{-1}$$

$$R^2 = 0.87$$

where

Y = current personal property collections
(thousands of 1968 dollars)

X_1 = linear time trend

X_2 = December Standard & Poor's stock market index

Correction factor for collection of delinquent taxes = 1.041

In the above equation the stock market variable is
lagged by one year to reflect the fact that collections in a given year are based on asset valuations

---

*It should be added that this tax is widely re-
garded as a joke and that most taxpayers understate
their assets by a wide margin. A vigorous enforcement effort using federal tax return information
could easily multiply the amount collected by several
times. To do so, however, would be self-defeating
because wealthy residents might well leave the City.

as of the close of the preceding year. The negative
sign on the time trend variable is notable in that
it reflects a declining asset base in the small city,
doubtless reflecting the flight of the more affluent
to the suburbs.

Based on linear extrapolation the Standard &
Poor's index was expected to increase by 4.4 points
annually. This estimate yielded forecasted current
revenues from this source of $4,908,000 in 1968 dol-
lars and $6,061,000 in inflated dollars for fiscal
1975/76, further corrected to a total yield of
$6,310,000.

Real Estate Tax

On examination of the deflated real estate tax
series it was immediately evident that no trend
existed in the yield from this revenue source.
Rather, it was found that after adjusting for rate
increases, the yield from the real estate tax had
with some variability just managed to keep pace with
the rate of inflation. The real estate tax return
was therefore projected to remain constant at
$104,486,000 in 1968 dollars. In current dollars it
was projected to increase at the rate of inflation,
reaching $129,040,000 by 1975/76.

No correction factor for delinquent accounts
collection was used.

Other Revenue Sources

With the exception of two items other City revenues were projected by regression against time of
the deflated series for the period 1958-68. The
equations and their estimated yields are listed below. In each instance X_1 refers to the time trend
variable and Y equals revenue collected in thousands
of dollars.*

───────────────────────

*For ease of computation the time trend variable
in these and succeeding regressions was centered
around zero, the value of the time variable equaling
-5 for 1958 and +5 for 1968.

Other Taxes.

$$Y = 5,536.841 + 175.579X_1$$

This equation yields a predicted revenue of $7,205,000 in constant dollars and $8,898,000 in current dollars for fiscal 1975/76.

Licenses, Fines, and Service Charges.

$$Y = 23,322.770 + 678.462X_1$$

Revenue predicted by this equation is $31, 803,000 in constant dollars and $39,277,000 in undeflated dollars.

Income from Leased Utilities.

$$Y = 16,447.138 + 576.485X_1$$

This revenue source should yield $23,653,000 in constant dollars and $29,211,000 in current dollars by fiscal 1975/76.

Income from Airport, Harbor, and Civic Center.

$$Y = 6,355.479 + 541.868X_1$$

Income from these operations should reach $13,128,000 in constant dollars by fiscal 1975/76 and $16,213,000 in current dollars.

Other Series. Additionally, income from reimbursement for commuter car debt service was expected to rise at the rate of inflation to $2,475,000, and income from additional self-sustaining bonds was estimated by the City's Department of Finance to reach $36,694,000 by fiscal 1975/76.

Summary

Overall, a substantial revenue increase was predicted by the City staff. The forecasted $304,365,000 revenue increase is, however, composed of numerous components, only one of which represents real growth in regular revenue series. If the 3 percent Philadelphia income tax rate had been applicable in 1968, revenue for that year would have been higher by $68,129,000. Inflation, moreover, is judged to be responsible for $125,936,000 of the increase. Additionally, $36,694,000 of the increase is accounted for by new self-sustaining bonds. Only $73,606,000, then, represents increase in real dollar income from normal revenue sources assuming the current level of tax rates.

Federal Reserve Bank Revenue
Forecasts Compared

The staff of the Federal Reserve Bank started from data for the fiscal year 1969/70, two inflation-packed years later than the Philadelphia Economic Development Unit started. They therefore found a higher rate of inflation and started their projections from a somewhat higher base.

Table 16 summarizes the projections of City revenues by both the Economic Development Unit and the Federal Reserve Bank staff for both fiscal 1975 and 1976 in current dollars. Data on 1968 revenue yields are included for comparison.

First, it should be observed that there is general agreement in the projections. The greatest differences appear where there is no rational method of projection, that is, in intergovernmental transfers, licenses, and fines and in new debt service on such facilities as the harbor, airport, and commuter transit system, for which plans change from year to year.

In spite of significant differences on these items the difference in toto is not great. The Federal Reserve Bank group projected annual revenue growth at $40.9 million, whereas the City staff projected a comparable value of $38.0 million. Thus, one would expect that the City total would exceed the Federal Reserve Bank total by about $40 million since it refers to a year later. Instead it is slightly smaller. Adjusting for the difference in years, there is a 7 percent difference between the two estimates.

TABLE 16

City and Federal Reserve Bank Projections of
Philadelphia City Revenues, 1968, 1970, 1975, and 1976
(millions of current dollars)

Revenue Source	City 1968	FRB 1970	FRB 1975	City 1976
Wages and salaries	112.0	178.5	239.9	258.2
Earnings	13.3	18.3	33.8	31.1
Net profits	11.0	15.3	21.0	23.0
Personal property	4.4	5.1	7.0	6.3
Mercantile license	21.9	23.4	29.8	29.8
Real estate	104.5	107.2	116.4	129.0
Other taxes	6.2	6.2	6.1	8.9
Leased utilities	18.2	24.5	35.1	29.2
Harbor and airport	10.1	12.6	30.1	16.2
New self-sustaining bonds				36.7[a]
Commuter car debt	2.0	2.7	6.8	2.5
Income from other governments	29.1	37.5	109.9	51.6
Licenses, fines, and service charges	24.9	31.1	33.0	39.3
Total revenues	357.5	462.5	667.1	661.8

[a]Most of this money applies to harbor, airport,
and commuter car investment.

Source: Prepared by the author.

Nevertheless, the Federal Reserve Bank figure is based on an inflation adjustment of 4.5 percent per year with only a small growth of real return from only four out of twelve of the revenue sources. Real growth as estimated by the City staff was considerably greater, from a larger number of revenue sources. Neither projection can be regarded as optimistic, but the one is a little less pessimistic than the other. Both, however, make the basic assumption that the tax yield will effortlessly grow with inflation. Neither bothers with an explanation of why this assumption is made. For the real and personal property taxes such an assumption seems unwarranted and for the other taxes it seems certainly something less than a foregone conclusion.

Economic Development Unit
Expenditure Forecasts

In the preparation of estimates of City expenditures it was early recognized that no rigorous statistical formulation, such as was made for the major revenue series, was feasible for this analysis. Whereas tax revenues fluctuate regularly with respect to local and national economic trends, City expenditures are most closely related to administrative expansion of departmental activities and to increases in City pay scales. (City pay scale changes are related to wage movements in the private sector, although in Philadelphia they generally had lagged behind.)

For these reasons the Unit's approach in estimating City expenditures was to predict the level of fiscal 1975/76 expenditures as they would exist if the current rate of expansion continued. Although such a procedure is not purely predictive in nature, it did permit reasoned judgments to be made about the City's fiscal outlook in 1975/76 if program activities were not expanded at a greater rate than they had been in the recent past.

Personal Services

The major characteristic of most City departments is their labor intensiveness. Total expenditures for most City departments can thus be forecast as a linear function of their personal service expenditures. Listed below are equations relating total expenditures to personal service requirements in 1968 dollars for those Philadelphia departments in which this method of estimation was deemed feasible. These equations are based on the years 1958-68, all data in thousands of 1968 dollars.

Police

$$Y = 126.847 + 1.064 \, X_1$$
$$R^2 = 0.99$$

Fire

$$Y = 2,195.246 + 0.974 \, X_1$$
$$R^2 = 0.96$$

Recreation

$$Y = 273.151 + 1.127 \, X_1$$
$$R^2 = 0.99$$

Public health

$$Y = 724.180 + 1.137 \, X_1$$
$$R^2 = 0.95$$

Free library

$$Y = 264.912 + 1.243 \, X_1$$
$$R^2 = 0.99$$

Fairmount Park

$$Y = 202.127 + 1.157 \, X_1$$
$$R^2 = 0.99$$

Streets

$$Y = 9,458.334 + 0.964 \, X_1$$
$$R^2 = 0.80$$

Other City departments

$$Y = 7,976.754 + 1.433 \, X_1$$
$$R^2 = 0.97$$

To obtain 1975/76 expenditure levels from these equations it was necessary to estimate the level of each department's personal service expenditures for

that year. Forecasts of personal service expenditures
are best obtained by estimating the two components
separately--the number of employees and the average
salary per employee. Whereas number of employees
should expand linearly with the creation of additional
programs, average salary levels are best represented
to increase logarithmically, that is, in percentages
rather than in dollar increments.

Average City employee salary levels were projected on the basis of data from 1959 through fiscal
1969/70. The average employee salary for 1959-68 was
estimated on the basis of Pennsylvania Economy League
data on full-time City employees and total personal
service expenditures as reported in the City's annual
financial reports.[2] Based on verbal information
supplied by the Department of Finance a 15 percent
increase in average salary level was allowed for fiscal 1969/70.*

Forecasting of average salary was based on a
logarithmic regression against time of the deflated
salary series obtained as above. The derived equation was

$$Y = 3.7215 + 0.0176X_1$$

where

Y = log of average salary in 1968 dollars

X_1 = time trend variable

Based on this equation the average City employee's
salary was forecasted to increase from the 1968 average by 35 percent in real dollars through fiscal
1975/76. Included in this 35 percent increase were

---

*A separate salary increase computation was not
made for uniformed employees, as a report in preparation by the Philadelphia office of the Bureau of Labor Statistics indicated that, historically, the
average percentage salary increase had been the same
for uniformed and nonuniformed City employees.

the somewhat substantial wage gains already budgeted
for fiscal 1969/70.

Based on data for the individual City departments from Pennsylvania Economy League documents,[3]
departmental employee levels for fiscal 1975/76 were
projected linearly on the basis of 1958-68 employee
numbers. For each department an average salary level
for 1968 was calculated and extrapolated to 1975/76
on the basis of the percentage salary increase forecast for all City employees.

The product of the above-estimated employee
level and average salary provided projections of fiscal 1975/76 personal service expenditures in constant
dollars. Substituting these estimates in the previously listed equations gave total expenditures in
1968 dollars. These were converted to current dollar
figures by the estimated 23.5 percent inflation.

Other City Departments

For several City departments the approach outlined above was not adequate. Expenditure levels
for those were based on service levels, differential
costs, or independent estimates.

Public Welfare. Only a small fraction of welfare expenditures are in the form of personal services;
rather, most of the expenditures are purchases of
services for welfare recipients. Departmental expenditures are thus best related to the number of welfare clients. The following equation was thus derived
to relate departmental expenditures in constant dollars to the number of welfare recipients:

$$Y = 3,724.941 + 0.133X_1 \quad R^2 = 0.95$$

By linear regression against time, welfare recipients
were projected to number 162,682 by 1975/76. The
equation yielded estimated welfare expenditures of
$30,107,000 in 1968 dollars and $37,182,000 in current dollars for fiscal 1975/76.

Philadelphia General Hospital. Neither the number
of patients treated by the Philadelphia General

Hospital nor the number of employees had shown significant increases; rather, the hospital's operations
had been subject to the same rapid rise in costs that
plagues all health organizations. Consequently, deflated expenditures were related to the ratio of increases in health costs as opposed to the general
cost-of-living index by the following equation:

$$Y = 3,074.839 + 96.281X_1 \quad R^2 = 0.98*$$

Based on logarithmic projection the index of relative
costs was expected to rise to 349 in fiscal 1975/76
from 245 in 1968. This index value gave predicted
Philadelphia General Hospital expenditures of
$36,678,000 and $45,297,000 for fiscal 1975/76 in
constant and current dollars, respectively.

Public Property. The Department of Public Property
provides building and equipment maintenance services
to the City. Its expenditures are thus most closely
related to the number of City employees. This relation is expressed by the following equation:

$$Y = 31,255.646 + 1.670X_1 \quad R^2 = 0.92$$

Substituting the number of City employees as projected
previously yielded estimated departmental expenditures
of $21,929,000 and $27,082,000 in constant and current
dollars, respectively.

Pension Fund. Anticipated pension fund costs for
1975/76, assuming current employment and salary levels, were supplied by the Department of Finance. Two
aspects of these costs--Social Security taxes and
City normal pension costs--increase proportionately
with increases in City total salary expenditures.
Adjusting for these increases yielded projected pension fund costs of $59,878,000 in fiscal 1975/76.

---

*The index was computed as the ration of the De-
partment of Labor's index of daily hospital service
charges to the Philadelphia Consumer Price index.
In computing the index the base year, 1953, was set
equal to 100.

Sinking Fund. An estimated increase of $38,193,000
in expenditures by the Sinking Fund Commission was
supplied by the Department of Finance. Only a small
increase was anticipated in the tax-supported segment.
Most of the increase was expected to occur in the
self-sustaining category and was compensated for by
an equal revenue provision in the general fund revenue section (shown in Table 16 as "new self-sustaining trends").

Summary

Total City expenditures were projected to nearly
double, from $389.8 million in 1968 to $706.5 million
in fiscal 1975/76. Of this $316,764,000 increase,
$134,452,000 is to be accounted for by the anticipated
rate of inflation. Since these expenditure projections were based on the rate of program expansion of
1958-68, any sharp speed-up in the rate of program
expansion over historical levels would make these
figures an underestimate and leave the City in considerably greater financial difficulty.

Federal Reserve Bank Expenditure
Forecasts Compared

Federal Reserve Bank staff projections of City
expenditures lumped together some of the separate
budgets projected by the City staff. But the text
of the Federal Reserve Bank report indicates that
the projections given are actually a summation of
considerably more detailed projections of major expense items within the departmental budgets than the
final data indicate. The welfare budget, for example,
includes child care (rising sharply), care of the
indigent aged (rising per person but declining in
number of persons), and custody of prisoners (similar
to the aged). In toto the departmental budget was
projected to rise rapidly (from $39 million to $85
million current dollars) in the five-year projection
period.

Table 17 summarizes the projections of City expenditures by both the Economic Development Unit and
the Federal Reserve Bank staff for both fiscal 1975

and fiscal 1976 in current dollars. Data for 1968
are included for comparison.

The sum of the Federal Reserve Bank projections
for the whole City budget, as shown in Table 17, is
a third higher than the total projected by the Economic Development Unit. Adjustment upward to make
the years comparable shows an even more remarkable
difference. The disparity is to be accounted for
partly by the more rapid inflation rate anticipated
by the Federal Reserve Bank staff. But the bulk of
the difference is found in four items: police, welfare, pensions, and other expenditures. This is to
be accounted for by the extraordinary increases in
pay and pensions for all City workers and the rapid
rise in welfare caseloads in 1969 and 1970. The former increase is related to the rise of militant
unionism among municipal employees and the presence
of a mayor in office whose main political base was
the union movement. The latter was related to both
increasing need for welfare and increasing awareness
of its availability in the City's disadvantaged population.

Both these themes have become familiar in the
past few years in the discussion of city fiscal
problems.

THE PHILADELPHIA SCHOOL SYSTEM
AS A SPECIAL PROBLEM

The school system in Philadelphia spends money
independently; but the City Council must levy the
taxes, and the city-county assessment and collection
agencies must collect them. Although the school
system does not draw on City funds, the revenue needs
of the School Board impinge directly on the City's
ability to raise revenues for its own purposes, for
the City Council must bear the taxpayer's ire. It
is difficult to conceive of a worse system for public decision making. Indeed, the City has in the
past been in the position of being forced either to
surrender some of its own taxes or to secure the
authorization for new taxes to meet the School

TABLE 17

City and Federal Reserve Bank Projections of
Philadelphia City Expenditures,
1968, 1970, 1975, and 1976
(millions of current dollars)

Administrative Unit	City 1968	FRB 1970	FRB 1975	City 1976
Police	70.0	80.0	175.0	135.0
Streets	33.0	40.0	81.0	48.0
Public health	11.0			11.0
PHILADELPHIA General				
Hospital	27.0			45.0
Subtotal: Health	38.0	40.0	65.0	56.0
Recreation	8.0			17.0
Fairmount Park	11.0			20.0
Library	7.0			15.0
Subtotal: Recreation (park and library)	27.0	32.0	62.0	51.0
Fire	25.0	30.0	54.0	40.0
Welfare	24.0	39.0	85.0	37.0
Pension fund	23.0	43.0	111.0	60.0
Sinking fund	49.0	59.0	102.0	93.0
Public property	18.0			27.0
Other expenditures	82.0			152.0
Subtotal: Public property and other	21.0	95.0	208.0	180.0
Total expenditures	390.0	465.0	1,000.0	707.0

Note: Empty cells indicate the absence of Federal Reserve Bank projections for the specific administrative unit listed.

Source: Prepared by the author.

85

Board's needs. The analysis of School Board revenues and expenditures below is thus extremely relevant to the City's fiscal 1975/76 outlook.

Economic Development Unit Revenue
Forecasts for the School System

Projections of the School Board's revenues were made following the procedure of the earlier analyses. In each instance estimating equations were stated in constant dollars to eliminate the erratic impact of inflation.

Real Estate Tax

As indicated above, the real estate tax, adjusted for changes in yield, had just managed to keep pace with the rate of inflation. Given the current tax rate the School Board's real estate revenue was expected to increase by the rate of inflation from $94,100,000 in fiscal 1968/69 to $116,214,000 in fiscal 1975/76.

State Appropriations

Appropriations from the State constitute the second largest source of revenue for the school system. This source was estimated to yield $87,015,000 out of a total general fund budget of $243,215,000 for fiscal 1968/69. Estimates for fiscal 1975/76 were made by regressing against time deflated 1959-69 State appropriations. The derived equation was

$$Y = 49.586 + 5,219.5X_1$$

This equation yielded revenue estimates from this source of $112,214,000 and $138,584,000 in 1968 and current dollars, respectively, for fiscal 1975/76.

Corporate Net Profits Tax

The corporate net profits tax was a new tax on business income authorized to meet the School Board's

fiscal 1968/69 financial crisis.* Although fiscal
1968/69 collections amounted to only $15 million, it
was estimated that if collection and enforcement efforts had been fully operable $22 million would have
been collected. Projections for this tax were thus
formulated on the assumption of a base yield of $22
million for the previous year.

Since there was not sufficient information to
project this revenue series independently, it was
projected to increase it the same rate as the City's
mercantile license tax. This implied an increase of
9.9 percent in constant dollars to $24,178,000. Ad-
justed for inflation this tax was projected to yield
$29,860,000 in current dollars by fiscal 1975/76.

Federal Appropriations

The School Board's general fund receives revenue
from all federal appropriations exclusive of special
federal poverty grants. In the past these appropriations have not constituted a large revenue source to
the school system, typically providing less than 3
percent of the general fund budget.

Estimates of revenue from this source were derived by regressing against time for 1958-68 the constant dollar sum of nonspecial federal grants. The
estimating equation was

$$Y = 4,239.273 + 596.454X_1$$

Adjusted for the assumed rate of inflation, nonspecial
federal grants were predicted to reach $11,397,000
by fiscal 1975/76.

Unearned Income Tax

In fiscal 1968/69 a 2 percent tax on unearned
income was authorized for the School Board as a

---

*The legislation authorizing the corporate net
income tax provided that the general business tax
would be discontinued after the current fiscal year.

higher yielding alternative to the old 4 mill personal
property tax, which it replaced. It is estimated
that the tax should have yielded $5 million in fiscal
1968/69, although, because of the lag in setting up
collection and enforcement machinery, actual receipts
amounted to only $3.2 million. In the estimation of
this tax's yield for 1975/76 a $5 million base yield
for fiscal 1968/69 was assumed. Because of the lack
of an adequate data series on the tax, its yield was
forecasted by assuming that its revenue would increase
by the same percentage as the City's personal property
tax. This method of estimation yielded forecasted
revenue of $7,194,000 in current dollars for fiscal
1975/76.

Parimutual Tax

In the four years preceding the study the parimutual tax showed no increase in yield after deflation by the Philadelphia Consumer Price Index. Thus,
the yield of this tax was forecasted to increase by
the predicted rate of inflation from $1,822,000 to
$2,250,000 in fiscal 1975/76.

Miscellaneous Revenues

In addition to its regular revenues the School
Board receives income from various additional sources,
such as income from school cafeterias and tuition
fees for nonresidents. For projection purposes these
revenues were treated as a group.

The following equation was derived by regressing
deflated income from this source against time for
the years 1958-68:

$$Y = 2,189.235 + 284.345X_1$$

This equation estimated constant dollar receipts of
$5,601,000. In current dollars miscellaneous revenues
were predicted to reach $6,917,000 by fiscal 1975/76.

Summary

General fund receipts were thus anticipated by
the Economic Development Unit to increase from the

estimated fiscal 1968/69 level by the relatively moderate amount of $88,001,000. Of this projected in-
crease $59,448,000 is to be accounted for by infla-
tion, growth in real revenues amounting to only
$28,553,000. Most of the growth in real revenue was
expected to arise from the projected increase in
State appropriations. Table 18, then, highlights
one of the School Board's most pressing problems--
the extremely slow rate of growth in real dollar
revenues yielded by most of the taxes on which it
depends.

Federal Reserve Bank Revenue
Forecasts for the School
System Compared

The Federal Reserve Bank staff was considerably
more optimistic than the Economic Development Unit,
principally with respect to state aid, as will be
seen from Table 18. Their figures, however, included
returns from the general business tax and the then-
proposed commercial occupancy tax. The City staff
had anticipated abandonment of the former and had
never heard of the latter. The anticipation of a
huge increase in State subventions was without foundation, as subsequent events showed.*

Economic Development Unit
Expenditure Forecasts
for the School System

Corresponding to its analysis of City expenditures, the Economic Development Unit's approach in
estimating school system revenue requirements was to
estimate what school expenditures would total in fiscal 1975/76 if the current rate of increase in costs
continued. Simple extrapolation of total general
fund expenditures was not deemed feasible for two

---

*Until the time of this writing (mid-1971) the
State was still struggling with a state aid formula
that was grossly unfair to the big cities and likely
to produce no more than $26 million to $28 million;
it had just barely managed to pass a constitutionally
sound income tax to pay for it.

TABLE 18

City and Federal Reserve Bank Revenue Projections
for the School System, 1969, 1970, 1975, and 1976
(millions of current dollars)

Revenue Source	City 1969	FRB 1970	FRB 1975	City 1976
Real estate	94.1	95.2	104.3	116.2
Corporate net profits	15.0	16.1	22.0	29.9
Federal government	4.7	6.0	8.0	11.4
State government	87.0	140.0	280.0	138.6
Unearned income	3.2	3.0	4.9	7.2
Parimutual betting[a]	1.8	4.4	2.5	2.3
General business	14.8	12.7	17.6	0
Miscellaneous[a]	4.0	2.1	2.5	6.9
Commercial occupancy[b]	--	0	19.7	--
Total revenues	224.4	279.6	461.5	312.4

[a]No explanation is available for the inconsistency of the figures for parimutual betting and for miscellaneous sources. After the project was completed, it was determined that flat racing would move across the City boundary into Bucks County in 1972, cutting the betting tax return by a half, but this move had not been announced at the time of the City staff's study.

[b]This tax was approved by the City in 1969 but declared unconstitutional by the courts (based on the uniformity provision). Another tax in the 1969 package, an across-the-bar liquor tax was vetoed by the Mayor.

Source: Prepared by the author.

reasons: (1) As a result of the School Board's proposed capital program, debt service requirements
would increase at a much faster rate than in the recent past and (2) the number of students also would
not expand at the same rate as in the past.

The methodology used, therefore, was to extrapo-
late general fund expenditures per pupil exclusive
of debt service costs, multiplying this figure by
the expected increase in the number of students and
adding to the result an independent projection of
debt service costs.

Noncapital costs per pupil in 1968 dollars were
projected from 1958-68 data on the basis of the following equation:

$$Y = 573.545 + 35.855X_1$$

This equation predicted real dollar expenditures to
reach $1,003.81 per pupil by 1975/76, an increase of
approximately $30 per year from the current level.*
This figure multiplied by the School Board's projection of a 307,100 enrollment by fiscal 1975/76
yielded noncapital costs of $308,269,000 in 1968 dol-
lars and $370,848,000 in inflated dollars.

The current School Board capital program envisioned total capital costs of $395.5 million through
1975/76. Based on figures prepared by the City Department of Finance and assuming a 6.5 percent average
interest rate, debt service costs were projected at
$51,132,000 by the end of the projection period.
Adding this amount to the projected noncapital costs
yielded 1975/76 total expenditures of $421,980,000
in current dollars.

---

*To a considerable extent the predicted rise in
real dollar costs per pupil reflected the judgment
that junior and senior high school attendance would
continue to grow more rapidly than elementary school
attendance. Costs per pupil are approximately a
third higher for junior high schools and a half higher
for senior high schools than for elementary schools.

Federal Reserve Bank Expenditure
Forecasts for the School
System Compared

The Federal Reserve Bank staff made estimates
of several variables within the general fund budget
of the School Board. By doing so it arrived at a
much higher estimate of total costs than did the
City staff, as will be seen from Table 19. With
costs rising at a rate of $72 million per year, the
Federal Reserve Bank figure would be $715 million
for 1976, 75 percent higher than the City staff estimate. Since the City staff did not supply its 1968
figures, however, a comparison of starting figures
cannot be made.

The Federal Reserve Bank staff estimated trends
of growth in number of pupils and cost per pupil in

TABLE 19

City and Federal Reserve Board Expenditure
Projections for the School System,
1969, 1970, 1975, and 1976
(millions of current dollars)

	City	Federal Reserve Board		City
	1969	1970	1975	1976
Administration and miscellaneous		(18.0)	(40.0)	
Education		(235.0)	520.0	
Elementary		(115.0)	(213.0)	
Secondary		(113.0)	(288.0)	
Vocational		(7.0)	(19.0)	
General fund		253.0	560.0	370.8
Debt service		29.0	83.0	51.1
Total expenditures	253.2	282.0	643.0	422.0

Note: Empty cells indicate the absence of City
projections for the specific items listed.

Source: Prepared by the author.

three levels of schools, both of which are rising.
And it is likely that spending will rise even faster
following the teachers' strike of 1971.

The largest projected growth rate in expenditures
was in debt service, 1975 spending being estimated at
almost three times the figure for 1970. Most of the
district's school plant was overaged when the new
School Board took over in 1958; and by 1970 it was
still far from the goal of having modern fireproof
schools for all pupils. This situation accounted
for the huge capital expenditures required, but a
near-doubling of interest rates was a major factor
in increased debt service figures.

The Gap

The projected growth in School Board expenditures
contrasts sharply with the anticipated growth in
revenues. The City staff projected a gap of $109.6
million by 1976; the Federal Reserve Bank, a gap of
$181.5 million in 1975. In each case expenditures
exceed revenues by something like a third.

And the projected crisis had already begun by
mid-1971. Fiscal collapse of the Catholic schools
is also threatened, and a probable rapid escalation
of enrollment in the public system as a consequence.
The School Board has canceled most of the projected
capital expenditures program and reduced school programs drastically, dropping athletics, most adult
education, music, and other fringe benefits of the
educational system. A new set of projections probably
would show a gap of 50 percent or more by 1975/76.

Closing the Gap

According to the estimates of the Economic Development Unit the Philadelphia School Board faces a
most pressing financial problem, namely, a projected
revenue deficit of $109,564,000 by fiscal 1976.
The City's general fund faces a similar, though less
severe, financial problem. Projected expenditures
of $706,584,000 will exceed projected revenues of
$661,835,000 by $44,749,000.

The Federal Reserve Bank staff projected the
gap for the City as much larger: $332.9 million in
1975. The School Board gap was estimated at $129.6
million and $181.5 million for 1975.

The revenue gap described above places the City
as the common taxing authority for both City and
School Board in the throes of an almost inexorable
dilemma. On the one hand, the City is trying to
stimulate an economic revival. On the other hand,
the City is burdened with a population most of which
is not self-supporting in its demands for public services. Increasing the tax on individuals will only
encourage the flight of the more affluent and indirectly stimulate the further decline of businesses
to the extent that the effect of the wage tax must
be compensated by higher wages in order to compete
with the suburbs for workers. Additional direct
business taxes can only further hasten that very deterioration of the business environment that the
City is dedicated to alleviating.

Clearly, then, the City must make every attempt
to obtain the necessary additional revenues from external sources so that it will not be further hindered
in attempting to implement the economic revival to
which it is dedicated. There are two avenues through
which such external funds might be obtained: (1)
revenue sharing on the part of the federal government
and (2) a more equitable distribution of State educational appropriations such that the major cities,
burdened as they are with a heavy load of other governmental activities, would receive a higher proportion of such appropriations.

Revenue Sharing

The provision of revenue sharing has long been
sought by city officials throughout the country.
It has been viewed as the one means whereby large
cities could meet the extensive public service demands occasioned by having a large number of city
residents who are incapable of paying for the public
services they need, while, at the same time, not
further worsening the competitive position of the

cities in attracting more affluent citizens so as to
balance their socioeconomic composition. It seems
appropriate, therefore, to examine the revenue-sharing
program proposed by the Nixon administration, but
shelved as part of the economic stabilization program,
to see how far it will help Philadelphia in meeting
its anticipated revenue deficit--if the legislation
is effected as proposed.

The amount of revenue reverting to the city is
based on a two-step procedure. First, the percentage
of the total distribution that each state receives
is based on the state's population and the ratio of
state and local taxes to total personal income of
the state's residents. Based on 1967 statistics
Pennsylvania would have received 4.96 percent of an
initial distribution of $500 million in fiscal
1970/71. Second, the amount of this sum retained
by the state is equal to the state's share of total
state and local taxes. For Pennsylvania this would
have amounted to 76 percent, or 18.8 million, in
fiscal 1970/71. The remaining 24 percent would have
gone to local governments. Philadelphia would have
been allocated 33 percent, or $2 million, of this
amount, since the City collects 33 percent of all
local taxes in the State.[4]

The revenue-sharing proposal thus recognizes
differentials of "tax effort" between states, and
its proponents make much of this. But there is no
recognition of this principle between jurisdictions
within the states; and while income differentials and
tax effort differentials between states are not large
--and are getting smaller--they are large and growing
between municipalities within the states.*

---

*The highest state per capita income is not dou-
ble the lowest, whereas minor civil division median
incomes (per capita data are not available) within
the Philadelphia metropolitan area vary by a ratio
of 3 to 1. Historic trends of change in income are
well known to produce a leveling effect among the
states and the opposite for the city and suburban
areas in any large metropolitan area.

Revenue sharing then, as proposed, will not go
far in plugging the expected revenue gap for the
City of Philadelphia. Even with the $5 billion fed-
eral distribution expected in fiscal 1975/76, the
City's share would amount to only $20 million. It
has been pointed out that part of the low yield is
occasioned by the fact that Philadelphia has an independent school district and that, therefore, its
revenues are part of the State's rather than the
City's total revenue effort. Even were the State to
pass through to the City the amount attributable to
the School Board's revenue effort, only $766,600
would be added in fiscal 1970/71 and $7,666,000 in
fiscal 1975/76. The maximum that the City could expect to receive is then approximately $27.6 million
in fiscal 1975/76.

Thus, revenue-sharing hardly constitutes the
hoped-for financial panacea for Philadelphia and
other hard-pressed central cities. The reason it
will be so little effective is that, in the interest
of gaining political acceptance for the program,
revenue has been provided for every hamlet throughout
the country. Indeed, it is to be expected that the
proposed aid formula would not help central cities
so much, proportionately, as the wealthy suburbs
least in need.[5] And clearly the major tax problem
of the decade is not to help the suburbs but, rather,
to provide an external source of funds whereby the
central cities can redress their population imbal-
ances, become less competitively disadvantaged with
respect to their suburbs, and become once again viable economic entities. The Nixon proposal does pre-
cisely the opposite: It rewards the suburbs for
being rich and promises to make moving to the suburbs
even more attractive than it is now.

Since the enactment of revenue-sharing legislation with such provisions would be so severely damaging to Philadelphia, the City's executives and
legislators, recognizing the peculiar problems of
urban core cities, should spearhead an urban coalition with the objective of obtaining a provision in
the revenue-sharing proposal such that a much more
significant percentage of the available funds would

be channeled into the decaying urban areas where
they are most needed.   Lacking such a provision, the
revenue-sharing proposal should be defeated.

Many other alternatives to revenue sharing have
been suggested; and one from a particularly respectable source should be considered here.   The Committee
for Economic Development proposes, after disposing
of revenue sharing on the grounds described above,[6]
that federal grants should be related to actual need,
should be limited to jurisdictions making a real effort to help themselves, and should encourage reform
and improvement of administrative structures.   General
revenue sharing meets none of those criteria.   On
the contrary it "will help to fix in perpetuity the
ills and contradictions that plague state and local
institutions everywhere."

By way of application of these principles the
Committee proposes improvements in the present systems of grants-in-aid and inclusion of state and
local income taxes as credits toward payment on the
federal income tax.   And, most important, it proposes
a shift of all welfare costs to the federal govern-
ment--which alone would relieve all but a few cases
of urban financial distress.

Welfare problems, in the Committee's view, are
national in character; and whereas the record of
the state and local welfare delivery systems is de-
plorable, the record of the federal administration
commands universal respect.   The problem arises from
"the nationwide effects of population movements resulting from changes in agriculture and in the nature of modern society," which are completely out of
the control of state and local governments.

The effect on Philadelphia of a shift of all
welfare costs to the federal government would not
immediately be very substantial.   The welfare component in the City budget historically has been less
than 10 percent of the total and is not growing proportionately.   The State, however, if relieved of
its heavy welfare burden, would be in a better position to assist the City and the School Board to a

greater extent. Moreover, if the welfare system was
better run and more generous, the City's poor would
have better incomes, would be less financially dependent in terms of services, and would eventually produce better tax yields. Such indirect benefits are
not to be dismissed lightly, but turning an $85 mil-
lion item (Federal Reserve Bank projection) over to
the federal government would not resolve the problem
of the $333 million projected deficit for the City
and would do nothing to offset the $180 million pro-
jected deficit of the School Board.

State Educational Appropriations

As does the Nixon administration in its revenue-
sharing plan, the State, in its provision of appropriations to local school districts, overlooks the
plight of urban core cities. Philadelphia, like
other central cities, has a higher percentage of its
population in low income groups and a considerable
deficiency in the middle and upper income groups as
compared with its surrounding suburbs. Philadelphia
thus has much higher public expenditure needs for
police and fire protection, health and hospitals,
recreation, and so forth than do the other counties
of the SMSA. These expenditures are so high that
Philadelphia has only a relatively small percentage
of its budget available for educational purposes.

A recent study by the Economic Development Unit
showed that the ring of suburban counties around
Philadelphia--Bucks, Chester, Delaware, and Montgom-
ery--had about 70 percent of their total direct general expenditures available for education, whereas
Philadelphia had only 30 percent so available.

The high level of other governmental expenditures
severely restricts the ability of Philadelphia to
provide quality education through increased taxation.
Taxes in Philadelphia thus have a distinct aspect of
income redistribution. This factor restricts Philadelphia's ability to raise further money for education as, beyond a certain point, resistance to further
income redistribution will be expressed either politically or through the maximally effective means of
the moving van.

The State in its aid allocation does not take
notice of the special situation of Philadelphia.
Rather, the school aid formula allocates aid on the
basis of real estate property value per weighted
average daily attendance.* A more realistic approach
would be to allocate aid on the basis of the real
estate tax base that would remain to support schools
after all other municipal expenditures were paid (assuming all local taxes were raised by a real estate
tax). If such was the case, Philadelphia would be
entitled to roughly twice its present proportionate
share of State funds, and the allocation of approximately $87 million would be very substantially in-
creased.

It is imperative, then, that representatives of
Philadelphia and other core cities within the State
exert every effort to publicize the plight of central
cities and obtain the proportionately greater share
of State appropriations that would enable them to
provide quality education comparable to that of the
suburbs. Such a judgment, however, unfortunately
runs afoul of the real power relationships in the
State and the City. The state aid formula is based
on "membership" (attendance), because a high proportion of the City's children go to Catholic schools
and upstate Protestant politicians use this fact as
an excuse to diddle the city slickers. The City's
strongly Catholic politicians go along with them in
the hope of getting state aid for the Catholic
schools,** arguing that if the Catholic schools col-

----

*In fiscal 1966/67 Philadelphia had 12 percent
of the State's public schoolchildren but received
only 8 percent of State appropriations. Subsequently
the percentage of State appropriations has increased,
but it remains below the City's percentage of public
schoolchildren.

**For many years the system was noted for its
penury, and its course of penny-pinching stored up
many of the overwhelming problems that the system
faces today. It was a common joke that the schools
were run at the convenience of the janitorial staff,
who were, in fact, better paid than the teachers.

lapse, the public schools will be swamped by a rise
in enrollments.

A campaign to revise the allocation system must
recognize these realities of power: the formula that
breaks the pattern must please at least two thirds
of the State's major power blocs. A resolution favorable to Philadelphia will probably not be achieved,
however, until the blacks develop a coherent political
grouping that is not easily deceived by ideological
issues and that can be delivered as a masse de
manoeuvre by black politicians with black interests
at heart.

Additional Tax Sources

If the attempt to obtain the needed revenue from
external sources fails, it must be raised by increased
taxation. And it was the responsibility of the Economic Development Unit to advise the City how needed
revenues could be raised in such a way that (1) the
increased taxes would cause the minimum possible dislocation to the economy and (2) the tax burden would
be distributed fairly among the population.

In one instance the concern for equity of the
income tax burden led to a study that demonstrated
that the highest income components of the population
paid only a minute fraction of their income in taxes.
This study was a major factor in the implementation
of the School Board's unearned income tax. Similarly,
concern for the possibly disruptive effects of the
City's business taxes resulted in a study that recommended that a value-added concept replace the gross
receipts business tax concept so as not to drive out
low-profit-margin businesses. This report was responsible for the School Board's new corporate net
income tax's being formulated on a value-added basis.
Finally, concern for the unfavorable economic impact
of the real estate tax resulted in a study of the
feasibility of a land value tax, an alternative to
the real estate tax widely favored in the professional
journals. In this instance, however, it was concluded
that the land tax would be an unacceptable alternative

because of the limited new revenue it could produce at a reasonable tax rate.*

Two factors are of vital concern if the large projected fiscal 1975/76 deficit must be compensated by additional taxation: First, the tax must be equitable and produce a minimum dislocation to the economy, and, second, it must produce continuing real growth in revenues. The second point is particularly important as part of the School Board's problem in that its major current tax source--the real estate tax--has exhibited no real growth in revenue at constant tax rates since the mid-1950s.

There are only two tax sources from which such a large revenue deficit can be met, that is, the Philadelphia income taxes and the real estate tax. To raise the necessary revenue by primary reliance on the real estate tax would require more than a 50 percent increase. A real estate tax rise of such proportions would substantially increase the gross rate of return necessary to justify new construction and improvements to existing construction. The effect would thus be to slow the City's efforts at urban renewal substantially. A priori, then, primary reliance on the real estate tax would cause considerable disruption to the City's attempts at economic revival.

A 1 percent rise in the Philadelphia income taxes seems, therefore, the logical primary source of revenue to bridge the gap if substantial external funds are not forthcoming.** Such an increase should provide an additional $104,110,000 in fiscal 1976. This increase plus the $27.6 million anticipated from

---

*This does not mean that the land tax as a reform of the present tax would not be a highly useful measure, over the long pull, in reviving the City's economy.

**The wage tax was subsequently raised by 3/8 percent to 3 percent.

revenue sharing, as proposed, would make up
$131,710,000 of the anticipated $154,313,000 deficit
total of the City and school district. The remaining
$22,603,000 would have to be obtained either through
additional business taxes or through the real estate
tax. Given that part of the wage tax is, in effect,
passed on to businesses in the form of higher wage
scales, and given the City's desire to implement a
business revival, a small increase in the real estate
tax is viewed as the less undesirable alternative.
A relatively moderate 9 percent increase in the tax
rate would achieve the desired revenue. Such an increase would be only half as large as the 18 percent
increase experienced in the seven years studied and
should not hinder attempts at urban renewal greatly.

Conclusion

According to the staff of the Philadelphia Development Economic Unit a modest note of optimism
is therefore justified: The gap can be covered
partly by revenue sharing and partly by relatively
modest increases in traditional taxes in combination.
The Federal Reserve Bank staff, on the other hand,
could not possibly be so optimistic, having projected
a total gap of more than a half billion dollars.
(Because of the lack of comparability of Federal Reserve Bank conclusions with City conclusions, the
former are printed, without comment, in the appendix.)

CAN THE PRESENT TAX PROGRAM
BE IMPROVED?

The Philadelphia Income Tax

Government should perform certain services for
the benefit of society. And people who do not pay
cannot be excluded from the benefits that result.
It is for this reason that contributions cannot be
left on a voluntary basis; coercive power must be
used to exact contributions. Some basis of alloca-
tions must be determined.

Any tax measure involves a decision about how
the burdens should be allocated among various payers.

Obviously the burdens should be distributed "fairly"
or "justly." But what, specifically, do fairness and
justice imply? Fiscal theory has traditionally distinguished between two approaches to financing gov-
ernment--the benefit approach and ability-to-pay
approach. These two approaches will be outlined and
the Philadelphia income tax will be related to these
approaches.

As to Philadelphia, the income tax applies both
to residents and to nonresidents employed in the
City. However, suburban communities are legislatively
prevented from taxing Philadelphia residents employed
in their jurisdictions--a fact that has led to storms
of protest from the communities surrounding the
City. Philadelphia has argued that it is simply
charging for the benefits provided by Philadelphia
to surburban residents. Further, the Philadelphia
income tax law defines taxable income as wages and
salaries and profits of unincorporated business, and
it levies a flat tax on these items with no exemptions
or other features that would lessen its impact on
low income taxpayers. It has thus been charged that
the Philadelphia income tax is regressive, at odds
with the ability-to-pay approach.

The Benefit Approach

According to the benefit approach the taxpayer
and government are seen as being in an exchange relationship. And since the relationship is one of
exchange, the rules of the public household are taken
to be more or less the same as those of the market:
the taxes paid by each person in the society should
be equal to the value of the services provided by
government activity. The benefits as a result of
governmental services must thus be allocated to individuals. And the traditional basis for estimating
the value of a governmental service is the cost of
providing that service, the implicit presumption being that there is neither an underallocation nor an
overallocation of resources to a service area. However, since most government costs are of the overhead variety, neither cost nor benefit can be allocated among citizens with a high degree of accuracy.
When the services are directly related to property,

such as water and sewage service, or when there is a
means test, such as with low rent public housing,
the recipient groups may be easily identified.   It
is less apparent how the services of the police department and public school system are to be imputed
to specific groups.   One approach to this problem is
to separate expenditures that result primarily in
benefits to individuals from those that primarily
benefit property.   Benefits are then allocated by
property value and income class.[7]

For Philadelphia, the benefit approach is used
as a justification for taxing the income of nonresidents who derive their income from activity within
the City.

> Despite their regressivity, payroll taxes
> are of some merit for core cities because
> they are a means of collecting some reve-
> nue from the commuting nonresident who
> works and earns his income in the central
> city.   Thus, payroll taxes--although they
> cannot be justified strictly on the basis
> of the "ability to pay" principal--are a
> means of recovering the costs of some of
> the benefits provided to the working com-
> muter (such as hospitals and health ser-
> vices, cultural centers and facilities,
> subsidized transit transportation and the
> like).[8]

The first argument for taxing nonresidents on
the benefit principle is, as stated above, that since
individuals, while employed in the City, receive services from the City, they should be required to pay
for those services.   Obviously, other municipalities
could present the same arguments.   And the argument
would, logically, lead to a taxing system whereby
both municipality of residence and municipality of
employment would be allowed to tax a person's income.
The prerogative would be shared between the two, and
the sharing would be in proportion to the benefits
provided by the two municipalities.   However, the
Pennsylvania legislation that allows municipalities
in the State other than Philadelphia and Pittsburgh

to tax income at the same time prevents sharing or
offsetting between Philadelphia and other municipalities. This relationship does not result if the benefit argument is rigidly followed.

It is argued in addition that nonresidents of
Philadelphia receive cultural advantages from Philadelphia and should pay for these benefits. And so
the income tax on nonresidents is a method of obtaining payment. Following the benefit principle strictly,
the nonresident users of cultural facilities should
be charged according to the degree of their use of
those facilities; admission or other fees should be
revised or instituted. Moreover, the nonresident employed in the City is not necessarily the user of
these facilities. And further, nonresidents who are
not employed in the City but use the facilities pay
nothing. Thus, payment for cultural benefits by the
means of taxing nonresidents employed in the City appears to be inequitable.

The second argument is related to the opportunities for employment that are provided by the City
for nonresidents: The City makes expenditures that
benefit employers and result in more demand for labor
in the City, and, therefore, nonresidents should pay
for these employment stimulants. However, following
the benefit principle, if employers receive the benefit, they should be the ones paying for the benefit.
Moreover, suburban counties could advance the same
arguments and claim the right to tax residents of
Philadelphia employed in their municipalities.

Arguing on the basis of employment opportunity
is too particularistic. The whole fabric of the nation's high income economy is dependent on the existence of orderly cities of enormous scale, inter-
change of a massive complex of skills among a huge
work force being the key to the efficiency of the
economic mechanism. More than any other political
units the central cities of the nation's metropolitan
areas have sustained and nurtured this growth--the
states and the national government more often than
not having been a hindrance rather than a help--and
crumble now under the strains of supplying the infra-

structure that supports the continued prosperity of
the metropolitan economy.

What could be a more appropriate measure of the
benefits accruing to the individual from this bearing
of burdens than the income derived from the metropolitan economy. Benefit, thus, is measured by the
taxpayer's ability to pay, which is identical with
income. And the State of Pennsylvania recognized
this implicity in a rare act of wisdom when it em-
powered Philadelphia to tax the commuter and precluded
reciprocity for income taxes at the home end of his
commuter trip. To describe this as an inequitable
way of paying for the benefits misstates the case by
miles. It was a matter of both utter necessity and
complete equity, and it saved Philadelphia from collapse for a dozen years. Along with Philadelphia,
it saved the structure of cushy incomes for suburban-
ites. (Of course it is inequitable for some subur-
banites to escape paying, and worse yet the tax fur-
nishes an incentive for high income workers to shift
both jobs and residence to the suburbs.)

Unfortunately the years of respite from fiscal
collapse have not all been spent wisely, and more
acts of wisdom are needed from the State and the national governments before another fiscal collapse
threatens to bring the very heart of the metropolitan
economy to a state of chaos.

In any case, the benefit approach in combination
with local government as it is now institutionalized
has a fundamental weakness. Rigidly following this
approach would restrict the scope and scale of local
government services--and so the benefit principle of
allocating tax burdens may be incompatible with
other objectives of society. There are some benefits
conferred by government that cannot, without defeat-
ing the very purpose of government, be made contin-
gent on the ability of the recipient to pay for them.
Common instances are education and welfare subsidies
to the underprivileged. Further, other services,
such as police and fire protection, of course would
not be withheld if people did not have means of paying the full cost of providing these services to them.

The State's preferential legislative treatment
of Philadelphia is not so much a matter of alloca-
tional equity as a matter of need. Philadelphia has
public finance problems that suburban communities
in the SMSA do not have, and a much larger proportion
of its population is composed of low income people.
This segment of the population requires more public
services than do more affluent groups, and it does
not have the resources that can be taxed to support
these services. The present Philadelphia income tax
is a method of shifting part of the support of such
public services to residents outside the City. For
providing needed public services for the underprivileged is not just a city problem; it is a regional
problem, a state problem, and a federal problem.
Providing such public services benefits all these
areas and in large part arises because of decisions
(or lack of decisions) made at the national and state
levels. However, only nonresidents employed in the
City pay for these basic public services while other
nonresidents do not pay. The benefit principle could
function on a theoretical level in allocating the
burden of local tax if there was not the concentration of the poor and the disparities in resources
between different communities. If there were full
subsidies from the state and federal governments for
providing all the services to the poor up to a determined minimum level, then the benefit principle
(barring the measurement problem) could operate as
an allocationally efficient taxing principle and the
income tax as a component of the total tax package
could be reviewed in terms of benefit received.

Ability to Pay

The ability to pay has been associated traditionally with progressive taxation, itself clearly
based on a utilitarian philosophy. Utilitarian
philosophy has justified progressive taxation by the
argument that marginal utility obtained by a person
from income diminishes as income increases: the
loss of utility from the loss of a dollar by taxation
results in less loss in total utility for an individual with a high income than would a proportional tax
system--and obviously a regressive tax system would

result in more loss of utility than either benefit
or progressive tax systems. However, in recent years
increasing doubt has been raised about the utilitarian
philosophy. Theoreticians have argued that the principle of diminishing utility does not necessarily apply to income as a whole, even with respect to one
individual. There also may be a prestige value that
hinders the operation of diminishing marginal utility
of income. As a consequence, it is difficult to
argue conclusively that additional increments of income yield persons less satisfaction than earlier
increments. Moreover, the utilitarian approach to
ability to pay assumes that each person has the same
capacity for happiness--that all persons receive
equal satisfaction from the first units of income
and that each increment of income adds the same satisfaction for each person. But it cannot be argued
that two persons who have the same income receive the
same total utility or marginal utility. And so it
is generally concluded today that interpersonal comparisons of utility are impossible. If this is so,
the disability that accompanies the payment of taxes
is immeasureable--and it is futile to base a tax system on utility.

But as one economist put it: Marginal utility
economics is the "curvelinear niceties of the obvious."
We should not throw away the obvious just because
the elaboration of the niceties is unconvincing.
Any tax is after all a social contract, in the pre-
Utilitarian sense, and there is a fundamental basis
for any such "deal" in a democratic society: the
belief that one man's needs are as good as another's.
Thus, it can be argued that the basis for any demo-
cratically determined tax is the implicit assumption
of equivalent utility for each member of society.

Present-day justification of the ability-to-pay
principle is more likely to be based on society's
nontheoretical attitudes toward the distribution of
real income--in effect, on unsophisticated value
judgments with respect to equity. It is indeed true
that taxation must be conceived as an instrumentality
for altering or correcting the distribution of income
or wealth, without which wealth would grow out of

control and the government would not have the means
to prevent anarchy, which would destroy the basis of
wealth itself. But, given this context, taxation
and disposition of revenues is a behavioral, not a
moral, problem. Taxation, even on the local level,
must affect the distribution of income, and it is
only sensible to face the issue and determine what
kinds of effects and results are desired.

First, income must be defined. Broadly the word
connotes the exercise of control over the use of society's scarce resources for one's satisfaction. It
does not deal with satisfaction but with the right to
command the use of goods that yield satisfaction.
The ownership of personal property constitutes control of society's scarce resources and yields a flow
of benefits in a given period of time. These benefits should be included as income. Also, the rental
value of a house should be considered income because
homeownership yields a considerable benefit to the
owner. If benefits of this kind are not viewed as
taxable, the person who has such wealth essentially
enjoys the same as tax-free income. Especially older
persons owning their homes and other assets have considerable nonmoney income.

Robert M. Haig has presented a definition of
income along the lines just suggested:

> Income becomes the increase or accretion
> in one's power to satisfy his wants in a
> given period insofar as that power consists
> of (a) money itself, or (b) anything suscep-
> tible of valuation in terms of money. More
> simply stated, the definition of income
> which the economist offers is this: Income
> is the money value the net accretion to
> one's economic power between two points of
> time.[9]

Such a definition could obviously provide a sound
basis upon which to judge a taxpayer's ability to
pay. However, data on the distribution of income as
above defined are generally not available for Philadelphia. Data on the distribution of income provided

by the federal government are based on the Internal
Revenue Service's definition of income. And, obviously, this definition has certain weaknesses. It
includes capital gains only when realized, and, then,
only half of them are included in the taxable base.
Further, neither income as the result of the ownership of personal property nor interest on municipal
bonds is included in this tax base.

These forms of income in all probability increase more than proportionally with total income
and must be kept in mind when judging the regressivity
of an income. Further, using a particular definition
of income, estimating the burden of an income tax
requires, initially, certain assumptions about the
incidence of the tax. (In the initial part of the
study of the Philadelphia income tax, for example,
it was assumed that the statutory incidence was the
actual incidence, that is, that the tax was not
passed on from one group to another but stayed where
it was levied.) Also, the regressivity or progres-
sivity of a tax may be judged in terms of a number
of varying taxing units. The tax unit may be the
family, the individual, the number of dependents, or
combinations of the above. And the federal income
tax, using both the individual and the family as the
tax-paying unit, introduces an element of family income.

Impact of the Philadelphia Income Tax

The Economic Development Unit began its study
of the Philadelphia income tax by defining the tax
base. The finding: Revenues from taxes on wages
and salaries were by far the dominant source of
revenue of the Philadelphia income tax. Therefore,
it was intuitively known that the Philadelphia income
tax was regressive. However, the extent of the regressivity was not known, and a purpose of the study
was to estimate the regressivity of the Philadelphia
income tax paid by residents of Philadelphia. The
results are presented in terms of the rate of taxation in 1964 for residents of Philadelphia in relation to their total income, if they had been taxed
at the current rate of 2 percent. (See Table 20.)

TABLE 20

Philadelphia Income Tax as a Percentage of Adjusted
Gross Income, Before and After, Allowing for
Deduction on Federal Tax Return,
Extrapolated from 1964 Data
(in percent)

Adjusted Gross Income	Before	After
Under $600	1.93	1.93
$600 under $1,000	1.69	1.69
$1,000 under $2,000	1.62	1.62
$2,000 under $3,000	1.69	1.69
$3,000 under $4,000	1.78	1.42
$4,000 under $5,000	1.84	1.47
$5,000 under $6,000	1.88	1.55
$6,000 under $7,000	1.90	1.56
$7,000 under $8,000	1.91	1.53
$8,000 under $9,000	1.91	1.53
$9,000 under $10,000	1.91	1.53
$10,000 under $15,000	1.87	1.50
$15,000 under $20,000	1.76	1.28
$20,000 under $50,000	1.58	1.10
$50,000 under $100,000	1.30	0.60
$100,000 under $500,000	0.77	0.26
$500,000 under $1,000,000	0.23	0.05
$1,000,000 or more	0.15	0.03

Source: Prepared by the author.

The definition of total income used was that of the
Internal Revenue Service for income tax purposes,
designated as adjusted gross income.

For residents having positive adjusted gross incomes, the estimated rate of taxation ranged from
1.93 to 0.15 percent. Residents having less than
$600 of adjusted gross income showed a rate of taxa-
tion of 1.93 percent, and residents with incomes of
$1 million or more showed a rate of 0.15 percent.
The rate of taxation for residents having adjusted
gross incomes of less than $600 was almost thirteen
times (12.97) the rate for residents having adjusted
gross incomes of $1 million or more.

Moreover, since local income taxes are deductible
on federal income tax returns, the additional tax
that must be paid as a result of Philadelphia income
tax on a net basis depends on the marginal tax
bracket of the taxpayer. For example, if a person is
in a marginal federal income tax bracket of 50 percent and pays $1,000 in Philadelphia income tax, the
additional tax that he pays because of the Philadelphia tax after allowing for deduction on federal income tax returns is $500. However, if he is in a
20 percent marginal tax bracket, the additional tax
paid is $800.   (The second column in Table 20 shows
the effect of federal tax deduction on the effective
rate of the Philadelphia tax.) After allowing for
deductions of the Philadelphia income tax on the
federal income tax returns, residents having adjusted
gross incomes of less than $600 showed an estimated
rate of taxation of 1.9306 percent, whereas residents
having more than $1 million of adjusted gross income
showed an estimated rate of taxation of 0.0342 percent. Residents having adjusted gross incomes of less
than $600 paid at a rate of taxation more than 56
times that of residents having adjusted gross incomes
of more than $1 million, after allowing for the de-
duction of the Philadelphia income tax for federal
income tax purposes.

Computations were also performed to estimate
the effect on the regressivity of the Philadelphia
income tax if the base was broadened to include interest and dividends.   (See Table 21.)

TABLE 21

Philadelphia Income Tax as a Percentage of Adjusted
Gross Income by Income Class,
Extrapolated from 1964 Data
(in percent)

Adjusted Gross Income	Tax Base Plus Interest	Tax Base Plus Dividends	Tax Base Plus Interest and Dividends
Under $600	2.00	1.97	2.00
$600 under $1,000	1.80	1.73	1.85
$1,000 under $2,000	1.75	1.68	1.81
$2,000 under $3,000	1.78	1.75	1.84
$3,000 under $4,000	1.84	1.83	1.89
$4,000 under $5,000	1.89	1.88	1.93
$5,000 under $6,000	1.92	1.91	1.95
$6,000 under $7,000	1.93	1.92	1.96
$7,000 under $8,000	1.94	1.94	1.97
$8,000 under $9,000	1.94	1.94	1.97
$9,000 under $10,000	1.94	1.94	1.97
$10,000 under $15,000	1.91	1.93	1.96
$15,000 under $20,000	1.81	1.88	1.94
$20,000 under $50,000	1.66	1.87	1.94
$50,000 under $100,000	1.38	1.87	1.95
$100,000 under $500,000	0.84	1.83	1.90
$500,000 under $1,000,000	0.28	1.46	1.51
$1,000,000 or more	0.16	1.60	1.63

Source: Prepared by the author.

With interest included in the income tax base, the estimated rate of taxation for residents with positive adjusted gross income ranged from 2.00 to 0.16 percent. However, with both interest and dividends included in the tax base, the estimated rate of taxation ranged from 2.00 to 1.63 percent. With the inclusion of interest and dividends, the Philadelphia income tax in terms of this standard would have been only slightly regressive. And so it is clear that the primary factor that causes the regressivity of the Philadelphia income tax to drop is that high income groups tend to derive a relatively higher proportion of adjusted gross income from dividends.

It should be kept in mind that adjusted gross income does not include many forms of income and that excluded forms of income tend to be more important as a source of income for high income groups. For example, long term capital gains are included in adjusted gross income at 50 percent of excess of long term capital gains over losses. Adjusted gross income may actually be more regressive when a broader definition of income is used. It must also be kept in mind that the study did not take into account the distribution of benefits as a result of using this tax revenue. When that is also taken into account the tax and expenditure package in combination may actually be proportional or progressive. However, income groups may be receiving more in benefits than they are paying in taxes. Thus, Philadelphia may be engaging in income redistribution.

There are serious questions as to whether local governments should engage in income redistribution. If local governments take into account federal policies affecting income redistribution—such as allowing the deduction of local taxes—the federal government may, in turn, adjust its position in the light of local policies. Thus, differences of opinion about income redistribution between federal and local government could lead to an unstable situation characterized by continued oscillation from one policy to another.

Besides the theoretical problem presented by having more than one level of government engaged in

income redistribution simultaneously, there are pro-
ductional problems. If a municipality engages in income redistribution through its expenditure-taxing
process, it is questionable whether it has the power
to "significantly" affect income redistribution because municipal government is restricted in territory;
an individual who finds the redistribution of income
not to his liking can migrate to an area where it is
more to his liking.

It must be kept in mind, however, that municipal
government can engage in income redistribution through
its expenditure process as well as through taxation.
By establishing locally financed programs that primarily benefit the poor, a local government is engaging in income redistribution just as if it were
taxing at a progressive rate. A municipality may be
in danger of losing its tax base, however, if it
spends "too much" of its revenue on programs that
aid the poor; again, more affluent residents may
move away. Beyond programs designed to aid the poor,
regular public services are expensive in low income
urban areas; such a regressive tax as the Philadelphia income tax may be charging low income residents
for services received. And charging low income residents for municipal services received and avoiding
redistribution of income may be necessary to avoid
adverse effects on the tax base--even though it may
violate most people's sense of justice.

Business Taxes

Two taxes that were repeatedly in dispute in
Philadelphia were the general business tax of the
Philadelphia School District and the mercantile license tax of the City of Philadelphia; they were
continually opposed by the business community as being discriminatory and harmful to the economy of the
City. Consequently, the Economic Development Unit
undertook an investigation of the economic implications of these taxes, with an eye toward their modification in the direction of greater equity and increasing returns, by employing the concept of value
added as the base against which the City would tax
business.

Provisions of the General Business Tax and the Mercantile License Tax

The general business tax of the Philadelphia School District and the mercantile license tax of the City of Philadelphia were basically gross receipts taxes, imposed for the privilege of carrying on or exercising for gain or profit within the City of Philadelphia any trade, business, profession, or vocation or any manufacturing, commercial, service, financial, or utility business or activity. Gross receipts excluded receipts or the portion thereof attributable to any item of sale or lease involving the bona fide delivery of goods, commodities, wares, or merchandise in a location regularly maintained by the other party to the transaction outside the limits of the City.

The general business tax was levied at the rate of 2 mills on gross receipts or 2 percent on net income. Previous to 1968 it was applied only to gross receipts at a rate of 1 mill. The mercantile license tax applied to wholesale dealers or wholesale vendors at the rate of 3 mills on each dollar of the volume of business transacted or, alternatively, at the option of wholesalers, at a rate of 3 percent of annual gross volume of business, less the cost of goods and labor. In manufacturing the rate was 3 mills on each dollar of annual gross volume of business.

Both the general business tax and the mercantile license tax exempted receipts from sales delivered to locations outside Philadelphia. This removed much of the hardship that would otherwise have been imposed on Philadelphia enterprises that had to compete in regional or national markets. More important, however, both these taxes, alternatively, could be paid as a percentage of net profit.

The general business tax allowed the option of being taxed at a rate of 2 mills on gross receipts or 2 percent on net income. The mercantile license tax allowed the option of wholesaler and manufacturer to be taxed on net income rather than on gross receipts at a rate of 3 percent and 2 percent, respec-

tively. For it to be more advantageous to be taxed
on gross receipts, a business needed to have a net
profit margin of more than 10 percent--and there are
very few business areas that have such a net profit
margin. Therefore, it was advantageous for most
businesses to be taxed on net income. However, firms
that tend to earn more than 10 percent on sales pay
less than 2 percent tax on net income--and this lower
rate of taxation is offered with no justification or
rationale.

For the great majority of firms (which earn less
than 10 percent) the two taxes add up to a hefty bite
out of net income, on top of the federal and state
taxes.

Problems of a Gross Receipts Tax

A gross receipts tax is a very unsophisticated
form of taxation. It discriminates against low margin and nonintegrated enterprises. The rate of taxation imposed by a gross receipts tax on a low margin
producer can reach confiscatory proportions. As an
example, if two firms have the same net profits but
one has net profit margin on sales of 3 percent, as
in the case of many apparel stores, while another
has a net profit margin on sales of 30 percent, as
in the case of many jewelers, the former will pay
ten times as much in taxes as the latter. A 1 percent tax on gross receipts in the case of the low
margin firm is equivalent to a 33.3 percent tax on
income. Profit margins of various broad industry
groups were calculated to show the variation in this
ratio between major industry groups.

In 1964 the motor vehicle and motor vehicle
equipment manufacturing industry earned 13.23 percent
net profit on sales. The wholesale grocery and related products industry earned 0.94 percent net profit
on sales. If one hypothesizes that both these industries are taxed at 1 percent on their gross receipts,
the profits of the wholesale grocery and related
products industry are completely wiped out, whereas
the auto industry merely has its net profit margin
reduced from 13.23 percent to 12.23 percent. Ob-

viously a gross receipts tax cannot be applied at a uniform rate to all industries. The variations so far pointed out are variations between industries. However, the variations within industries are even greater. In any industry there are surely firms that earn more than 13.85 percent and others that have sizable losses.

An additional problem of a gross receipts tax is that it discriminates against the nonintegrated concern. The amount of tax imposed on a product varies with the number of market transfers or turnovers that take place. Part of the tax is avoided when market transfers are eliminated through the combination of independent business firms. And so it is obvious that the gross receipts tax subsidizes integration.

On the other hand, there are two advantages to a gross receipts tax. First, it does measure and charge for, somewhat crudely, the benefit that accrues to a firm from its exploitation of a location in an orderly city that has such services as police, courts and laws, fire protection, and the upkeep of public streets--the use and benefit from which are roughly proportional to the volume of business done by the firm. Second, revenue does not disappear, as it does with a profit tax, when profits decline, with the result that the yield is more stable than that of a profits tax or a value-added tax.

Effects of Business Taxes

The effect of Philadelphia business taxes is to place Philadelphia firms at a competitive disadvantage when they are competing for sales within Philadelphia with firms located outside the City. They may be a particular hardship on retail firms that sell durable consumer goods, such as major appliances and automobiles, for which items locational advantage is not very great. The tax has to be absorbed by these firms. For example, on the basis of national data, automotive dealers and gasoline service stations earn 1.13 percent net profit on sales, and since they have to absorb Philadelphia business taxes, their net

profits after local taxes are considerably less than
can be earned in other areas. The result is that
such firms will tend not to expand or, alternatively,
will continue to leave the City until they can earn
the same profit on invested capital after paying the
tax as they can earn elsewhere.

   In that portion of the retail sector in which
the market is a small neighborhood area, the tax is
probably passed on to consumers, because the demand
for the products and services of these firms are inelastic; a potential customer will not shop outside
of Philadelphia to avoid the tax. These taxes thus
have the aspect of a sales tax for services and products bought only in a local neighborhood market.
The wider the markets are, the more the tax will be
absorbed by the enterprise. Since poor people tend
to spend the greater part of their money on goods
that have a small local market (food, pharmaceuticals,
clothing, and so forth) and also tend to shop in a
smaller market, they have to absorb more of the tax
as a percentage of their income than do higher income groups. Thus, to the extent that these taxes
are passed on to the consumers, they become extremely
regressive sales taxes. Moreover, they do not have
the advantage of a sales tax that can be treated as
a deduction on the customer's federal income tax.

   The only saving grace of these Philadelphia taxes
was that they were levied at a relatively low rate.
However, these taxes at a higher rate would compound
the present problems. The present taxes have been
modified so that some of the injustices of a gross
receipts tax have been mitigated, the modifications
adding to the complications of legislation and further adding to the cost of compliance and enforcement.
Even if many modifications were made, there would
still remain inequities because of the ill-defined
tax base. If business is to be taxed--and perhaps
at a higher rate--a more equitable basis of taxation
should be chosen.

The Value-Added Tax as an Alternative

   The efficacy of a tax is usually judged by one
of two criteria: ability to pay or benefit. However,

in the taxation of business, the ability-to-pay doctrine has no relevance. According to the ability-
to-pay doctrine, a firm that earns twice as much income as another firm has the capacity to pay more
than twice as much in taxes. However, the more
profitable firm may be owned by thousands of low income stockholders, and the less profitable one may
be owned by one very wealthy individual. As this
illustration points out, to tax the first firm at a
higher rate obviously bears no relationship to
ability to pay.

It is the view of many economists that local
governments should tax business on the basis of the
benefit principle; that is, government should be
viewed as a productive factor employed within an enterprise, analogous to labor and capital or as an
external supplier of services resembling an independent business firm. In order to charge business for
the use of these productive services, there must be
a unit of measure of public services to business.
Creating such a measure is, of course, of necessity
a very imprecise process, primarily because most public services cannot be allocated to any one particular group; that is, benefits of the kind that make
for a better environment benefit both business and
residents. Further, benefits that may be allocated
primarily to a particular group often generate exter-
nalities, benefits that accrue to people other than
the direct recipient of the services. With regard
to education, for example, most of the benefits accrue to the recipient of the education, but other
benefits accrue as well, such as increased productivity of the labor force, a better educated electorate, reduction of social unrest, crime, and so forth.

The staff of the Economic Development Unit
took the position that the best base for gauging the
value of local government services to a firm was
value added to the firm's products in the course of
its business in the City, value added being defined
as the difference between the sales proceeds of a
firm and its expenditure in purchasing inputs from
other firms. The value-added tax would apply to all
firms in production and distribution channels on the

measure of value added by the firm. In effect, then,
the value-added tax would be a tax on the use of
labor and capital in the municipality to produce a
product.

Value added may be determined either by a subtractive or by an additive process. It can be determined by subtracting value of goods purchased from
other firms from total sales, or it can be determined
by adding profits and depreciation to wage and salary
payments. But the two processes do not yield pre-
cisely the same results. In the subtractive process
capital expenditures are, in effect, deducted immediately. In the additive process--assuming relatively
easy Internal Revenue Service rulings on depreciation
--capital depreciation is distributed over a period
of time. Thus, the additive process would probably
be much easier to administer on a local level; and
the definition of profits could be that of the Internal Revenue Service.

The value-added tax has been used by the State
of Michigan, where it is used instead of corporate
income tax, and it is used extensively by European
countries. Further, it was recommended by the Shoup
Mission and adopted by Japan after World War II. In
Germany and Japan the value-added tax replaced a
gross receipts tax. And, currently, the value-added
tax is the subject of increased interest in this country.[10] It even has been proposed by a former Treasury
Department tax expert as a substitute for the federal
corporate income tax.[11]

The value-added tax avoids most of the problems
of a gross receipts tax. Particularly, it avoids
the subsidy to integrated firms afforded by a gross
receipts tax. It also eliminates the problem of the
low profit margin of some retail sellers. A retailer
would pay only on the additional value that accrues
to the product because of the operation; he would
not pay on his total sales, but on value added,
which, in most cases, is approximately 20 percent of
sales. In other industries, where value added may
be as much as 80 percent of sales, the tax would be
greater.

The value-added tax base of the City of Philadelphia was estimated to be equal to $2.87 billion
in 1967--on the assumption that the current provisions of the general business and mercantile taxes
relating to deliveries outside of the City prevailed
and excluded value added to deliveries outside the
City from the tax base. The value-added tax base
was estimated at approximately 29 percent of a tax
based on sales. Thus, a tax rate of 3.44 times the
gross receipts tax rate would be needed to obtain
the same revenue using the value-added tax instead
of a gross receipts tax. Similarly, as a further example, a value-added tax of 6.88 mills would produce
the same revenue as the general business tax of 2
mills, without the option allowing business to be
taxed on net profits. The following table presents
the estimated tax that would have been produced by a
value-added tax during the calendar year 1968.*

Tax Rate (percentage of sales)	Revenue (millions of dollars)
2.00	59.2
1.75	51.8
1.50	44.4
1.00	29.6
.75	22.2

*The estimate of the value-added tax base of the
City of Philadelphia was based on data for 1967 general business tax payments by industry SIC code. The
tax receipts were divided by the tax rate to obtain
taxable sales by SIC code. Taxable sales for each
industry were multiplied by the ratio of value added
to sales of the industry. The ratio of value added
to sales for manufacturing was obtained from the 1966
Philadelphia County Industry Report, Pennsylvania Department of Internal Service Affairs. Wholesale, retail, and service relationships of value added to
sales rates were obtained from Statistics of Business
Income--1964, U.S. Treasury, Annual Statement Studies
--1968 Edition, Robert Morris Associates.

It was estimated that a tax of 1 percent on value
added delivered within Philadelphia would have resulted in $28.7 million in tax revenue for 1967 and
$29.6 million for calendar year 1968, as compared
with mercantile license tax and general business tax
revenues of $21.2 million and $8.7 million, respectively, in 1967.

The value-added tax does have certain defects.
First, since in most firms wage and salary payments
constitute the bulk of the tax base for the value-
added tax, it is primarily a tax on earned income
levied flat at the employer level. It is therefore
regressive in effect, and it has the additional disadvantage (like several other taxes on earnings) of
tending to discourage the hiring of marginal workers,
a matter of considerable importance in a city with
great problems of hard-core unemployed, unemployed
youths, and discrimination against minorities. Moreover, unlike the wage tax, it is not deductible in
the employee's federal tax return. Second, the value-
added tax is just as effective in driving business
across City boundaries as any other business tax.
It is useful only so long as the effective rate is
very small. (A rate of 2 percent is certainly too
high.) Finally, there are also considerable difficulties in the separation of value added in business
done with customers inside City boundaries from that
in business done with customers outside City boundaries. Since the tax rate must be kept very low in
any case, however, it would be sensible to enlarge
the tax base considerably by abolishing this distinction.

With all value added as the base for Philadelphia, the yield of $28.7 million noted above could
probably be gotten from a 0.5 percent rate, which is
well below any businessman's threshold of incentive
to move.

Conclusions

The two gross receipts taxes--the mercantile
license tax and the general business tax--were judged
by the Economic Development Unit not to meet the
criterion of a fair and equitable tax that produces

minimum disruption to the City's economy. And it was
concluded that replacing these two taxes by a value-
added tax would produce an equivalent amount of revenue without placing an insupportable burden on the
City's low-profit-margin business.

The Real Estate Tax

As of the first of 1969, when the Economic Development Unit began its study of the real estate
tax in Philadelphia, it amounted to 4.475 percent on
the assessed value of all nonexempt real property.
Total assessed value of taxable real estate was
$4,546,895,360. Applying the 4.475 percent rate to
this total produces a potential tax revenue of $203
million. This high yield remains the only aspect of
the tax above criticism.

The primary objection to the real estate tax
stems from the disincentives provided by the tax.
As one improves his property, the property is assessed
upward and one pays more taxes. Consequently, the
effect of this tax is to raise the price of improvements to property and new construction. That a tax
encourages or discourages certain expenditures is
not a priori undesirable, as long as the incentive
provided by the fiscal policy is consistent with the
avowed goals of the system. However, in the case of
property tax just the reverse holds. At a time when
the City of Philadelphia is deeply committed to urban
renewal, the taxing policy hinders its accomplishment.

While such criticism is appropriate, it is not
enough simply to suggest abolition of the tax. In
order to eliminate it, another tax must be substituted. And, consequently, the Economic Development
Unit undertook to evaluate the magnitude of the disruption actuated by the tax and to weigh it against
the potential drawbacks of the suggested alternatives.

An Evaluation of the Real Estate Tax

The proper approach to evaluating the real estate tax would be to trace the demand curve for improvements; then, the actual effect of the property

tax on housing and improvement expenditures would be
apparent. However, such a procedure is very costly;
therefore, estimates made by others were relied upon.
Margaret Reid concluded in her landmark study of
housing "that demand for space, as represented by
rooms, is quite inelastic, whereas demand for quality
housing is quite elastic."[12] In other words, holding
real income constant, a small change in the price of
quality housing results in a large change in the consumption of quality housing. In addition, she found
that "the demand for quality housing is highly elastic with respect to income."[13] Hence, as real income
increases, the consumption of quality housing rises
more quickly. When one adds the price and income
elasticities, the result is a highly elastic demand
schedule for quality housing. From Reid's analysis
one can infer that the effect of an ad valorem tax
on property is to decrease greatly expenditures on
quality housing and improvements to structures.

Further evidence comes from George Sternlieb,
who studied the declining areas of Newark. He con-
cludes: "There is no question that the fear of tax
increases plays a major role in inhibiting improvements. This is perhaps more a function of tax rates
than of assessment increases. . . . A more enlightened
tax policy would probably secure its greatest results
from the two ends of the ownership spectrum--the very
large owners and the individual parcel holders."[14]

In addition, the real estate tax creates an even
greater disincentive in slum areas, especially for
rented dwellings, than prevails for less risky classes
of real estate. The decision to improve a property
is based on the expected profitability of the expenditure. And, since slum housing is a rather risky
asset, the expected return on investments in slum
housing must exceed the return for other investments
in order to compensate for the risk. Moreover, the
additional tax liability incurred because of the improvement is essentially a cost on which a return
must also be made. Consequently, improvements that
are profitable with respect to one class of real estate are not profitable for the more risky slum real
estate. This dichotomy is aggravated by the inflation

of the cost of improvements by the real estate tax.

For commercial enterprises, locational mobility is the primary consideration. Tax burden is unquestionably important in the firm's decision to locate within Philadelphia. Once the decision has been made, the real estate tax tends to discourage construction and improvements by effectively increasing the price of such structures. Consequently, the firm tends to put less money into physical facilities than it might otherwise do.

Another criticism levied against the property tax is its alleged regressivity. Dick Netzer attributes this shortcoming to the fact that nonresidential property taxes are shifted forward to the consumer and, like any general consumption tax, fall most heavily on low income groups.[15] But this argument is unconvincing. The tax depends on the values in the real estate market created by the commercial uses. Those that serve high income uses typically generate much higher value than those serving low income customers.

In addition, some studies have shown expenditures on residential housing to be a decreasing proportion of rising income. Again, however, expenditures and values are not necessarily the same. The values accorded to higher income neighborhoods, particularly those that can claim racial exclusivity, tend to be far above what one would expect from the greater cost of development. Thus, the general effect of the real estate tax may well be progressive rather than regressive, in accordance with popular opinion on the subject. And, in addition to having this virtue, the tax has the related advantage of being levied on the basis of a fairly good measure of the benefits derived from several important urban services--fire protection, policing, and the upkeep of street and transit systems.

Further objection to Philadelphia's real estate tax arises from the very magnitude of the levy. Since the assessed value of property represents ap-

proximately 60 percent of sales value, the tax rate
of 4.475 percent constitutes an effective rate of
about 2.68 percent of property values. This is equivalent to a 26.8 percent tax on annual housing expenditures, assuming the rate of return is 10 percent.
This is considerably higher than the 6 percent tax
Philadelphians must pay on other purchases, thus
making other consumables cheaper than housing. Again,
to discourage one type of expenditure through fiscal
policy is not necessarily unsound and, in fact, can
be a very useful device when the effects are consistent with social and economic policy goals of the
system. However, discouraging housing expenditures
is not consistent with Philadelphia's economic and
social policies, and so reconsideration of the real
estate tax from this point of view is in order.

The administration of the real estate tax has
also been subjected to criticism, in that assessments
are not made on a uniform basis. The "Report on Real
Property Assessments and Real Estate Tax Revenues"
prepared by the Office of the Director of Finance in
1969 showed that the ratio of assessed value to sales
value for wards ranged from 40.6 percent to 72.1 percent. Such a substantial variation in ratios is indeed undesirable; however, there is of necessity
some variation. According to law properties are to
be reassessed annually. But because of the shortage
of qualified personnel available to the Board of Assessors, annual assessments are impossible; instead,
reassessments are made triennially. In a dynamic
economy property values are not constant; some decline as others appreciate in value. One would then
expect divergent ratios to reflect the progression
of economic life.

Certainly the difficulties associated with administration could be overcome without radical reform
measures that change the substance of the real estate
tax, but the occasion of a substantial revision of
the whole tax law would create the atmosphere needed
for improvement of the assessment and collection systems. Reform is also needed in the related fields

of the handling of delinquent properties, the collection of delinquent accounts, and tax exemption.*

A sweeping reform of the real estate tax is in order, but one that substantially reduced income from the tax could not be tolerated. The new form of the tax should not be a disincentive to development, and it should discourage speculative holding of vacant land or underdeveloped properties for long periods of time. It should expand the tax base if possible, and it should continue to utilize the measure of benefits mentioned above to some extent.

A Land Value Tax Proposal

The ad valorem tax on land alone has been proposed by many as a satisfactory alternative and, indeed, as a solution for solving every conceivable urban problem. The primary advantage of a land tax is that it does not interfere with human economic incentives; the most profitable use before the tax remains the most profitable use after the tax has been imposed.

> Provided that demand permits, it [the land
> value tax] would encourage owners to develop
> their sites more intensively, in an effort
> to minimize tax liability as a percentage
> of current receipts, since additional in-
> vestment in buildings would not increase
> tax liability. Within the individual ur-
> ban jurisdictions, taxes on vacant land
> would tend to rise, thereby increasing the
> holding costs of vacant land and making
> the speculative withholding of land from
> development a less attractive proposition.
> Thus, a switch to site value taxation is

---

*Interest and penalties, for example, are fixed by statute and for several years have been lower than the rate at which many taxpayers can borrow money. Thus, they can, in effect, borrow cheaply from the City by not paying their taxes, while the City must borrow to cover the loss.

likely to have its maximum impact in two
parts of a metropolitan area--in the central
areas, where it would encourage more investment in buildings, and in the outlying sections on the fringes, where it would tend
to discourage land speculation and resulting discontinuous patterns of land development (less "leapfrogging" over sites withheld from the market).[16]

There is no dispute with this argument in favor
of the land value tax. However, arguments that are
basically sound when applied to the classical theoretical model may lose meaning when applied to Philadelphia. The effect on vacant land, for example,
will be slight (for there is virtually no vacant
land left in the City) unless there is a simultaneous
reform in the suburbs. There are vast areas of obsolete structures and underdeveloped property that
cannot attract investment capital. In large part
this situation is the outcome of social conditions
that have nothing to do with taxes. Probably a
third of the black ghetto, housing 200,000 people,
and a quarter of the white residential area, housing
perhaps 200,000 people, are so unsafe as to be ruled
out for private investors except in the most unusual
circumstances. Public investment in these areas is
possible, but is hamstrung by the prices public agencies must pay to acquire land and buildings that
are now utterly useless. But two thirds of the City's
populated area and its major business and industrial
areas are available for private investment, and many
properties in these areas lie fallow largely because
the owner can sit on them cheaply and wait for rising
values to reward his inaction. If it was costly to
sit on them over a period of time, the prices of
these properties would fall and owners who lacked
the ability to improve them would have to sell out.
The objective in setting the land tax rate should be
to reduce the market price of land in old unchanging
neighborhoods substantially and prevent any further
price rises in progressive areas. By this means the
City's precious resource of highly accessible space
would be turned over to active developers rather than
be held by passive speculators.

The rate needed, assuming that land values are realistically assessed, is probably about 9 percent, which is three times the present 2.68 percent mentioned above. This would exceed the present rate of inflation of all values (about 4 percent) by enough (5 percent) to make speculative owners uncomfortable about being forced to double their invested capital input every fifteen years.

This rate would immediately triple the return from the quarter of the assessment role that represents land. But because the tax would arrest the rise or actually cause the decline of land value, new income from this source would tend to disappear over a period of time. Thus, no great increase in tax yield from the land tax would be anticipated. Indeed, it would work contrary to any great increase in yield, and it should be adjusted upward if land values rise more than proportionately to the general price level or downward if the rapid inflation of the currency slows down appreciably.

The tax on improvements should not be abandoned, for it offers a good measure of some of the benefits provided by City services and of the external costs imposed on the City by the improvements to property. However, it should not be so high as to form a substantial cost differential in comparison with competing municipalities, either by itself or in combination with other local taxes.

The current rate, by itself, does not compare unfavorably with the majority of suburban jurisdictions. But residents also pay the wage and unearned income taxes and businesses pay the City business taxes. Thus, the rate should be reduced as much as possible within the envelope of the total real estate tax yield. Simple arithmetic tells us that if the rate has been tripled on one fourth of the tax base, it can be cut by two thirds on the remaining three fourths of the base and preserve the same total yield.

Cutting the 2.68 percent rate on improvements to 1 percent would go a long way toward encouraging the improvement of vacant and obsolete properties if the current rate really is an obstacle. But it seems doubtful that it has been a great barrier since any improvement must produce gross returns on the order of 18-25 percent to cover financing and risk premiums. But the reduction would undoubtedly make feasible many marginal projects.

The effect of reduced land prices combined with a reduction of taxes on improvements--and compared to suburban areas that probably will not make any changes in their tax structures--could bring about a large resurgence of development in the City.

Since by far the largest number of properties show a ratio of improvements to land value close to the City average, most tax bills on houses would be only slightly changed. Many apartments and highly developed business properties, such as office build-ings, would be reduced. The taxes of the many small "taxpayer" shop buildings and gas stations, garages, and parking lots, which clutter the major streets in outlying sections of the City, on the other hand, would probably be raised. Manufacturing establish-ments, such as oil refineries having large land areas and taxable structures of relatively small value, also would face increases, but those located in loft buildings would enjoy reductions. Such establish-ments as parking lots and junk yards would feel the full effect of the tripling of the tax on land; some it is to be expected, would be unable to pay the tax, and, therefore, their properties would be put up for sale or go on the delinquency rolls. The City should therefore be prepared with new delinquency procedures. And among these should be a provision for leasing the land back to former owners, or new occupiers, for rentals less than the taxes on the land. Such leases would run for short terms so that the City could turn the land over for more economically viable uses when the opportunity arose.

If large areas turn delinquent under a higher tax rate and the City can find no new users who can pay the taxes, then it is clear that the City has overvalued the land. For such a contingency there should be a court-supervised revaluation and recapture procedure. But the history of assessment practice argues that this is an unlikely contingency; assessors habitually undervalue land in the face of the slightest doubt about its usability for the more intense urban uses. Indeed, the real danger is that the assessor would wipe out the effect of the reform in a few years by revaluing land further downward from its already general undervaluation on the tax rolls.* To prevent such a contingency a study commission of distinguished economists and other business and real estate experts, as well as assessment professionals, whould be charged with making recommendations for the modernization of the law and operational rules of assessment practice in the City. And another commission is needed to recommend a restructuring of the assessment and collection offices to rid them of abuses and prepare them for more efficient and timely service to the taxpayers and the City.

SOME FURTHER THOUGHTS

Fiscal analysis shows that the current tax-and-spend arrangements of the City of Philadelphia, fourth largest city and focal point of the fourth largest metropolitan population concentration in the United States, are rapidly approaching a crisis. Analysis of alternative taxing arrangements indicates that there is slight hope of increasing the rates on all the available tax sources without driving away

---

*Undervaluation is quite deliberate in many rural and suburban municipalities, even though everyone concerned will pretend that it does not exist, because it is quite illegal. But it is in everyone's interest--at least everyone who is privy to such affairs in these areas. The reasoning is that if assessments actually reflected real land prices, owners would be forced to sell and would be in a poor bargaining position. Development would then accelerate uncomfortably for the town government and the entire population of the town. Thus, everyone present has the same interest at stake.

the tax bases, namely, business activity, land development, and consumer incomes.

The revenue-sharing proposal put forward by the
Nixon administration is likely to make the situation
worse because it does more for the suburbs than for
Philadelphia; it would make the move to the suburbs
more attractive for the mobile tax sources without
in the least affecting the suburban governments' desire or ability to restrict movement of tax liabili-
ties into their jurisdictions.

It was hinted at in the concluding part of the
Federal Reserve Bank report that shifting of certain
cost loads to a more equitable metropolitan tax base
might give the City taxpayer some small measure of
relief. The policy statement of the Philadelphia
Economic Development Unit included another such
proposal. The Unit staff contented itself with proposals for better distribution of education subventions from the State. Those hints and half-a-loaf
proposals should be carried to their logical conclusions.

There should be a broad scale review of all of
the functions of government and related citizen activities and of the geographical distribution of
those land uses in the metropolis that support those
activities. From such a review it would be possible
to develop a fresh assignment of costs and benefits
and matching geographical jurisdictions to serve as
taxing districts for specific costs.

To provide an example of such a review, one
City government service system will be examined:
policing. For this purpose the policeman's function
is very broadly defined: The policeman is the government's Johnny-on-the-spot, the man who observes
or is first at the scene of a crime, an emergency,
or any violation of the public interest by man or
nature. He may correct the situation himself, call
in other services, refer the matter to other helpful
agencies, perform extensive investigations and sub-
mit his findings to enforcement agencies that have
broader powers, or actually restrain (arrest) citizens.

Policing functions can be generally characterized on the basis of the level of government that can perform them most effectively, the interests affected and the level of government that pays for the function. Functionally, eight groups emerge:

1. Beat-level social work: dealing with family quarrels, with drunken, psychotic, or sexually deviant behavior, with juvenile delinquency, and so forth and making referrals to appropriate social agencies as principal backup; providing emergency assistance in medical and behavioral emergencies, in case of fire and disaster, and so forth; providing information and an image of authority to the citizenry; reporting conditions for action to the City's housekeeping agencies, such as the sanitation department; and, as a by-product, reporting information for analysis and planning at the local government level.

2. Beat-level protection of persons and property: providing protection of persons and property from failures in functions 1 and 3; reporting facility failures and operation and maintenance problems (streets, trees, lights, signs, water and drainage pipes) and taking immediate protective measures; providing a protective presence of authority; reporting incidents and state of facilities for analysis and planning at the local government level.

3. Control of professional crime: controlling the work of professional criminals, including all usual activities defined as felonies and many additional ones now defined only as cheating the consumer or polluting the environment, except as covered in function 5.

4. Control of nonprofessional crime: dealing with amateur crime and crimes of passion.

5. Operation and protection of major facility systems: traffic control and accident assistance in the motor vehicular system; transit policing; protection and monitoring of utility systems, such as gas, water, electric, telephone, and drainage; air pollution control; airports; museums; stadiums and similar

places of assembly; schools and universities; rail-
ways and port facilities; defense establishments;
factories; shopping centers and business areas; hospitals, institutions, and recreation areas; fire and
housing code enforcement and property development
regulation; other environmental protection enforcement; boating, fishing, and hunting control.

6. Control of social unrest and social group
rivalry: control of riots and demonstrations; protection of minority groups, public figures, public
buildings and monuments, and other symbolic targets
in situations of social unrest.

7. Internal control: guarding against internal
police corruption and inefficiency.

8. Protection of the state apparatus: guarding
against corruption of government and protecting the
machinery of democracy; protection against subversive
plots and secret foreign intervention in domestic
affairs.

These policing functions are performed by a
variety of agencies, or not performed at all. But
most large police forces acknowledge some kind of
responsibility for some items under each of the eight
major headings, or the corresponding district attor-
ney's office does so. Most have several squads that
deal with riot control (function 6), vice (function
3), homicide (functions 3 and 4), and so forth separate from the body of patrolmen that constitutes
the majority of the force and performs the beat-
level functions (1 and 2) plus the initial steps of
investigations of the major crime control functions
(3 and 4), usually badly. In respect to the protection of facility systems (function 5), the patrol
force is usually loaded with traffic control and enforcement of traffic regulations on the street system and business area policing, but special guard
forces or other official agencies perform most of
the remaining functions, or they are not performed
at all. There is a tendency to gather a large force
of ill-trained and poorly led patrolmen to control
riots and large crowds (function 6). The "detective"

force is the second general-purposes group within
the typical police organization, which does everything at a relatively complex level, but focuses particularly on controlling crime (functions 3 and 4).

That such a simple police organization faces
modern crime accounts in good part for the fact that
most crime goes unrecognized and that of the crime
that is recognized only a minor part is punished.
For crime prevention the highest standard is simply
to manage to pursuade the criminal to go away into
some other jurisdiction to commit his crime. The
"correctional system," which is supposed to back the
efforts of the police, for the most part tends to
train the amateur offender to be a professional
criminal (fortunately without much success) and to
furnish profitable work for attorneys, bail bondsmen,
and the like.

Such as it is, nevertheless, spending on police
work is a major factor in every city budget and one
of the fast-growing items on the list. Institution-
alization of offenders is another substantial cost,
but not a growth industry.

It is clear that every function that could jus-
tifiably be charged to a larger taxing jurisdiction
should be defined as such and either shifted to a
force supported by it or supported by a subvention
of funds from the larger body. And so an examination
of the functions from this point of view is called
for--which is made, in reverse order, below.

Functions 8, 7, and 6, almost without question,
should be paid for or performed directly by the federal and state governments. Function 8 is constitutionally specified as a federal responsibility, and
function 7 is clearly the responsibility of the state
with respect to its creatures, the local governments.
Social unrest (function 6) is also, in most cases, a
national responsibility because the national policy
on migration is clearly responsible for the intrusion
of socially different groups into the cities.

Function 5 presents a mixed picture. Each of
the facility systems must be considered separately.

Traffic and accident services are the largest item,
and there is a prima facie case for shifting the burden onto some level of government that can effectively
collect taxes on the use of the streets by automobiles and trucks. Many of the other systems and facilities have direct revenues that can easily pay for
self-policing, and most do so now--though the city
should object when the effect of their revenue structure is regressive, as it generally is. A particular
problem is presented by those systems that are in
financial trouble but are of such nature as to make
local government subsidies seem reasonable. Such is
the case of the transit system. But the transit system as a whole should be subsidized by the whole
metropolitan region, not the city alone. Thus, the
extra burden of transit policing should be shifted
to a larger jurisdiction by the process of region-
alizing the transit system's deficits.

Similar logic applies to a number of other items
on the list: Art museums, zoos, auditoriums, thea-
ters, major recreation and historical parks, and
stadiums, for example, should be supported by regional agencies out of general taxes that have a
progressive impact on incomes (since they are generally of more interest to high income groups than
to the poor or the lower middle class residents of
the city). The concealed subsidies of police "presence" and crowd-handling without tax payments should
be eliminated by providing specific payments for
such services in lieu of general taxes.

Function 4 covers the majority of recognized
crimes and absorbs a major fraction of all police
budgets. The population prone to such unorganized
and often neurotic crime is concentrated in the grey
belt of the metropolis by factors beyond the control
of local governments. Its extraordinary incidence
and resulting high cost per thousand population
should be recognized by a system of subventions from
the state government. Since the states themselves
suffer differentially in the same way, there should
also be a system of subventions from the federal to
the state governments.

Function 3 relates to a class of crime that little is known about. Professional criminals are organized in something like trade associations, but they do not issue glowing statistics to the press; and police admit that they know only the peak of the iceberg of professional crime.* Successful professional criminals, quite sensibly, do not live in the grey belt although they frequently work there because the poor and downtrodden are easy marks. Thus, it is protection <u>from</u> crime that the grey belt particularly needs and should get from the larger community. However, it is the high mobility of the professional criminals and the complexity of the task of catching and convicting them that demands a regional organization. At the present time the cost of chasing them is not large because it is not being done, and it is pointless to speculate what it will cost when it is done effectively. When it is done, it will have to be done by a regional or superregional organization backed by an effective national intelligence network.

Beat-level policing functions must be controlled locally to be effective. If they are shorn of the duties specified under function 6 (riot control) and function 5 (principally traffic control and protection of major business centers and factory areas) and any but the reporting phases of functions 5 and 4, they can be performed at the expense of even the poorest local government.

The higher levels of government should provide assistance in providing training, sophisticated communications, and capital for stations and the like and also supervise record-keeping and information systems and provide internal control (function 7). It should be kept in mind, however, that the beat policeman supported by the local government must be backed up by effective social service institutions.

---

*The picture is confused by the silliness of laws defining crime. If gambling and prostitution, for example, were not defined as crime, much of what is called organized crime would be just another business.

These cannot be supported by communities with above-
average concentrations of poor and disadvantaged
groups and must be supported by large jurisdictions
with broad taxing powers.

There emerges from this discussion both a new
police administration system and an appropriate fiscal system. (Chart 7 shows a simple version of this
proposal.) Obviously very substantial changes are
required in the structure of the laws that assign
responsibilities and organize local governments, for
the effect of the proposed system is to shift about
two thirds of the cost of policing a city like Philadelphia onto other taxing jurisdictions. This does
not mean that City residents would pay substantially
lower taxes, for the other jurisdictions (state and
regional) would continue to collect taxes on residents
and on activities in the City. But the taxes would
apply in a way that would not encourage flight from
the City.

To be politically palatable, however, such a new
system would have to do something for other munici-
palities--which does by providing a more efficient
police system in suburban and rural areas that are
now almost unpoliced. Since these areas are being
affected by an unprecedented rise in crime rates and
will soon be calling for more state-supported policing, the regionalists should be making every possible
effort to press their cause.

The foregoing analysis of police functions has
been intended to show the way to an examination of
every major function of government in relation to
the social, economic, and physical development of
the metropolitan urban region, to make it possible
to assign major portions of expenditures of local
governments of low income sectors to regions or to
the federal government. There is, as a consequence
of this logical analysis, a basis for demanding that
the higher levels of government assume the financial
burden of carrying out certain functions now paid
for by local government--obviously welfare; certainly
street functions (except trash and garbage disposal),
which should be supported by road-user taxes; and
also certain health activities.

CHART 7

A Proposed System of Police Administration and Funding

Functions	Organization	Funding
1. Beat-level social work; image	} Local police	Local property taxes plus minor subventions
2. Beat-level protection; presence		
3. Professional crime control	Local police → Regional or subregional police[a]	Regional income, property and business taxes
4. Nonprofessional crime control	Local police → Regional or superregional police[b]	Regional income, property and business taxes
5. Special facility "presence" and major crime control	Special force / Special force → Regional or superregional police	Facility revenue and facility subventions and user taxes (particularly road-user taxes)
6. Riot control	Regional riot police	Regional income tax
7. Internal control	State police	State income tax
8. Protection of state	Federal police	Federal income tax

[a]For example, the city or county unit.
[b]For example, a superregion covering the eastern third of Pennsylvania, southern New Jersey, and Delaware.

Note: The arrow indicates that the local force is the first on the scene but that it calls in the higher level force to perform the function.

Source: Prepared by the author.

If debt service on related facilities and pension costs on related (former) employees were shifted
with current expenditures, it is possible that Philadelphia could live within its present tax system--
as could other cities faced with similar fiscal crises.

THE PROBLEM

The stark facts of Philadelphia's fiscal plight are clearly evident from the analysis in Chapter 3. Too many people need too many things. Philadelphia does not--and most other cities in the United States soon will not--have enough available resources to meet demands for public services and goods. To further exacerbate the situation, public employees are demanding and winning parity in wage levels with the private sector. (Thus, at this writing, Fall 1971, cities must be in the absurd unarticulated position, of course, of hoping for the slowest possible recovery in the general economy because a rapid advance will mean advancing wages in the private sector followed by yet another push from the public sector.)

Thus, city officials are in an unenviable and more hard-pressed position than ever before. They know they must hold the line on expenditures; yet the wage demands of city employees and the expectations of the public will not abate. Clearly, the situation demands a more satisfactory approach to choosing more carefully those programs that will make local government more responsive to public need and at the same time more efficient and effective in delivering its product. Obviously the budgeting process is one of the strategic devices for control and planning expenditures, and so a critical examination

of traditional city budgeting methods and procedures
and innovative approaches is called for.

TRADITIONAL BUDGETING

For years budgeting public expenditure has meant
continuing each year what was done the year before
with only minor changes. The traditional line item
budget submitted by a department or agency head would
show headings such as the following:

Salary and wages
Contractual services
Supplies (consumable)
Workmen's compensation
Equipment (purchased or rented)
Employee retirement
Repairs and maintenance.

But little or nothing would be said about the actual
functions being executed or how the city was expected
to benefit from the outlays. Furthermore, where traditional budgeting operates, a game (albeit a very
serious one) is played out each year between the
chief administrator of the city's finances and the
department heads--a game that conspicuously reflects
the lack of clarity and definiteness about public
objectives inherent in the entire budgetary planning
system.

About six months in advance of the beginning
dates of calendar or fiscal years, the budget chief,
finance director, or city manager issues a memorandum
or letter setting a schedule for submission and review of the forthcoming year's proposed budget. A
key part of the letter is the request that restraint
be used in requests for funds in the face of limited
resources. In response, without much hesitation,
the department heads request funds in excess of the
previous year's allotment. They do so not out of
perversity but out of a conviction that they are doing their jobs. In doing so, they are also relieving
any anxiety generated by a sense of professional responsibility and placing the onus of fund limitations

or refusal on the mayor and the city council insofar
as answering to the community is concerned. Thus,
the struggle begins. On one side are ranged the professional administrators and technicians seeking en-
largement of or innovation in the previous year's
program. These are the spenders, and in playing
their role they ignore constraints. Their documents
are delivered for review and analysis to budget officers, the cutters, who ignore program and service
considerations and generally see to it under orders
from the "chief" that the current year's expenditures
will be held to generally the same level as the previous year's--though some increases might be allowed
if a department is doing an outstanding job.

This model of the traditional city budgeting
system, with minor variations, has been until recently fairly prevalent. Despite the fact that it
is now being severely criticized, it has a number of
advantages. A few of the more cogent ones are these:

1. In the absence of highly skilled analysts
to advise the chief executive, it is an excellent
device for administrative control over expenditures.

2. It holds expenditures in line with revenues
--all other considerations notwithstanding.

3. It commits department and agency heads to
a fixed sum.

4. It is a direct means for rewarding good
work.

All this is to say that the existing system does
work. If nothing else it serves to hold expenditures
in line with revenues--and therein lies its principal
strength. Another strength is that key men in local
government--the mayor and the city councilmen--must
be served in the budget document to the extent that
they can easily identify proposed expenditures by
departments; for they are the people who are ultimately responsible and accountable to the electorate.
The more complex the document, however, the greater
the possibility of misunderstanding and lack of
support by key officials.

Though much more study is required, it is argued here that this system is irreversibly intertwined with the traditional political mode in which the elected city official operates: he is responsive solely to what is expedient and most visible to his constituency. For this reason he requires a document in which he can quickly identify his interests and those of his allies in the city council and elsewhere.

Thus, any serious proposal to change budgetary procedures must take carefully into account the political realities alluded to above before instituting sweeping changes. Unless a carefully thought-out education program is undertaken that clarifies the direct advantages to city officials and councilmen, along with the technical and managerial benefits, innovation in budgetary planning will find itself on a very rocky road.

PROGRAM PLANNING BUDGETING

In many states, counties, and cities sophisticated technicians, with the support and encouragement of the chief executive, have introduced in rapid succession substantial changes in the budgeting process --changes that follow precepts emerging from a body of thought and experience called Program Planning Budgeting, or PPB.

PPB is actually not new. Both the British and the U.S. armed forces used it in a certain form (operations research) in World War II. In 1949 the Hoover Commission recommended a "performance budget" for the federal government based on PPB principles. In 1954 David Novick of the Rand Corporation developed the system further in association with the U.S. Air Force. Charles Hitch, Comptroller of the Defense Department during the Kennedy administration, introduced the idea, expecting implementation would take several years; but Defense Secretary McNamara put the system into operation at once. In August 1965 President Johnson ordered the system to be applied throughout the major executive agencies of the federal government.

PPB can be looked upon as the halting beginning of rationality on the part of all levels of government that are using it both in allocating limited funds and in endeavoring to institute an accurate accounting and evaluation of results achieved for money and effort expended. In effect, it seeks to have the government act like the rational consumer in theoretical economics who knows the price and utility of everything he buys.

It should be stressed that PPB is not an automatic producer of ideal decisions. Its appeal rests on the feeling that traditional budgeting, and its advantages, described in previous pages is obsolete in that it is oriented to internal management rather than to problems.*

As a process PPB can be viewed as a total system, a closed loop, in terms of generating information output, action, and ultimate feedback. The chief executive responds to demands of the electorate and social pressures or in fulfillment of election promises. He, in turn, gives directives to his staff and department heads. They, in conjunction with their technicians, refine these into a program report consisting of statements of problems (reflecting specific difficulties, deficiencies, malfunctions, needs, and so forth), statements of objectives, cost-effectiveness analysis, a program structure, and a budget.

---

*Perhaps the proof of this lies in the Philadelphia experience described in a later section. As working committees representing bureaus, agencies, commissions throughout City government attempted to follow the programming approach in their budget planning effort, technicians guiding those giving directions found themselves having to stress again and again that statements of "problems" and "objectives" should reflect the problems of the City that the office was constituted to deal with or the service it is expected to render and that the internal administrative, management, or supply problems of the office were not relevant.

Statements of Problems
and Objectives

Obviously the more clearly and accurately a
problem is stated, the easier it is to specify the
objective to be sought, which will, presumably, either
diminish or resolve the problem. Statements of objectives flowing from statements of problems answer
such questions as these:

What is the condition or state we are trying to achieve?

Why is this necessary, and who is to benefit?

What approach is being employed?

Staff members then posit alternative ways of achieving
specific objectives. They also delineate specific
results the achievement of which will signify that
objectives have been achieved or are being achieved.
The evaluation of these alternatives is based on
measurements to determine costs and benefits, or
cost-effectiveness.

Cost-Effectiveness

Cost-effectiveness is taken to mean analysis to
determine the direct and indirect effects or impact,
measured in both monetary and nonmonetary terms, of
an expenditure made in one functional area as compared with another. For instance, money spent on
the construction of an inpatient hospital facility
will achieve one objective, namely, provision of
hospital beds and surgical facilities; in contrast,
money spent on health education and preventive medi-
cine will have many direct and indirect effects and
cost less than a hospital in the long run.

Program Structure and Budget

From an intensive evaluation of alternatives a
program structure emerges. This is the vehicle for
the description of the hierarchy of activities of a

city, beginning with output objectives and working
back to activity components of the administrative
structures of the city. In the Philadelphia system
these activities were called programs, subprograms,
elements, and subelements.

The Philadelphia program budget, embracing the
entire array of agencies and administrative functions,
developed eight general programs and approximately
200 subprograms. The activity on which this book
focuses, economic development, found its position in
the budget structure, according to this nomenclature,
as follows:

Program: Community Development

Subprogram: Economic Development

Element: Economic Development Planning

Subelement: Minority Enterprise Development

Viewing government or any institution in this
manner not only forces a recognition of structural
relationships but also permits managers to see how
their participation and activity relate to the overall objectives of the organization. It also permits
directors of subunits and individual staff members
to identify with the overall goals and objectives of
the organization. In lay terms, the program structure is the skeleton of the system.

Finally, along with program structure come costs
grouped according to objectives or purposes. The
relative amounts in such a display illuminate the
priorities that the entire PPB process has assigned
to each objective, whether or not such ranking of
priorities was intended.*

---

*It should be noted, as a practical matter, that
implementation of PPB does not require, for programming purposes, that expenditures be grouped in terms
of output-oriented objectives rather than in terms
of line items. Some jurisdictions, like Los Angeles,

PROGRAM PLANNING BUDGETING
IN PHILADELPHIA

The Adoption of PPB

In the spring of 1966 several management studies
were carried out to determine the feasibility of PPB
for the City of Philadelphia. Most important of
these was that of the Office of the Director of Finance, which resulted in a proposal to the Mayor that
a PPB unit be established under the Director of Finance in the Budget Bureau. This report also cited
two major problems. The first was the need for additional staff to provide technical assistance to
the departments. The second was the anticipated
need for the preparation of two budget documents for
some time to come--one to satisfy the City Council's
preference for line item budgets. The report concluded that, despite these difficulties, the advantages of PPB far outweighed the disadvantages. And
thus began the PPB effort in Philadelphia--without
specific directives from the Mayor but with his tacit
approval. Primary responsibility for developing and
coordinating the City's PPB efforts was assigned to
the Chief of the Operating Budget and the fiscal and
cost analysis staff. Work began in September 1966,
the goal being to produce a program budget by September 1967. After preliminary analysis and discussion,
problems were identified and strategy outlined.

A memorandum dated September 30, 1966, for example, listed the following as some of the problems:

1. Obtaining cooperation from all City agencies
involved

2. Providing adequate training of all personnel
directly involved in the program

---

have done so, but Philadelphia, while establishing
such a program structure, retained the line item
system.

3. Recruiting systems analysts for the program

4. Determining the program structure

5. Handling long range operating budget projections

6. Making changes in the accounting and data-processing systems to record expenditures in line with the program subcategory structure

7. Providing a smooth transition from the traditional method of budget preparation to the PPB system.

A general strategy for the City to follow in the implementation of PPB was also outlined:

Phase I: To develop an output-oriented program structure reflecting major problem areas

Phase II: To redesign budgeting and accounting systems to incorporate program planning language

Phase III: To conduct program analysis, make program choices, and develop long range plan; base the budget on the plan

Phase IV: To record and report output measures reflecting progress toward program objectives

Phase V: To take corrective action where progress is not satisfactory

Phase VI: To reevaluate annually program objectives, reproject costs, recalculate effectiveness, and revise the long range plan.

As an aside it became immediately clear that in any such project the commitment of the chief executive can be an important determinant. On his commitment depends, at least in part, the size and scale of the effort and nature of the response of the staffs of the departments that make up a city government. At the same time, small scale incremental efforts

become heavily dependent on career professionals who
may or may not have the weight of the mayor behind
them. On an incremental basis implementation of PPB
in Philadelphia contrasted sharply with implementation of New York's PPB, which was initiated by the
Mayor and moved forward with his active involvement
and support. One explanation of Philadelphia's
Mayor's reluctance to imitate Mayor Lindsay may have
been his view of PPB's potential public impact; he
may have anticipated that, once problems were defined,
a critical or opposition press might publicize them
as the result of the Mayor's ineptness. The Philadelphia effort, which originated among professionals
in government, was furthered largely by the spirit
of cooperation at the agency level.

To assure that the structures developed by the
agencies would have an overall rational relationship
to each other, general agreement on a broad basic
framework for the entire City was reached initially
between the Philadelphia Department of Finance and
operating agency officials.

Phase I strategy produced a program structure
containing eight program areas:

1. Community development

2. Transportation

3. Judiciary and law enforcement

4. Conservation of health

5. Public education

6. Culture and recreation

7. Improvement of the general welfare

8. Services to property.

Under Phase II agencies were requested to specify
subprograms and program elements within program areas.
They were also instructed not to limit themselves to

any one program element of a subprogram if a contribution was expected to be made to other programs.
In order to further infuse agency statements with
PPB language, the 1967 operating budget forms requested statements of program element objectives and
a statement of the relationship of program element
objectives to subprogram and program objectives. In
addition, a statement of expected output was requested.

For Phase III a separate program analysis committee of eight members was established for every
major program area of the program structure. These
committees were so constituted as to have representatives from each City and quasi-public agency showing a program element in a major program. Personnel
participating in the committees were expected to be
of that rank or have that level of responsibility
that would permit them to make decisions and formu-
late policy recommendations.

The major function of the program committees
was to analyze each program area as a total system.
The ultimate product was to be a series of policy
recommendations to the Mayor and the City Council.
The steps they agreed to follow in executing program
analysis are:

1.   To define and rank major city problems
within each program area

2.   To establish long range program objectives
that were concrete and specific

3.   To delineate present and alternative methods
of achieving objectives

4.   To estimate costs and outputs of present
methods and each alternative so that a judgment about
effectiveness in achieving objectives could be made

5.   To select the best method and establish a
long range plan of action

6.   To prepare a program analysis report to
serve as basis for a budget.

PPB in Action: The Work
of the Subprogram Committee
on Economic Development

Following is a chronicle of the effort to implement PPB in the area of economic development, just
one of the scores of subprograms established for
Philadelphia. This effort, the work of an ad hoc
interagency subprogram committee, is a cogent example
of what can be done under PPB.

The budget Director and the City Economist, in
the role of analyst, generated interest and momentum
by giving considerable time to explain carefully the
entire concept and the critical path to be followed
to its realization. In a campaign of personal diplo-
macy they sold the idea to agency heads and their
staffs on an individual basis so as to obtain the
level of participation and accompanying candor necessary to begin.

The committee met as a body for the first time
in April 1969. Representatives of seventeen agencies
were present. (See the Appendix, page 327.) The
first tasks undertaken were limited to the accomplishment of steps 1 and 2 of the program analysis
process outlined in the preceding section (page 150).

The Subcommittees

Because of its size the Economic Development
Committee divided itself into four temporary subcommittees: Industrial, Commercial, and Institutional
Development; Convention and Tourism Service; Manpower;
Airport and Port. This breakdown provided the opportunity for committee members to focus on smaller
components or segments of economic development, essentially their assigned area of concern, while at
the same time extending their involvement to the
general economic development picture of the City.
Then, with the assistance of the Office of the City
Economist acting as staff, subcommittee deliberations
began in earnest in June and continued throughout
the summer of 1969.

Industrial, Commercial, and Institutional Development
Subcommittee. The Industrial, Commercial, and Institutional Development Subcommittee addressed itself
to those problems traditionally viewed as components
of economic development--land and floor space supply,
creation of job places, capital investment, management, and business services. Because of overlap in
the responsibilities of committee members (see the
Appendix, pages 328-33), separate caucuses were set
up to deal with the following:

> Economic Development Planning
> Industrial, Commercial, and Institutional
>   Development
> New Business Development
> Services to Business.

Despite the lack of data the participants emerged
from deliberations with specific problem and goal
statements. And it was understood that these would
be a guide for future research by the City Economist's
staff and for committee members.

Convention and Tourism Service Subcommittee. Data
on the exact magnitude of the different types of
tourist and convention markets were not immediately
available to the committee. And it was recognized
that future planning programming and budgeting would
require (1) knowledge of returns on investments in
new tourist and convention facilities and (2) an evaluation of these activities representing the best potential for the City of Philadelphia. Quantification
of the standard services required to bring more
visitors and to extend their stay was given substantial thought.

Manpower Subcommittee. The unique aspect of the Manpower Subcommittee's functioning was its willingness
to admit agencies outside government to the deliberations. Problem and goal statements produced by the
group clearly reflected awareness of overlapping and
duplication in manpower programs throughout the City.
It was estimated that at least twenty five separate
organizations were dealing with this problem, and

it was agreed that PPB could reduce inefficiencies
by reviewing the totality of the problem to the end
of defining a single system that could take an unemployed individual and place him in a job.

Airport and Port Subcommittee. For the first time
agencies involved in airport and port development were
brought together to review their common problems.
With technical guidance from the City Economist, committee members were eventually able to recognize
problems common to both functions. Planned and orderly development of adequate facilities and services
to meet the transportation needs of all economic activities was recognized as a major goal. This posed
the problem of establishing adequate services and
facilities for both airport and port, including marketing, research, and planning and coordination as
well as development and maintenance of physical facilities. The committee recognized that, in order to
quantify problems further, there was a need for additional marketing and technical research to obtain a
greater understanding of the potential the City had,
to take advantage of future opportunities presented
by a growing economy.

One of the most important ideas to evolve from
committee discussions was the formulation of a joint
planning program to produce a port authority for
port, airport, and bridge operations.

The Wheels Begin to Turn

The report of the Economic Development Committee
(Appendix, pages 328-42) indicates that success was
achieved to the degree that complex problems were
successfully separated into component segments so
that each could be studied in detail.

With respect to the planning and budgeting procedures of agencies concerned with economic development, three changes have since occurred. The first
and most important change is that through this combined effort the various government and quasi-govern-
ment agencies now view their individual program areas
in terms of an overall economic development program

for the City. This change is reflected in the care
given formulation of subcommittee goals so as to cor-
respond with the general overall economic goals for
the City.

The second change observed is that, in addition
to defined committee efforts to develop a comprehensive economic development program, joint efforts
were also made by agencies in the subcommittees to
analyze their common problems and goals. In some
instances it was the first time that government agencies had collaborated in this way, and in other instances it was also a first opportunity for government and nongovernment agencies to work together in
a planning effort. And it is to be hoped, of course,
that this cooperative effort among concerned agencies
to plan and develop economic resources for the future
will continue.

The third change brought about by PPB program
analysis is that agencies are beginning to view economic problem solving in terms of output rather than
management efficiency. This concern for output, however, is still in its conceptual form because the
input data necessary for quantification of goals is
in the process of being developed. Certainly the
experience of the Economic Development Committee has
shown that the committee, as made up of departmental
administrators and staff, responds to technical
guidance.

With the completion of problem and goal analyses,
the next phase of the PPB program will be the identification of alternatives to achieve the objectives
formulated and a comprehensive cost-benefit analysis
for each alternative. These two processes are the
key outputs of the PPB system. This phase of the
program will draw heavily upon the analytical tools
of the professional disciplines, including mathemat-
ics, economics, operations research, engineering,
and computer sciences. A staff experienced in these
areas has been requested to work with the committees,
to apply technical expertise to the research and
computation necessary to project costs and estimate
output, and, also, to guide committee members in

their planning and budgeting efforts.

First Results

After several months of analysis each subcommittee of the Committee on Economic Development emerged with a problem statement at the level of specific issues (program elements and subelements) and a corresponding goal statement indicating the desired condition or state to be achieved by the measures to be taken, that is, the condition that would either correct or improve the situation cited in the problem statement. Statements of problems and goals were then reviewed by the director and staff of the City Economist's office and consolidated into a comprehensive form so that all concerned City interests--public and private--would have a clear picture of the totality of problems and challenges before them:

> After discussion with agency heads in the public, nonprofit, and private sectors of the Philadelphia economy, along with intensive study of available statistical data, reports, and analyses, we conclude that the following symptoms of social and economic disorganization exist but are not unique to the city of Philadelphia and urge that instruments capable of reducing their intensity be designed and activated at the earliest possible time:
>
> 1. Out-migration: Prosperous businesses have moved in a never-ending stream to suburban industrial parks and modern shopping centers, which has produced increased job opportunities where they are least needed and at the same time made it more difficult for those who do need them to reach the place of employment.
>
> 2. Low labor skills: A large number of workers cannot be employed in high-wage-paying industries because of lack of skills, meaningful employment experience, and discrimination. Job opportunities for the less skilled continue to decline.

3. Inadequate personal incomes.

4. Slow growth of industry mix: The complex of businesses and services making up
the economic base has not yielded growth
in the past decade comparable to that in
other major urban centers over the nation.

5. Low quality production facilities and
infrastructure: Obsolete buildings, inefficient street systems, substandard services, delayed delivery, and inadequate
size of industrial and commercial sites
reduce business willingness to remain or
relocate in the City.

6. Malfunctioning capital markets: There
is export of locally generated savings, in-
sufficiency of venture or risk capital, and
inadequate supply of competent managers.

7. Insufficient positive action by responsible governments: The City has not used
its powers to draw economic sectors together. It has not exhausted available federal tools or the resources of the private
capital markets. The State provides inadequate aid for development that could reverse
business out-migration and/or stimulate new
economic activity and, in fact, makes low
interest loans for industrial development
in suburban areas, all to the detriment of
the City's tax base and the unemployment
problem.

8. Inadequate transportation system: Heavy
traffic congestion, parking congestion, slow
movement of traffic, high accident rates,
poor accessibility in areas demanding rapid
and easy access are all in evidence. Increasingly more important is the absence of
an adequate system for reverse commuting.

9. Polarization of land use: Spatial separation of white and nonwhite and affluent
and poor has produced a distortion in land

values and, consequently, location patterns
of commercial and industrial development.

10. Fiscal crisis: The City government
is lurching from one fiscal crisis to
another because of rising wage demands by
civil servants, inflated construction
costs, and increasingly burdensome welfare
roles.

11. Insecurity: Danger to persons, property, and vehicles prevail, and a reputation for crime and danger persists that
may be much worse than the reality.

12. A counterproductive tax system:
Existing taxes on individuals, businesses,
and property are damaging to the City's
economy.

According to the next step in PPB procedure
these problem statements were translated into a statement of two primary, general long range goals: to
maximize income and to maximize development. Detailed
elaboration of these in the form of shorter range
objectives, which can be programmed, are stated below and consolidated in the accompanying chart:

1. To keep, develop, and attract business from
outside the area

2. To develop and enhance productivity of human
resources through training and education (special attention should be given to enhancing the supply of
management and entrepreneurial talent)

3. To provide employment and income at a level
necessary to reduce poverty and social disadvantage

4. To assure an adequate and continuing supply
of land and/or floor space to accommodate new, expanded, or relocated businesses

5. To provide adequate financial resources for
investment in business enterprise, both existing and
new

CHART 8

Relationships Among City Goals, Objectives,
and Economic Development Programs

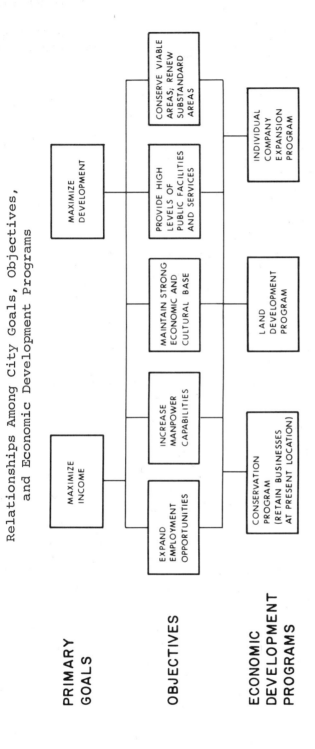

PRIMARY
GOALS

OBJECTIVES

ECONOMIC
DEVELOPMENT
PROGRAMS

161

6. To reduce inefficiencies in the infrastructures and expedite renewal and other supportive programs

7. To resolve the problem of community participation in decision making (optional).

Something New Emerges

From these summary statements of problems and goals it became clear that the loop should be completed and the feedback characteristic of systems analysis introduced.

It also became possible to state the general problem of the City clearly and succinctly: Inner city areas are obsolete and decaying; more specifically, they do not meet the essential market criteria necessary to bid effectively for capital in the private and even the public investment market as we know it. It also became possible to propose the following comprehensive goal statement as a matter of policy for final adoption by the Mayor and City Council:

> Local government must assume, in a planned,
> deliberate, and determined fashion, the role
> of entrepreneur, directly intervening in
> markets to become a preserver, promoter,
> and funder, if necessary, of public enter-
> prise. In doing so it accepts responsibil-
> ity for reversing physical deterioration and
> providing the stream of funds, land ser-
> vices, and human resources necessary to the
> task. Recognizing that it cannot achieve
> this goal alone with the private sector,
> it will seek support and participation from
> State and federal subventions designed to
> enhance the economic base of the City.

5

**TOWARD
MORE COMPREHENSIVE
ECONOMIC GROWTH INDICATORS
AND A
POLICY MODEL**

THE NEED FOR INDICATORS

Since the mid-1960s we have witnessed the number or cities with economic development objectives and the creation of organizations to effect these objectives. But, generally, attempts to influence the private local economy by use of public sector activity are still embryonic.

The current "state of the art" is such that there are no systematic and reliable measures of economic change through time as related to the urban metropolis. Considering that changes in the local gross metropolitan product (the microeconomic equivalent of the GNP) directly influence the supply and quality of housing, property support, and maintenance services of local government and the supply and quality of educational services and of medical services, the failure to attempt to effect economic growth in a meaningful way implies a fatalistic acceptance by local government of the constraints imposed by taking current economic conditions as given.

While measures of change in a consistent way are really not available, there is, as indicated in the labor demand measurements discussed in Chapter 6, sufficient research to establish that manufacturing out-migration is a phenomenon characteristic of nearly all the cities of the industrial North and of many of the other older cities in the country. The consequent out-migration of jobs has produced in each instance geographic areas within cities that are major pockets of continually growing, persistent, and substantial unemployment. The failure of opportunity to increase incomes by obtaining jobs in the private sector implies growth in welfare dependency and deterioration of the public services required to reverse such a cycle.

The cities so far engaged in economic development efforts, because of the practical pressures to produce practical results, have been forced to utilize such traditional resources as have been available to them--coordination of city departmental resources, utilization of existing manpower programs, and the occasional help available when a city can qualify for the assistance available under the Public Works and Economic Development Act of 1965. Where these resources have been used in efficient manners, they have no doubt been effective; but the principal effects have been to stem the tide of manufacturing out-migration and, under the best circumstances, to produce stable or (less euphemistically) stagnant economic conditions.

The major federal response to the pockets of persistent and substantial unemployment within cities has been in the field of manpower training. Since 1961, when the Area Redevelopment Act provided special training funds for designated redevelopment areas, there has been a succession of laws that have provided a variety of funds and programs to undertake manpower training. The Manpower Development and Training Act (with its subsequent amendments), the Economic Opportunity Act, and Model Cities legislation have been principal among these tools. But there is substantial research to indicate that none of these measures has had any important effect on reducing unemployment in areas of substantial oversupply. At the same time survey research suggests that unemployment rates are impacted by significant changes in national economic conditions.

What has been distinctive, then, about the application of existing manpower resources is that they all relate to affecting the supply of labor and are not responsive to changes in the demand for labor. Since there is such overwhelming documentation of loss of jobs from central city areas, it is not surprising that measures designed to affect the supply of labor should be so impotent to reduce rates of unemployment. At the same time the field of urban economic development is currently in such an embryonic state that urban policy makers are helpless to know what measures to apply to stimulate the private sector. Clearly, the assumption made by the U.S. Department of Labor that a labor market area comprehending as many as six or eight counties is a region where labor really is mobile, is unwarranted. Substantial industrial growth in the suburbs does not produce jobs accessible to inner city workers. Research identifying policy variables that govern geographical areas of potential growth is essential if effective measures of reducing central city unemployment are to be undertaken.

University researchers have heretofore assumed that the condition of a local economy is principally dependent on two things: (1) national economic conditions and (2) comparative advantages to that region flowing from geography, location, and other factors. While this may be true in regard to the total product, or gross metropolitan product, of a given region--or even if it is true in large part--what may be more important is where jobs are generated within the region in relation to areas of supply.

No one has ever systematically studied the effects of local government taxing or fiscal actions in relation to private sector development, nor have local public works been programmed to contribute to the stabilization of local economies or agglomerated to stimulate the development of industrial parks. The design of local transportation systems has been influenced in large measure by federal priorities because of funding arrangements and has not necessarily been related to stimulating local growth. It is quite evident that there are numerous tools that might conceivably be made to contribute to the objectives of urban economic growth. In addition, however, to the articulation of such tools, data must be systematically collected to develop consistent and reliable indicators of economic change, on both the supply and demand sides of the ledger. In fact, not only the development of indicators but also the definition of all policy variables that have applicability to most cities in the nation are required.

DEVELOPING URBAN ECONOMIC INDICATORS

A prerequisite to the development of tools that can be relied on to have a positive impact on the economy is the identification and structuring of measurements that are relevant and accurate indicators of economic change. A set of proper indicators is necessary both in a static sense (in order to get a meaningful grip on existent problems) and in a dynamic sense (in order to develop good measures of the empirical effects of implementing policies and programs).

At the outset the selection criteria for such indicators might include a great number of provisos. But the task then might be so formidable as never to be begun. In order to begin, only two are suggested as necessary: (1) Initial indicators should relevantly reflect important supply and demand conditions in the local economy and (2) indicators initially selected should be available and practically collectible among as wide a range of cities as possible so as to permit comparison and development of programming vehicles applicable to many urban areas.

In general, the goals of economic development programming, though complex, can be abstracted into some simple measurable statistics that will constitute yardsticks by which program implementation can be evaluated. Nevertheless, two of the real deficiencies attributable to a host of programs implemented during the 1960s were the failure to specify the scale by which success might be measured and, consequently, the failure to try to measure the output or benefits of programs that were implemented.

Recognition of these deficiencies in the public sector led to the beginning of PPB systems to define measures of cost-effectiveness and to other kinds of systems planning. That these systems have as yet really failed to take hold is in part attributable to the fact that parallel work on the development and collection of data on indicators has not taken place, with the result that measuring cost-effectiveness is often well nigh impossible. It is also in part attributable to the fact that one group of interests has focused on the refinement of systems planning while other "schools" have focused on determining what kinds of indicators are appropriate, leaving policy makers and program planners in the lurch so that decisions must continue to be made by an intuitive process.*

In the field of theoretical economics and economic development per se, there are signs of acceptance of the necessity both to implement systems approaches and to determine what kinds of indicators should be developed. Key measures of economic progress that have been most frequently discussed are these:

1. Measures of gross metropolitan (or gross urban) product

2. Measures of (change in) per capita income levels

---

*The notion that the use of intuitive programming is doomed to fail is, however, patently wrong. As is shown at the beginning of Chapter 4, its success depends on the intuition of the policy makers, many of whom are highly artful in developing a feel for the appropriate technique and program. The problem that stems from reliance on these approaches consistently is that the lack of systematic progress makes it impossible to ascertain which approaches have impact and which do not.

3. Measures of distribution of income levels within urban areas

4. Measures of unemployment.

These indicators, if consistently compiled in time series from both information on secular trends in each area and effects experienced consequent to the business cycle, constitute an accurate measure of local economic change. Nearly all the economic programs that have been or might be implemented are intended in the final analysis to affect some combination of the four aggregate indicators specified, that is, per capita income levels or per capita income levels along some range of the income distribution. Moreover, these data are already collected and might be made available in the aggregative sense without compromising the confidentiality of Internal Revenue Service records.

The long range goal of such a program would be to develop both methodology and cost estimates that the federal government would require to publish the time series of aggregate parameters for various sizes of subdivisions of selected urban metropolitan areas. Having these data available on such a basis would permit studies to determine which action programs do in fact yield positive changes in the economic well-being of a city.

Demand Side Indicators

As suggested at the beginning of this chapter, a principal deficiency in the attempts to develop policy and program tools is the presumption that the labor markets of metropolitan areas are relatively homogeneous with respect to the mobility of labor. Not only has every recent serious attempt to research this matter proved such a hypothesis to be patently false but the continuation of data collection procedures on such a basis has led to the continued development of program approaches doomed to ineffectiveness. Data appropriate to the creation of effective programming vehicles must penetrate the current concept of the labor market as related to urban areas

and be amenable to distinguishing geographic, transportation, or socioeconomic rigidities or barriers
in the movement of labor. What is proposed here is
a selection among a series of possible demand-side
indicators, both leading and current, which might be
available in a wide range of cities selected for
study.

Among the types of indicators from which selection could be made, the following should be included
as a minimum:

1.   Industrial and other private sector investments, (a) by type (industry--two-digit code, residential, and so forth), (b) by geographic area, and
(c) by dollar and space volume

2.   Employment (a) by geographic areas within
each urban framework, (b) by industry type, (c) by
occupation type, (d) by skill and education levels,
and (e) by changes in wage rates

3.   Transportation relatedness within metropolitan areas, (a) by areas of excess demand by needed
skills, (b) by areas of excess supply by available
skills, (c) by transportation relatedness, and (d)
by available resources to relate potentially marginally related skills to potentially marginally related demand.

Supply Side Indicators

If the goal of local policy as related to the
economy implies both the reduction of rates of unemployment in areas where these rates remain persis-
tently and substantially high and the raising of income levels in impacted communities, then the assumption that such unemployment is structurally based in
deficient training, skills, and productivity must be
closely examined. A shift from this assumption does
not deny its partial validity, but policy must address
other barriers not founded in this presumption. That
gaps exist not founded in the structure of available
skills is established by research: John F. Kain of
the Joint Center for Urban Studies, MIT-Harvard, has

developed an econometric model that produced the estimate that approximately 40,000 manufacturing jobs were lost to Chicago's black community because of the distribution of available housing to that community; the model when applied to other cities--for example, Detroit--produced similar estimates. And these findings tend to be substantiated by the work of Ira Lowry, Beverly Duncan, and others in their studies of skill-related commuting patterns.

The implications of these studies are not subtle in their relationship to effective policy development. Barriers to employment not related to training must be identified. Among the supply side indicators of the type necessary to develop policy, the following would be included in the list from which appropriate indicators would be selected:

1. Measures of surplus labor, (a) by geographic areas, (b) by available skill levels, (c) by barriers to employment, (d) by unemployment and dependency rates, and (e) by improvement in private sector income level necessary to make private employment a realistic alternative

2. Measures of labor force entrants, (a) by termination of educations experience and (b) by migration by area migrated from.

DEVELOPMENT OF POLICY
AND PROGRAM MODELS

Even given the assumption that the total of gross metropolitan or gross urban product is not significantly influenceable by any set of policies or programs that might be undertaken by any municipality, such an assumption does not carry with it the implication that rates of unemployment or areas of surplus labor cannot be affected by local policies. By public actions municipal governments may be able to shift private sector production functions so as to induce them to use more labor and less land, for instance, than they do currently. While such a possibility may on first examination seem outside the

realm of possibility, it was in fact exactly a set
of public actions that induced the reverse private
sector actions and made possible manufacturing out-
migrations. The implementation of the federal interstate program led to manufacturing decentralization
by making it feasible to substitute land for labor
and to make widespread use of the one-story land-
based or extensive manufacturing facility.

Though there are real gaps in the existing data,
there is sufficient research to establish both the
fact of manufacturing out-migration from central
cities and the consequences of suburbanization. Jobs
developed in suburban corridors are not accessible
to inner city workers. While in theory there are
three potential alternatives available to correct
this situation, in fact only one is really within the
policy prerogatives of central city municipal policy
makers. First, theoretically, housing might be made
available in suburban areas on a nondiscriminatory
basis to low or moderate income workers, placing them
within commuting distance of areas of suburban job
growth. Second, it is conceivable that mass urban
transit systems might be developed to permit reverse
commuting to suburban factories. The problem with
the first theoretical alternative is that neither
the federal government nor individual suburban governments have shown a willingness to take the initiatives required to make available the kind of housing
required in the suburban rings because of the anticipation of political resistance to such initiatives.
The second alternative is perhaps even more compli-
cated. Even if adequate mass transport systems were
developed, the problem of transporting workers from
the nodules of such corridors to factories in decentralized suburban areas are substantial because these
areas have not replicated the public transportation
infrastructure of the central city. The costs of
doing so across a much more widespread and less populated area would be prohibitive--not to mention the
complication of sustaining intergovernmental suburban
cooperation.

The problems inherent in these first two alternatives suggest the practicality of pursuit of a

third solution. Stimulation of job growth within
the central city in areas accessible to neighborhoods
with labor surpluses seems really to be the only
practical approach both to reducing unemployment and
to increasing income levels in such areas. Both economics and the physical constraints implied in doing
otherwise suggest a national stake in maintaining
"central places" with high degrees of public access
and potential for economical movement of people.
The reasons to pursue such a goal relate not only to
economic welfare but also, importantly, to the maintenance of the environment. The implications of
substantial increased decentralization are really
increased per capita consumption of power and increased reliance on private modes of transportation,
with even larger amounts of space devoted to highways
and greater problems in monitoring the implied environmental output. And those who suggest that the
problems of modern life are a by-product of increased
population density in central cities are controverted
by the facts: the population density of most of the
major central cities of the industrial North is about
equal to or less than what it was during the 1930s.

It seems likely that the failure to provide avenues through which impacted populations can improve
the quality of their lives is more critical in explaining urban problems than is population density.
Moreover, the development of such avenues has been
founded historically in providing real economic opportunity. The policy and program alternatives that
need more comprehensive study in pursuit of this objective include:

1. Fiscal tools

   a. designation of areas where private sec-
      tor investments and manufacturing loca-
      tion should be encouraged

      i. taxation policies
         temporary freezes of property tax
            bases
         tax credits for creation of employ-
            ment

        federal, state, and local investment credits

   ii. spending policies
       agglomeration of public works to develop infrastructure to leverage private investments in industrial parks and so forth
       development of transportation-related corridors combining public transportation with other modes related to freight movement

   iii. development of programs to offset costs associated with hiring of target population groups

2. Business cycle stabilization policies

  a. reserves of public works projects implemented in times of loose labor market conditions when they are cheaper publicly do not contribute to inflationary pressures and reduce unemployment

  b. income, maintenance, and manpower

    i. local income maintenance programs during downtrends in the business cycle

   ii. training programs focused on long run skill development

   iii. manpower focused on private employment-related programs during tight business cycle conditions

A PROJECTION OF DEMAND
FOR LABOR BY INDUSTRY
AND OCCUPATIONAL SKILLS

Projected measures of demand for labor have
particular value in programs purporting to assist
and guide economic development. Several sources of
historical and current data exist, but, until the
time of the Philadelphia Economic Development Unit
study, no attempt had been made to amalgamate these
into a comprehensive statement of demand. Nor had
the admittedly tedious and technically forbidding
task of detailing this demand over time by area, by
industry, and by occupation skills been given serious
thought.

Analytic comparison of two data sources--the
Pennsylvania Bureau of Employment Security's yearly
series entitled "Employment and Wages of Workers
covered by the Pennsylvania Unemployment Compensation
Law" and the U.S. Bureau of the Census reports entitled "County Business Patterns"--led to the selection of the latter as the best available historical
data base for projection. County-by-county and year-
by-year data from this source were structured on a
two-digit SIC coded industry basis. Separate metho-
dologies were developed to estimate data points missing because of disclosure considerations and to

estimate the employment data for 1963, a year not included in the data source.

The actual employment projections were then performed. The basic logarithm was a least squares linear regression of the independent variable time against the logarithms of the dependent variables employment, taxable wages, and number of reporting units. This approach allowed the use of a linear methodology for determining the equation of a regression curve of higher order than a straight line. However, several supplementary projection techniques were employed where it was determined that the data base was not regular or complete enough to support the linear semilogarithmic regression approach.

These projections of employment by industry were run against industry-occupation coefficients produced by the linear interpolation of two industry-occupation matrixes from U.S. Bureau of Labor Statistics sources for 1968 and 1975.[1] (The summarized results are shown in Tables 22-25 and Charts 9-12.)

Slow Growth in Jobs
for Philadelphia Residents Expected

A look at projections for Philadelphia give little cause for complacency. There is almost no growth projected for the manufacturing base. Further, 1970 census figures published after the study was made showed that there were 12.1 percent fewer factory jobs in the City of Philadelphia in 1968 than there were a decade earlier; this amounted to a loss of 35,000 jobs.

In contrast, there were 28 percent more factory jobs in the seven counties surrounding Philadelphia than in the City in 1970. That gain amounted to 66,500 jobs. As a result of this substantial difference in growth, by 1970 only 44 percent of all factory jobs in the Philadelphia SMSA were located in the City.

The projections indicate the jobs in the seven surrounding counties will increase by 126,000, or 45

TABLE 22

Employment Demand by Industry Group, City of
Philadelphia, 1968 and 1975

Industry Group	1968	1975	Percent Change
Construction	31,917	54,371	+71
Manufacturing	249,564	248,782	-5
Transportation and utilities	48,648	69,582	+43
Trade	168,254	110,098	-35
Finance	65,231	105,603	+62
Services	157,989	176,655	+12
Government	153,500	155,000	+1
Total	875,103	920,091	+5

Source: Prepared by the author.

TABLE 23

Employment Demand by Industry Group, Counties
Surrounding Philadelphia, 1968 and 1975

Industry Group	1968	1975	Percent Change
Construction	32,468	54,251	+70
Manufacturing	279,187	405,890	+45
Transportation and utilities	25,286	35,594	+37
Trade	162,334	232,672	+45
Finance	25,960	35,594	+37
Services	108,628	170,088	+1
Government	115,100	116,500	+58
Total	748,963	1,050,370	+41

Note: Burlington, Camden, Bucks, Chester, Delaware, Gloucester, and Montgomery counties, in Pennsylvania and New Jersey, are included.

Source: Prepared by the author.

TABLE 24

Occupational Demand by Occupational Skill Category, City of Philadelphia, 1968 and 1975

Occupational Skill Category	1968	1975	Absolute Change	Percent Change
Professional, technical, and kindred workers	90,023	106,044	16,021	+17.8
Managers, officials, and proprietors	91,582	96,509	4,927	+5.4
Clerical and kindred workers	137,324	164,879	27,555	+20.0
Sales workers	71,393	84,873	13,480	+18.8
Craftsmen, foremen, and kindred workers	96,244	105,458	9,214	+9.5
Operatives and kindred workers	176,870	175,837	1,033	-0.6
Laborers (except farm and mine)	30,920	29,128	1,792	-5.8
Service workers	75,321	82,720	7,399	-9.8
Total	770,215	845,943	75,728	+9.8

Note: Estimates do not reflect occupational categories in the government sector.

Source: Prepared by the author.

178

TABLE 25

Occupational Demand by Occupational Skill Category, Counties Surrounding
Philadelphia, 1968 and 1975

Occupational Skill Category	1968	1975	Absolute Change	Percent Change
Professional, technical, and kindred workers	77,131	120,434	43,303	+56.2
Managers, officials, and proprietors	77,753	100,491	22,738	+29.4
Clerical and kindred workers	101,926	144,991	43,065	+43.2
Sales workers	57,273	78,627	21,354	+37.0
Craftsmen, foremen, and kindred workers	105,032	145,155	40,123	+38.7
Operatives and kindred workers	161,754	214,800	53,046	+32.4
Laborers (except farm and mine)	31,173	34,490	3,317	+10.1
Service workers	65,225	92,933	27,710	+42.5
Total	677,625	931,921	254,296	+38.0

Note: Bucks, Burlington, Camden, Chester, Delaware, Gloucester, and Montgomery
counties, in Pennsylvania and New Jersey, are included; estimates do not reflect occupational categories in the government sector.

Source: Prepared by the author.

CHART 9

Employment Demand by Industry Group: Philadelphia Compared with Surrounding Counties, 1968

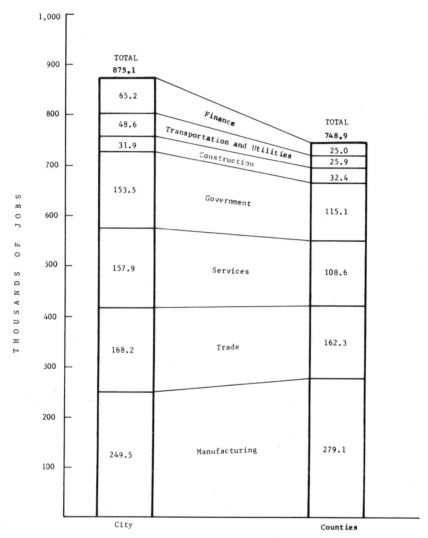

Note: Burlington, Camden, Bucks, Chester, Delaware, Gloucester, and Montgomery counties, in Pennsylvania and New Jersey, are included.

CHART 10

Employment Demand by Industry Group:
Philadelphia Compared with
Surrounding Counties, 1975

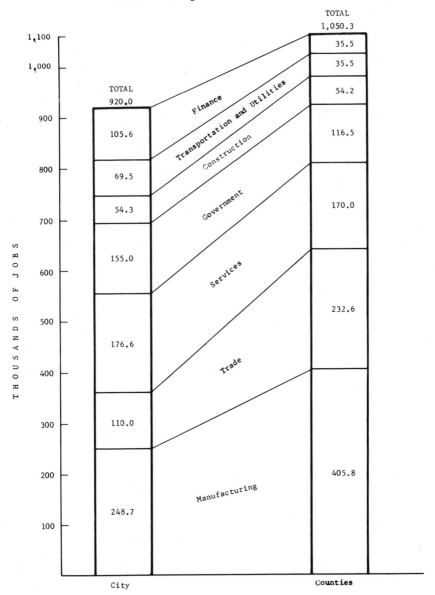

CHART 11

Occupational Demand by Occupational Skill Category:
City of Philadelphia, 1965 and 1975

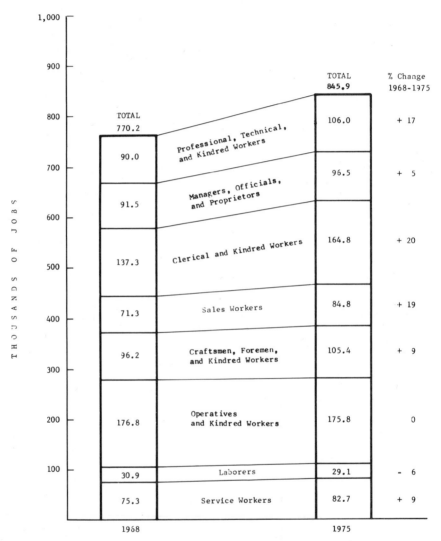

Note: Estimates do not reflect occupational categories in the government sector.

CHART 12

Occupational Demand by Occupational Skill Category:
Counties Surrounding Philadelphia, 1968 and 1975

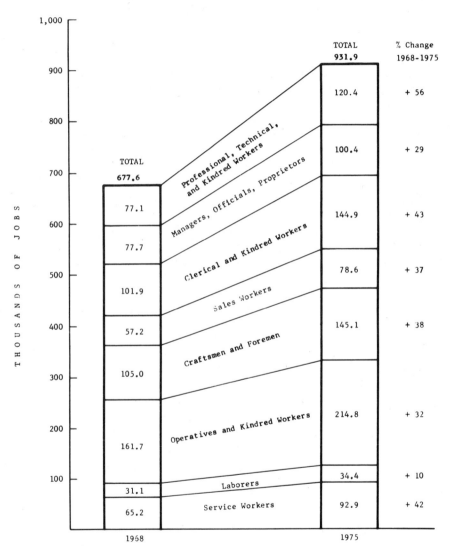

Note: Bucks, Burlington, Camden, Chester, Delaware, Gloucester, and Montgomery counties, in Pennsylvania and New Jersey, are included; estimates do not reflect occupational categories in the government sector.

percent, by 1975; this means that by the middle of
the 1970s 62 percent of all manufacturing jobs will
be located in the suburbs. In all likelihood, new
industry will come into the area and choose the suburbs instead of the City as the place of operation.

In trade, retail stores particularly follow customers. Philadelphia's population dipped by 2.7 percent in 1960s, but the population of the surrounding
counties rose by 24 percent. Wholesalers follow retailers. The result: Philadelphia for the first
time in its history witnessed a decline of employment
in this field, which is so vital to and characteristic of urban centers.

The picture is brighter for Philadelphia's service industry jobs. But the fact remains that the
picture is not so positive when compared with that
in the surrounding area. A 12 percent growth by the
mid-1970s is anticipated, but this is completely
overshadowed by the anticipation of a 58 percent increase in the remainder of the metropolitan area.

Governments--municipal, state, and federal--are
the fourth biggest employers in the City and in the
metropolitan area. Along with service jobs, government has been a growth industry in the Philadelphia
SMSA, as elsewhere--the federal government accounting
for 44 percent of all government payrolls, as an employer in numerous defense establishments and in the
regional administrative center. However, considering fiscal difficulties facing all levels of govern-
ment--city, state, and federal--and the policies of
austerity that have been introduced in the face of a
lagging economy, it is doubtful that significant increases in employment in this area can be expected.

The data show the construction industry moving
up by 70 percent outside the City limits, as opposed
to 9 percent inside them. With the adjoining areas
growing so much faster than the City, this is not
surprising.

The City of Philadelphia, of course, still
clearly dominates the SMSA's finance, real estate,

and insurance employment, accounting for 71 percent
of the jobs in that area; significantly, in that
sphere, its growth rate leads that of the seven surrounding counties. Predictable also is the City's
heavy percentage of the SMSA's total employment in
transportation and public utilities.

Summarized, these data tell the familiar story
of the relative stagnation of the inner city and the
rapid growth of the suburbs. Simultaneously there
is evidence that the city of the future, acting as
an administrative communications and managerial center, is evolving. But it is too early to tell whether
or not the centripetal forces developing will maintain their strength or at some point the disincentives
to central locations for such functions will become
so overriding that the process of decentralization
will affect them also.

Occupational Demand
by Type of Skill

The general direction of changes in the types
of skills demanded are determined by changes in the
nation's economy, which is affected by changing demands for products and services as well as by changes
in the technology of production. And what has been
known intuitively for some time is documented by the
analysis: A shift in demand from lower to higher
levels of skill is projected, particularly strong
growth being noted in the managerial, professional,
and clerical groups, both in the City and in the surrounding areas.

Increasing demand for operatives in the suburbs
is accompanying the growth in manufacturing and construction.

Of great concern is the rate of deterioration
of employment opportunity for relatively unskilled
workers. The decline is much higher and the rate
faster in the City proper than in the surrounding
counties. While services show promise in the suburbs, the rate of increase within the City again
seems too limited to provide the needed number of

opportunities for those who are in need of such employment.

THE DILEMMA AND A CLEAR
MANDATE FOR ACTION

Even superficial application of systems thinking to the problems the foregoing data disclose clearly indicates that change from within is essential, that new policy positions and solutions are called for by the labor supply-demand picture if the human condition of a large part of Philadelphia's population and labor force is to be prevented from further deterioration.

A good starting point is a definition of some of the specific objectives for a worker:

1. To obtain, through employment or self-employment, an adequate amount of money, at reasonably regular intervals

2. To find a job when unemployed or a new job when the job or activity in which he is employed is no longer satisfying--and to do so quickly and cheaply

3. To be able to go to the place of employment or self-employment reasonably quickly, simply, and cheaply

4. To have access to ways in which he can become more productive so that, with time, his income can grow, in real terms, at a reasonable rate--and to be able to do so relatively easily and cheaply, without being discriminated against

5. To work in a place that is safe, healthy, and fair

6. To have a reasonable degree of choice in the number of hours and time of day he works

7. To have a way of obtaining a reasonable amount of money when--temporarily or permanently--

for reasons beyond his control, he is unable to find
employment or self-employment--and to be able to do
so reasonably quickly, without having to go a long
distance or yield too much privacy.

And it is also essential to define some of the
many implicit and explicit assumptions regarding the
functioning of the manpower system, the fundamental
groundwork underlying policy decisions:

1. Most people find jobs in a rather haphazard
fashion, never fully aware of the alternatives available to them and thus compromising interests and
abilities to take whatever job is available.

2. Most employers hire people in a less than
systematic fashion, not having adequate knowledge of
the skills, interests, and abilities of the available
labor force and thus having a work force imperfectly
matched to the tasks to be performed.

3. Earning a living and sustaining oneself are
part of a work ethic that proclaims these activities
to be intrinsically fulfilling to the individual.
This ethic is present in the culture today; it has
been present in all industrialized and competitive
cultures and will continue for several decades to
come.

4. The economic fluctuations of an economy
create periods and isolated instances of unemployment.

5. The longer a person is unemployed, the less
employable he becomes.

6. Most job growth--upward, lateral, and ob-
lique mobility--happens in an unstructured and whimsical fashion.

7. Most jobs (collection of tasks) have been
created in an informal fashion--marginally related
to the technology and processes involved and completely without regard to the worker.

8. Most career and growth patterns are limited
by (a) the size of the employer and jobs available,

(b) the opportunity and ability to learn new skills,
(c) the lack of relevancy of job composition, and
(d) the lack of relationship between job qualifications and job requirements.

9. The economy of Philadelphia is not an enclosed one but one that is characterized by (a) a
relatively high degree of commuting in and out of
the area and (b) a relatively high degree of trade
in and out of the area.

The first and most important step is the turning
of the economic tide. This must be accomplished
through continuing solid data analysis, systems planning, and competent management of a group of aggressive entrepreneurs that will retain current business
and attract new business to keep pace with the minority population needs.

Moreover, in view of assumptions 1 and 2, it is
obvious that some system must be devised that will
provide employers and employees with the maximum
feasible choice in being hired and hiring, so that
both will achieve the greatest satisfaction.

This is the objective of YOUNGPLACE--a sophisticated model of job and applicant information exchange
using "state-of-the-art" technology.

Assumptions 3, 4, and 5 would indicate that without sufficient jobs attainment of the fundamental objectives would be impossible. An operational system
that would on one hand curb some of the economic fluctuations while on the other hand create jobs when required is the fundamental background of MEDC--a job
creation model.

The unsystematic and whimsical nature of job
growth is found in assumptions 6, 7, and 8. A method
whereby employees can maximize their potential while
employers maintain their return on invested capital
is presented in Employer Training Consortiums.

Assumption 9, that the area is interdependent
within itself and with other regions, is the reason
that regionwide models with local delivery systems
were designed.

Other key elements are the concepts of discrimination and training. The former is dealt with by an operating arm of MEDC that provides intensive technical assistance to employers while encouraging law enforcement, and the latter through a detailed analysis and dissemination of meaningful job information to all groups.

METHODOLOGY FOR LABOR DEMAND STUDY AND PROJECTION

Data Preparation

The first step in developing the labor demand study and a basis for projection was the selection of a suitable data base. Only two data series could be considered. The first was found in the yearly series entitled "Employment and Wages of Workers Covered by the Pennsyvlania Unemployment Compensation Law by County and by Industry, First Quarter 19--," issued by the Bureau of Employment Security (BES) of the Department of Labor and Industry of the Commonwealth of Pennsylvania. The second was the data contained in the series "County Business Patterns" produced by the Bureau of the Census of the U.S. Department of Commerce. Both are statistical by-products of employer reports under employment-related social programs, the former being from the quarterly reports of Pennsylvania employers under the Pennsyvlania Unemployment Compensation Law, the latter being from Treasury Form 941, Schedule A, whose filing is required by the Federal Insurance Contributions Act, plus a special survey of multiunit companies needed to provide the necessary county and industry detail.

The scope of employment covered in these data sources seemed largely equivalent, with one exception. The forms of noncovered employment for both included farm workers; domestic workers; employees of the federal, state, and local governments; self-employed persons; and workers in interstate railroads and ocean-borne vessels. But the BES source excludes employees of nonprofit organizations, while "County Business Patterns" picks up the vast majority of these workers. These exclusions are quite sizable; the Social Security Administration estimates that in March 1967 only

68.4 percent of total paid civilian employment was covered by the scope of the "County Business Patterns" and that in previous years this percentage was even less. However, there are sources for many of these excluded categories; and it was decided to pursue a methodology that would allow ready entry of these categories if and when it was felt that the improvement in the results would warrant the necessary additional resource investment.

The BES data source has two apparent advantages over the census data source. The BES statistical information bulletins containing the series in question have been produced yearly since the early 1950s. The BES series also offers complete disclosure within each two-digit industry category, while the census source has many industries for which it will report only the number of reporting units and not disclose wages so as not to violate the confidentiality of identifiable tax-paying enterprises. However, the census source also enjoys two apparent advantages. One is the ready availability of "County Business Patterns" reports for the New Jersey portion of the Philadelphia SMSA, assuring coverage for the entire SMSA in exactly the same statistical terms. The second is the previously mentioned broader census definition of "covered employment" to include the employees of nonprofit organizations.

In view of these countervailing advantages and drawbacks it was not at all obvious which data source would be superior. It was recognized that the most serious drawback of the BES information would probably be the lack of BES data for New Jersey. It was decided to attempt to compare the Pennsylvania data series and see whether the BES data were good enough to warrant a search for comparable New Jersey data. Each of these data series contains thousands of data points (employment, wages, and number of reporting units for eight counties; sixty- or seventy-odd two-digit industries; and a number of years) and it was quite apparent that one would not be readily able simply to glance over the two data series and decide which series was a superior data source. Therefore, it was decided to write a program that would run the two data decks against each other and generate a variety of aggregate measures of coverage of the work force by

the two data sources, so that an objective comparative
evaluation could be made.

The program written for this purpose calculated
the following indicators for each of the data decks:
the number of two-digit industries represented, the
number of these that lacked employment data because
of the disclosure problem, the number of industries
that had zero employment listed, the total number of
employees explicitly enumerated over all industries,
the number of reporting units explicitly enumerated,
the number of industries in the given data series that
had a disclosure problem data gap but matched with the
same industry in the other data series that had employment data given, the total number of employees
listed for the given data series in industries that
also had a listing in the other data series that had
a complete data disclosure, and the total number of
reporting units in the given data series that also had
a matching reporting unit data point in the other data
series. Six comparative indicators were also generated, namely, the number of matching industries, the
number of matching industries having complete data in
each series, the number of industries in the complete
data matching subset in which the number of employees
listed for the second data series was greater than
that for the first data series, the number of industries in this subset in which the number of employees
listed for both data series was equal, and two indicators similar to these last two but relating to the
numbers of reporting units rather than the number of
employees.

Runs were made for all five counties of the Pennsylvania portion of the SMSA and totals developed for
the sum of the five counties. The results generally
showed that the BES covered greater numbers of reporting units and industries (this was probably because of
definitional differences) while the census source generally covered greater numbers of employees, even
though there were a significant number of employees
that were not included in the census totals because of
disclosure problems. In a couple of the smaller counties the BES totals were greater, probably because of
the greater severity of the disclosure problem in
smaller samples, while in the larger counties and in
all five of the counties in respect to the matching

industry totals the census data source displayed significantly greater coverage than the BES source. This
superiority was especially pronounced in Philadelphia
County, the area of particular concern in the study.
Since these data were based on a point-in-time measurement of the actual number of persons for whom taxes
were being paid, it was possible to equate "more employees" with "better data" as the major data problem
would be short counts, not overreporting. For the
SMSA as a whole the census reported an additional 7.1
percent employment for the Pennsylvania portion of the
matching industries, while in Philadelphia alone the
corresponding figure was 7.6 percent more reported employment. In absolute numbers of employees this came
to 77,806 additional employees for the Pennsylvania
portion of the SMSA and 51,786 additional employees
for Philadelphia proper. Even after writing off the
considerable number of employees in the disclosure
problem industries (who could eventually be included
after an estimation step) Philadelphia's census listing of employees included 40,032 more workers than the
BES data source. Evaluation of these and the other
computed indicators suggested a clear-cut superiority
for the census data source. Coupled with the difficulty expected in finding good, comparable data for
the New Jersey portion of the SMSA and the fact that
there was considerable evidence that the census methodology was superior to the BES approach in several important respects, it was decided to proceed with
"County Business Patterns" as the principal data
resource.

The next step was to have the rest of the data
for the eight counties of the SMSA coded, punched, and
verified for 1962, 1964, 1965, 1966, and 1967. (No
"County Business Patterns" was produced for 1963.) A
simple program was then written that took these decks
and merged them into one deck per year with a four-
digit SIC code field added for use in sorting in correction cards for the disclosure gap estimation process. These correction cards were then prepared.
They were coded on the same format as the two-digit
data cards and presented any three- or four-digit detailed employment data available from "County Business
Patterns" for industries for which two-digit data did
not include employment and wage data because of non-

disclosure considerations. These cards provided both
right- and left-justified SIC codes (the latter the
four-digit new field) to allow manipulation both by
electronic computer and card-sorting apparatus.

Decks of the statewide totals by industry from
the "County Business Patterns" were also prepared. A
program was then written and run to provide estimates
of data missing because of disclosure problems. The
methodology of the program is as follows: The program
first reads and stores tables of state totals of employment, wages, and number of reporting units by industry. Then it begins to read through a merged deck
of two-digit data cards and related correction cards.
It reads a two-digit data card, and, if there is no
disclosure data gap, it punches out a similar card for
the new deck. If the card does have employment data
missing (a negative number is entered in the appropriate field in these cases to ensure recognition of this
condition), a search is made behind the card for all
associated correction cards. If none is found, an estimate is computed directly by applying the statewide
average of employees and taxable wages per reporting
unit to the number of reporting units recorded on the
incomplete card. These values are punched into a new
card for the new deck being prepared on the same format as the other cards, with the exception of a signal
punched in a special field to allow future identification of all cards containing estimated information.

If the incomplete card is followed by related
correction cards, the program constructs a file of all
correction cards relating to the industry under consideration and scans this file to construct totals of
employment and taxable wages of as large a portion of
the two-digit industry as can be covered explicitly
by complete data on the three- and four-digit level,
along with a total of the number of reporting units
for which these explicit data are available. Then,
the remaining data gaps are filled with an estimation
process based on the use of statewide average employment and wage levels per reporting unit. In certain
cases where certain detailed information on industries
and reporting units is desired to be recorded there
are correction cards without any explicit employment
data. In these cases the entire industry is estimated
on the basis of the statewide totals.

The use of statewide totals to compute average employment and taxable income per reporting unit for use in estimating nondisclosed data will in the average case lead to underestimation, for the average metropolitan enterprise is larger than the average enterprise on a statewide basis. This systematic underestimation complements other aspects of the study, such as the nature of the data base and certain computational wrinkles found elsewhere, that tend to produce results that might be described as "bed-rock" figures, that is, results that are known to be lower than the actual numbers by an indeterminate--though, it is hoped, small--amount. For many of the potential uses of this study this sort of result--the presentation of a firm minimum number of occupational and skill positions that should exist at some point in the future-- is a useful or even especially desirable form that can prove of great value in hand program planning.

These new decks of employment data by industry, years, and county with disclosure gaps estimated covered 1962 and 1964-67. A program was written to estimate the data for 1963 from the corrected data from 1962 and 1964 and the state totals from BES sources that provided 1963 data as well as totals for 1962 and 1964. If the program came upon an industry with data for both 1962 and 1964 (the general case), it would estimate 1963 employment so that it would be based on the 1962 and 1964 data but adjusted by the state totals for all three years so that the 1963 estimate for the county would bear the same relationship to the 1962 and 1964 data as the 1963 statewide total would bear to the 1962 and 1964 state totals. It was felt that this more complex algorithm would make allowances for cyclical and other variations within the given industry better than a simplistic averaging scheme.

After the 1963 employment figure was calculated, the average taxable wage rates within the given industry for 1962 and 1964 were computed. The 1963 wage rate was then estimated by taking the mean of these two rates, and the estimated 1963 taxable wage rate was computed by multiplying this estimated wage rate by the newly calculated 1963 employment. The number of reporting units for 1963 was computed by a weighted algorithm that gave 60 percent weight to the average of 1962 and 1964 reporting units and 50 percent weight

to the deviation of the 1963 estimated employment from
the simplistically computed mean based on 1962 and
1964. This was done because it was felt that fluctuations in employment reflect influences that affect the
number of reporting units to a certain degree but that
the inertia of the number of existing reporting units
is also a strong effect. More recent reflection suggests that good weights might be up to 70 percent for
inertial effects as represented by straight means and
down to as little as 30 percent for fluctuations from
the mean.

If only one card (1962 or 1964) was found for the
given industry, it was judged that this fact could be
interpreted as meaning that the industry was either
just entering or leaving a period of dormancy and that
the 1963 estimates would be the mean of the one explicit data point and the implicit zero data point, that
is, one half of the one point available. An additional
feature assured that the estimated number of reporting
units was at least one. This feature was not inserted
in the other section of the algorithm, but the results
suggest that it should have been, and after floating
point round-down several cards had to have their reporting unit entry manually changed from 0 to 1.

Projection Technology

Thus, at this stage a complete, regularized data
deck for the eight counties of the SMSA for the six
years from 1962 to 1967 was in hand, and the time was
ripe for the generation of an actual projection of
the demand for labor in the Philadelphia SMSA. A program was written for this purpose. Its control features were designed so that it could be readily used
in the future with different data, for different periods of projection, with different periods of data
base, and so forth. The actual projection algorithm
used was the least-square methodology as laid out by
Ezekiel.[1] However, it was decided to reform the dependent variables (number or reporting units, employment, and taxable wages) into their logarithmic form
for the projection process. This device, similar to
the use of semilog paper for graphical linear extrapolation, allows a linear projection mechanism to project
a higher order curve than a simple straight line.

The completed projection program contains about 370 lines of Fortran instructions and comment cards and is really too complex to discuss in detail here. In brief, it reads through the available data and decides whether enough of a data base is available for the projection of each industry in each county. Basically three sorts of projection are available: a projection of zero employment in industries that seem to have dwindled to zero employment during the period of the data base; a level projection of the last available employment and reporting unit figures, plus a nominally level but conservatively inflated taxable wage indicator for industries for which there is not enough of a data base available for a regular projection but which seem to be thriving in the last year available; and the previously described linear projection of logarithmic data, the general case. In early test runs of the mechanism it was discovered that in some cases the latter projection method would blow up. This was generally because of the projection process' making an unwarranted sustained projection of the dramatic percentage-wise growth of certain small industries. This problem proved difficult to deal with, but eventually a mechanism was developed whereby the projections being generated were constantly being compared to a simultaneously generated "ceiling" rate of growth. Whenever the projected rate of growth exceeded the ceiling rate of growth, the latter was substituted for the former. The algorithm for the ceiling rate of growth allowed for different suitable growth rates for employment, wages, and number of reporting units and included a term that made one year's employment, for example, a function of the square root of the previous year's square root of its employment, a function that allowed very high percentage growth rates while industries were small but made percentage growth rates drop sharply as the industries in question became larger. This limitation is both realistic and necessary.

The program generated and punched out yearly projections to 1975 of employment, taxable wages, and number of reporting units by SMSA county and two-digit industry. The projection then had to be translated into occupational and eventually skill-level breakdowns. As before a program was written to accomplish this task. The program utilized two industry-occupa-

tion matrixes presented by the U.S. Bureau of Labor
Statistics.[2] These two matrixes as presented in the
cited source gave percentages of total industry employment of almost 200 occupational categories for
about 160 industries on the two- and three-digit SIC
levels for 1960 and 1975. The former is from the
detailed data of the 1960 census; the latter was estimated by BLS analysts from a variety of sources.

From these two large matrixes two smaller ones
were derived, each giving employment percentages for
ten major occupational categories over about 75 two-
digit SIC industries. These small matrixes for 1960
and 1975 were punched up as decks, and the occupational distribution program stored these matrixes and
produced a set of working percentages for any year
from 1960 through 1975 on demand by linear interpolation. This was considered sufficiently accurate because these percentages are gross technological coefficients, not data points, and they tend to change
slowly and smoothly over time. Before they could be
applied to the year in question one other adjustment
of the data was necessary. A characteristic of the
projection process was that the sum of the projected
individual industries varied significantly from the
SIC industry category 0, that is, the total covered
employment for the county in question. Generally the
sum of the projections was greater than the projected
total. This effect was most pronounced in the smaller
counties and most likely is a product of the residual
tendency for small, growing industries to "blow up"
upon projection to a certain extent, despite the damp-
ering ceiling device described previously. The solution was to divide the projections of the individual
industries to the projected totals. This problem
had been foreseen, and one of the functions of the
projection program was to total and punch the sums
of the individual industry projections. This correction process implies that the projection of the
county totals can be relied upon; every indication
is that the projection of these large, complete data
points is completely in control and quite reliable.

After this correction process the matrix of working employment percentages for the year in question
was applied to the corrected employment projections
for the year in question, and the occupational levels

were totaled for county and metropolitan summations.
Then the occupational sums were broken down into
skill levels and these were totaled. This process
was done for 1968 and 1975. The last process was
done by hand as it was judged the most efficient
approach. The details of this process, especially
the rationale of the skill-level breakdowns, will be
presented in the discussion of results, since it is
a matter central to the usefulness of these results.

Spotlight on the Construction
Industry

Reconstruction and renewal in Philadelphia carried the label "Top Priority." Legislation on all
government levels provided funds and programs. Political leaders and neighborhood groups alike demanded
action. Yet, no label, program, or politician can
ever raze a slum or build an apartment. This task--
implementing the grand schemes of city planners or
renewal technicians--can only fall on the laborers
and craftsmen of the construction industry. This
single fact raises a question not often asked: Can
the construction industry do the job?

The answer is no! The local construction industry simply cannot satisfy both the ongoing private and
public demand and the additional requirements of rebuilding immense areas without making revolutionary
changes in its nature, size, and structure. This
structural revolution may occur as the industry rises
to the challenge, but only if it does can the job be
done.

Available Construction Labor

The total supply of qualified workers at any
point in time is the total of several definable labor
force classifications. Between 1961 and 1967 roughly
13,000 full-time production workers were added to
the ranks of the employed. To help explain who these
workers were, where they came from, and implications
for the future, an analysis of the classifications
from which the employed labor force is derived will
be helpful.

The first group, and by far the largest and most important, is composed of the regular full-time dues-paying members of the local member unions of the Building Trades Council. Although precise membership data are unavailable, reliable sources have indicated that membership in these unions has remained relatively stable at approximately 43,000. However, these same sources also indicate that nonreporting or overreporting by local unions might run as high as 10 percent, or approximately 4,000 workers.

The second group is composed of workers who normally work on a permit basis. Since special union work permits are issued to qualified workers when seasonal high demand or other special conditions make it impossible to fill contractors' needs through regular union membership, the union work permit has the same effect as temporary union membership. However, the temporary nature should not be overemphasized because reliable sources indicate that many permit holders are in fact full-time permanent members of the work force. Again, few hard data are available, but reliable sources estimate that the permit holders' group is normally composed of from 10,000 to 15,000 workers.

The third major worker group is composed of nonunion full- and part-time workers. Both union and nonunion sources indicate that this group has grown significantly over the past few years. The two sources, however, differ about the absolute magnitude of this group, estimates from union sources being considerably below those from other sources. On balance, it can be reasonably estimated that in 1967 this group ran between 10,000 and 15,000 workers.

Summarizing these three groups gives the following 1967 estimates:

Regular union members	43,000 to 47,000
Permit holders	10,000 to 15,000
Nonunion workers	10,000 to 15,000
Total workers	63,000 to 79,000

In 1967 actual seasonal employment of production workers varied from approximately 57,000 to 76,000. In 1962, a relatively bad year for construction, only 67,000 total workers and 57,000 production workers were employed. Seasonality caused the range of production worker employment to run from 46,000 to 64,000. An examination of the three groups above gives the following 1962 estimate:

Regular union members	39,000 to 43,000
Permit holders	5,000 to 12,000
Nonunion workers	7,000 to 12,000
Total workers	51,000 to 67,000

Various sources and assumptions lead, therefore, to the following estimated change from 1962 to 1967:

Regular union members	no change to +8,000
Permit holders	+5,000 to +12,000
Nonunion workers	+3,000 to +8,000

From these ranges it is obvious that the great bulk of the employment expansion probably occurred under union auspices. If the 13,000 workers added on an annual average basis were distributed among these groups, point estimates of increases would be as follows:

	Number	Percent
Regular union members	2,737	21
Permit holders	5,816	45
Nonunion workers	4,447	34

Regular union membership rolls can be increased from five sources: (1) increased apprentice enrollments, (2) reactivation of inactive members, (3) transfers from other areas, (4) mass inclusions of the work force of contractors brought under union contracts, and (5) individual applicants who can pass examinations to qualify as journeymen.

Reliable sources indicate that of the above five methods of increasing membership rolls, only

methods 2, 3, and 4 could be considered significant
between 1962 and 1967. Of these three, by far the
most important category was the second, the reactivation of inactive members. These individuals are
considered to be re-entrants into the industry's
labor force. Two facts argue well for the proposition that these re-entrants were in fact the prime
source of increased manpower. First, a special
study by the U.S. Department of Labor indicated that
the early 1960s had extremely high interindustry mobility for persons in the construction trades. Second, during the period 1953-67 employment in construction averaged approximately 79,000 and then fell to
65,000 in 1961; therefore, a ready pool of fully
trained potential re-entrants existed as construction expanded in the period from 1962 to 1967. Reliable sources indicate that the other significant
sources of increased union membership each accounted
for, at most, a few hundred additional workers. Supporting evidence for this proposition is to be found
in the fact that only one manpower area in eastern
Pennsylvania and New Jersey showed a decline in employment during the period being studied, and that
decline was relatively small.

     In addition, the 1962-67 period found the unions'
organizing efforts exceptionally passive, and only a
handful of new contractors were brought under union
contracts.

     The growth in permit holders can be accounted
for in much the same manner as union membership increases, the bulk of such workers being re-entrants
into the industry in response to high wages and
strong demand conditions.

     The growth in the nonunion sector can be ac-
counted for by two factors; the growth of minority
contractors and the passive organizing efforts of
the trade unions. It is almost axiomatic that organizing efforts are strongest in periods of falling
demand, when a nonunion contractor poses an immediate
threat. In periods of rising demand, such as the
period under study, no threat is felt when marginal
nonunion contractors are hiring, and often training,

their own nonunion labor force. The growth of the
minority contractor poses a special problem for the
unions. If they bring him under a union contract,
his minority workers immediately become full journeymen. The countervailing internal forces within the
union have, in general, left such contractors in the
nonunion category even after they become a competitive challenge to union contractors. In 1967 two
such minority contractors, employing together less
than 50 journeymen in all trades, were brought under
union contracts. At present there are more than 90
minority general contractors and subcontractors
operating in the Philadelphia area.

On balance, it can be reasonably asserted that
the great bulk of the net increase in the construction labor force under union auspices came from re-
entrants to the industry and only a very small
proportion from persons not previously in the industry
and therefore requiring training. Conversely, the
great bulk of the net increase in the nonunion sector
came from new entrants into the industry from related
industries (for example, carpenters from furniture
making) or from new entrants, especially minority
workers, who required training and learned their
skill or craft on the job.

Finally, it is reasonable to assume that the
supply of new workers from the re-entrant category
is undoubtedly almost wholly depleted. This is probably true for several reasons. First, the magnitude
of the assumed re-entrants between 1962 and 1967 accounts for the bulk of the 1956-61 employment decline
of approximately 11,000 production workers. Second,
the firm demand and high wages continued for the
five full years of the period studied, and, therefore,
persons who left the industry between 1956 and 1961
and failed to return between 1962 and 1967 can be
reasonably presumed to be either better situated or
retired. Third, unemployment in 1967 in the Philadelphia area reached an all time low for the period
after World War II.

The obvious conclusion from the foregoing is
that the total actual supply of skilled construction

labor in the near future will only expand as training
programs, especially union apprentice programs, expand to meet future labor requirements. If the
trends of the five years studied continue to hold,
the total annual average production labor force in
1972 will be approximately 75,000. On a seasonal
basis the available labor force should run from
69,000 to 85,000.

Construction Demand

Two estimates were made of the level of construction activity between 1967 and 1972 and in 1972.
The first projection was a simple linear trend on
total construction value, calculated on a constant
cost basis (1967 dollars). The eight-county Philadelphia area total construction value rose from $639
million in 1961 to $810 million in 1965 and settled
in the tight money years of 1966 and 1967 at approximately $760 million. The trend established by the
seven years yields a 1972 projection of construction
value of approximately $900 million. To this $900
million must be added the additional impact of the
City's new housing programs and the School Board's
stepped-up school construction. In 1972 these two
additional factors will add approximately $115 mil-
lion to the projected total, bringing the grand total
for new construction to slightly over $1 billion.

The second estimate of the total value of construction was based on projecting residential and
nonresidential construction independently. To estimate the number of housing units likely to be constructed by 1972 within the SMSA, the following
projection methodology was employed.

First, the population of the SMSA was projected
to 1970 and 1975. This projection was based on the
relationship between State of Pennsylvania population and SMSA population. Both were available from
series P-25 Current Population Reports (CPR) from
1960 to 1966. Over this period the SMSA changed
from 38.3 percent of Pennsylvania's population in
1960 to 40.5 percent in 1966. This ratio increased
each year at a slightly declining rate over the

period. By 1970 the trend of this ratio would indicate a figure of 41.1 percent and by 1975, a figure
of 41.6 percent. These figures were then applied to
the CPR projection of Pennsylvania population in
1970 and 1975. Both high and low estimates were employed, using an SMSA figure of roughly from 4,780,000
to 4,830,000 for 1970 and from 4,880,000 to 5,050,000
for 1975.

To estimate the number of households, it was
necessary to project the household size ratio. First,
a ratio was drawn with the Pennsylvania and U.S. persons per household data over time and projected.
The SMSA data showed an increasing divergence from
the Pennsylvania data over time from 1950, when both
State and SMSA were equal to 3.60 persons per household. By 1960, the persons per household figure had
diverged by 0.044, the state being lower. Some data
were also available for 1965, and increasing divergence was indicated. For 1970, the CPR indicated
that the state figure would be approximately 3.29
and for 1975, 3.25. Using these changes as given,
the SMSA household ratio was preliminarily projected
to be 3.354 in 1970 and 3.337 in 1975.

Second, the SMSA data were compared with the
U.S. series. From 1950 onward this series showed an
increasing convergence. In 1950 Philadelphia's persons per household differed from the United States
by 0.072. By 1960 it had converged to 0.049 and in
1965, to 0.017. Therefore, a second preliminary estimate was that complete convergence would occur during the projection period. This would yield an estimate of 3.321 in 1970 and 3.28 in 1975.

The third series of preliminary figures was
also estimated. This used a differential rate of
change analysis on all three series. This method
produced 1970 and 1975 projections of 3.337 and
3.297, respectively.

Inasmuch as the three estimates of persons per
household differed insignificantly for 1970, the
state divergence series was employed. Because of a
value judgment on the part of the writer that census

series projection I-D--which is based on an assumption of declining fertility rates and therefore yields lower numbers--is somewhat more realistic than series I-B--which yields higher results because of the assumption of increasing fertility--the base series I-D was employed.

Applying these figures to the projected population yields a household projection for 1970 of from 1,437,000 to 1,452,000 and for 1975 of from 1,508,000 to 1,561,000. Thus, net household formation in the 1965-70 period would equal from 72,000 to 82,000, and from 1970 to 1975 would be from 71,000 to 109,000.

Next, it was necessary to project relationship of net household formation to new housing starts. On an annual basis, using national data, this ratio varied during the 1956-67 period from approximately 1.2 to nearly 3.0, making the annual relationship series highly unsuitable. It was hypothesized that this variation was possibly the result of cyclical fluctuations in such areas as interest rates and consumer buying habits. Therefore, to smooth these variations, three-year moving averages were calculated for both housing starts and net new household formations. When the ratios between the moving averages were calculated, an excellent and consistent relationship was established. Only three periods-- 1958-60 (recession of 1959), 1960-62 (the recession of 1961), and 1965-67 (the exceptional tight money market of 1966)--showed significant deviations. Outside these years the ratio moved steadily and consistently upward. Applying a linear trend to the ratio, it is expected that the 1968-72 period should show, in general, a ratio of new housing starts of approximately 1.80 housing starts per net household formation. The experience in the SMSA has not, however, matched the national figures, the period from 1950 to 1960 showing a rough equality between net household formation and new housing and the period from 1960 to 1965 showing a ratio of approximately 1.3 rather than the national 1.65. Assuming that this general pattern continues, a projected 1968-72 ratio of approximately 1.38 would result for the SMSA instead of the 1.80 to be expected nationally.

Applying this ratio to the projected net increase in households in the SMSA the five-year period 1966 to 1970 shows between 99,000 and 120,000 new houses constructed in the SMSA in the 1966-70 period and from 97,000 to 149,000 in the 1971-75 period.

Of the first five-year projection period two years' data were already available. In 1966 building permits were issued to 26,160 new housing units, and in 1967 permits were issued to 22,323 new housing units. Assuming that 95 percent of the permits issued actually resulted in new housing, this would mean that approximately 46,000 new housing units were started in 1966-67, leaving a residual for the projection period to 1970 of from 53,000 to 74,000. In 1971-72 between 39,000 and 60,000 new houses should be constructed. Thus, the five years 1968-72 should see the construction of from 92,000 to 134,000 new housing units.

In the years 1965-67 the deflated value of the average Philadelphia area housing unit held steady at $13,100. If the years 1967-72 show no significant change (outside of cost changes) in this average value, then the housing unit projection above will mean an annual average residential construction value (in 1967 dollars) of from $241 million to $351 million. For point estimations the midpoint of the range, $296 million, was employed. This relatively low value per unit figure is consistent with the demand projections of the CPR. The Gladstone Report (CPR Technical Report $14) projected the low cost housing deficit to be 60,000 units by 1970.

Nonresidential construction over the past twenty years has expanded almost constantly on both a constant dollar and current dollar basis. Because of this consistency a linear trend seemed highly appropriate for projection purposes. Using the nine years 1959-67 as a base, an expansion in 1967 dollars from $222 million to $469 million was observed. Thus, the trend would yield for 1967-72 a total nonresidential construction value in 1967 dollars of $2.8 billion, or an average of $560 million per year.

The trend also yields a point estimate for 1972 of
$621 million. Again, looking backward in the 1959-67
period, an average deviation of ±5.6 percent from
trend was observed, and the maximum range of deviation from trend was from -9.1 percent to +11.5 percent, which occurred in consecutive years. Using
the 5.6 percent deviation would yield a range of from
$586 million to $656 million for 1972.

Total construction vlaue, aside from the City's
special housing program and the School Board's expanded school construction program, was therefore
estimated to be $917 million in 1972, with a devia-
tion of no more than $90 million likely. Adding the
City's new housing programs and the School Board's
school construction program raised the estimated
1972 total value to approximately $1 billion.

Since both estimating procedures yielded almost
identical results of approximately $1 billion, it
was next necessary to independently estimate the
labor force required to produce this total value of
construction.

In 1967 the average construction value per production worker in the Philadelphia area was approximately $11,400. If this value was to apply in 1972,
88,000 workers would be required to meet the demand
projected for that year. However, if productivity
increased by 2 percent a year during this period,
total value per production worker (a reasonable proxy
for productivity) should increase to roughly $12,500.
At these levels annual average demand for labor would
be only 81,000 workers. It is interesting to note,
however, that during the period 1963-67 the value
per worker measure remained stable in the eight-county
area and grew only slightly--that is, at less than
2 percent per year--in the nation. Because normal
seasonality within construction labor usually runs
in the vicinity of plus or minus 10 percent of the
annual average, it becomes relatively clear that regardless of the exact level of productivity change,
demand for labor will fluctuate between roughly
73,000 and 90,000 workers.

Supply Versus Demand

The table below compares annual average low seasonal and high seasonal labor supply with the corresponding demand estimates for 1972.

	Annual Average	Low Seasonal	High Seasonal
Available labor	75,000	69,000	85,000
Labor demand	81,000	73,000	90,000
Labor deficit	6,000	4,000	5,000

Thus, in spite of assumed increasing productivity and assumed labor force growth consistent with past trends, 1972 should see a rather severe labor shortage. In 1967 the high seasonal showed unemployment of roughly 4 percent, or 3,000 workers, and contractors considered the labor market extremely tight, available workers in some crafts being non-existent. Since the 1972 projections show a minimum high seasonal deficit of 5,000 workers, it can only be concluded that many construction jobs will be delayed or canceled because skilled workers cannot be found.

In summary, the following has been shown:

1. Increasing levels of new construction will result in a demand for at least 11,000 additional production workers in the industry by 1972.

2. The major element in recent labor force expansion was the re-entry of skilled workers into construction trades after an absence of from three to ten years. There is little possibility that such re-entrants will be a significant factor for expansion in the future.

3. The existing size of apprentice programs and apprentice enrollments are not significantly different from current retirements, resulting in a union work force generally stable in size.

4. Productivity in the construction trades has
not appreciably improved in the past five years, and
no notable increase is expected to occur in the near
future. Increasing productivity cannot therefore be
expected to offset the anticipated increase in labor
demand.

The conclusion is that although natural labor
force expansion can meet the anticipated demand for
construction labor, whether or not this will actually
take place will be largely decided by the policies
and procedures of the Building Trades Council and
its individual member unions. Without significant
changes in present policies, the reluctant and pain-
ful conclusion is that this will not occur.

The policy role of the City government should
take into account the following possible positions
and actions:

1. Vocational education programs to produce
more qualified journeymen

2. Review of contracts with the City government
for minority participation

3. More intensive studies on productivity increases in relation to wages with contract negotia-
tions.

The Need for Managers

The Problem

As an economic input the importance of management personnel has successfully avoided any attempt
at accurate measurement. There are, however, very
visible signs of the chronic shortages in this manpower category. Recent salaries for business school
graduates and for holders of postgraduate business
degrees have skyrocketed in response to unprecedented
competition among public and private employers for
their untested skills. The unprecedented growth and
proliferation of executive recruiting agencies is
only one indication of increased mobility accorded

the experienced management specialist by the inter-
company struggle to obtain experienced personnel.
So common are attempts to lure executives and lesser
managers away from other employment that the term
"executive piracy" has become the name of a highly
profitable business rather than a pejorative for the
practices of an unscrupulous minority.

There is no indication that these problems will
in any way be elevated from existing sources in the
foreseeable future; in fact, the American Management
Association estimates an additional unfilled need
for in excess of 200,000 qualified managers by the
mid-1970s. Indeed, locating, training, and retain-
ing sufficient numbers of management personnel is a
well realized national problem--and the City of Philadelphia is no exception to the rule. With this in
mind, the Economic Development Unit, in a two-pronged
approach, explored this situation for both small and
large business through surveys and interviews in an
attempt to determine the need for, and potential
acceptability of, a local management training center
to provide previously unavailable training and to
allow employers to expand their own management programs.

To assess management needs in the Philadelphia
area economy a study of demand for managerial talent
was conducted on two distinct levels. The first was
the preparation and distribution of a questionnaire
directed toward evaluating the feelings of larger-
scale employers toward the management situation in
the area. The second was a series of direct interviews with various small business agencies and entrepreneurial training programs in an attempt to get a
firsthand feeling for the problems of this chronically
management-scarce subsection of the economy.

Although management problems for larger-scale
employers, as revealed by the survey, were, as expected, less than for small-scale employers, management skills emerged as one of the greatest single
problems across the spectrum of the economic foundation of the economy. None of this is startling information, but it does suggest the very definite

need for investigation into additional facilities
and methods for recruiting and training management
candidates. It is imperative that this training be
made available to the small-scale businessman for
his survival in an increasingly competitive and involved business community, and it can be an extremely
valuable addition to the programs of most large-scale
employers. Competently administered, such training
could have far-reaching effects in that it would allow for the upgrading of skills of able persons who
may be overqualified for the positions they hold but
excluded from ascending the employment ladder by educational deficiencies. One benefit that would arise
from providing access to upward mobility would be in
relieving the pressure upon, and consequent tensions
of, currently employed persons who see the hiring of
minority and hard-core persons as a threat to their
security, finding themselves without the ability to
advance their own positions.

The Survey of Large Corporations*

The survey was prepared by the Economic Development Unit in cooperation with the Office of the Director of Commerce and was mailed to the 738 employers in the Philadelphia area. The mailing list was
compiled from the City wage tax files of the City's
Department of Collections and was verified and up-
dated by the staff of the Economic Development Unit,
using corroborative information made available through
the Greater Philadelphia Chamber of Commerce.

Selection of the mailing list was made on the
basis of a number of criteria. The first was favorable experience encountered in previous distribution
to this sample. Second was the desire to achieve a
maximum coverage within the limitations imposed both
by time and financial considerations. Third was the
fact that this taxpayer list insured a high degree
of accuracy and timeliness dictated by the necessity
of maintaining current status for efficient collec-

---

*See sample of survey questionnaire in Appendix
to Chapter 6 (pp. 343-50).

tion of revenues. Finally, the Philadelphia City
wage tax is collected from all persons employed in
the City and all Philadelphia residents regardless
of location of employment. Thus, major employers
within the City and in the immediate surrounding area
would be included.

To ensure maximum response the questionnaire was
addressed directly to the ranking personnel officer
of the concern or, failing this, to the senior person in the Philadelphia area office. In addition,
the Department of Commerce supplied a covering letter
over the signature of S. Harry Galfand, City Representative and Director of Commerce, whose name is well
known and respected throughout the business community.

The survey was designed by the Economic Development Unit with the advice of Bertram Zumeta, Economist for the Philadelphia Electric Company, and Walter
Powell, Vice-President of the Auerbach Corporation.
Detailed instructions for completion of the questionnaire were included, and a telephone information line
was maintained by the Economic Development Unit.

The questionnaire was organized into four basic
categories: analysis of current sources of management personnel, present and future demand for management personnel, possible additional sources of management, and program approaches for possible management training. Again, in the interest of simplicity,
the number of questions was rigorously confined to
encourage a prompt and complete response.

The results were tabulated and coded by the Economic Development Unit and compiled in conjunction
with the Water Department Computer Center. Of the
738 questionnaires mailed out, 157 returns were received, a 21.3 percent level of response for the
sample. In excess of 193,000 persons were employed
by respondent firms, representing over 20 percent of
total covered employment for the City.

In the interest of clarity, the results will be
considered in the order of the questionnaire to

facilitate cross reference to the questions and directions.

The first table gives a comparison of the answering employer's current management situation with that of two years previously, in the interest of determining the general short term trend in the availability and supply of management personnel. As shown in the table the experience of the majority of the respondents reveals an improvement in their situation, only a small minority, 5.8 percent, indicating a negative experience.

Management Situation	Number of Respondents	Percentage of Total
Improved	90	57.9
Remained static	57	36.5
Detrimental	9	5.8

The second table shows the relative importance of commonly accepted sources of management personnel. Pennsylvania State Employment agencies were included in the questionnaire to determine what acceptance this agency enjoys in such a generally high level employment classification. The table indicates the ranking accorded the various sources on a weighted basis showing the percentage of total response given each category.

It was assumed that college recruiting would generally be considered a personnel department function, but the response did not support this conclusion. Redistributing college recruiting to personnel would result in the ranking in Column A, Rank A. A point of interest is that, although the respondent was allowed to eliminate any choice not employed, the various State Employment agencies, contrary to common belief, do enjoy significant acceptance as a source of management candidates, indicating that they might realistically be expected to be helpful in providing job opportunities to persons completing meaningful training programs in management.

Rank	Source of Personnel	Percent-age of Total Respon-ses	Col-umn A[a]	Rank A[a]
1	Internal	19.2	19.2	2
2	Other (primar-ily college recruitment)[b]	18.4	18.4	3
3	Personnel	15.4	23.7	1
4	Direct advertising	14.1	10.1	6
5	Private employment agencies	12.9	12.9	4
6	Employee referral	12.3	12.3	5
7	Pennsylvania State Employ-ment agencies	7.7	7.7	7

[a]Column A and Rank A represent, respec-tively, the percentile response and rank-ing if the proportion of the responses allo-cated to "other" that was respondent-desig-nated as college recruiting is allocated to personnel.

[b]Parenthetic qualification added to indi-cate respondent commentary under "other" was not included in question as presented in the survey.

The next table presents the results of respon-dent ranking of five categories of employment in lo-cation decision making. As in the table above the replies were grouped and are presented in percentile figures. Combined management--middle and lower plus executive--although usually considered the most mo-bile group appears to rank surprisingly high in mak-ing the decision to expand or locate in a particular area.

Order of Importance of Manpower Categories in Site Location	Percentage of Total Response
1. Production	24.2
2. Middle and lower management	22.1
3. Clerical	19.8
4. Executive	18.2
5. Unskilled	15.7

In the following table the expectations of future employment for the sample as a whole are shown. Figures were requested covering current employment (mid-March 1969) and estimated employment for mid-March 1971 and 1974. (The figures do not represent the sample as a whole. They are compiled only from those returns complete for the two years being compared. Therefore, the comparison between 1969 and 1971 was based on 129 returns complete through 1971, and the comparison of 1969 with 1974 was based on 122 returns complete through 1974.)

Also requested was an indication of anticipated deficits in the form of an estimation of the difference between expected actual employment and that necessary for optimal operation. Unfortunately so few returns were received complete in this respect that no meaningful conclusions can be presented. Projected employment expansion appears to run at about 3 percent a year. Figures for management run similarly to those for nonmanagement. However, short term expansion in the area of management training appears to outrun that in all other areas, indicating that the demand for trainees will remain high and that chronic shortages of qualified replacement personnel will be a continuing problem.

Question 8 revealed that 29 percent of all respondents (45 out of 155) were using programmed instructional materials and that none had found these materials to be unsatisfactory. Of the 45 respondents who employed such programs, 15 felt they were receiving successful results and 13, satisfactory results; 17 found the results currently unascertainable.

Manpower Category	1969	1971	Percent-age Increase
Executive management	2,732	2,936	7.5
Middle and lower management	15,269	15,654	2.5
Management training	2,881	3,282	13.9
Other employment	145,420	154,707	6.4
Total employment	166,302	176,579	6.2

Manpower Category	1969	1974	Percent-age Increase
Executive management	2,651	3,133	18.2
Middle and lower management	15,048	16,813	11.7
Management training	2,881	3,457	20.7
Other employment	145,420	167,120	17.4
Total employment	162,498	190,523	17.2

The following table ranks four sources of personnel for entry-level management positions. In this case "other" was predominantly designated as college graduates or persons in the process of completing their degrees, indicating that, at least for the sample representing larger industry, there remains a significant degree of resistance to considering alternatives to college graduate managers or

managerial candidates. Yet thought is obviously being given to alternative choices, and realistic
training may prove as beneficial for the advancement
of these persons as for entrepreneurs.

Alternative Sources of Management	Number of Responses	Percentage of Total
Current high school graduates	6	3.5
Employees in lower skilled jobs selected for interest and ability	41	23.8
Combination of the above	55	32.0
Other	70	40.7

The last table, below, shows the ranking assigned
four management training formats to upgrade employee
skills for entry-level management positions. Internal on-the-job training ranked highest, 33.8 percent
of the total response; and this result was reinforced
by the answers received in Question 7, which almost
exclusively supported the fact that experience showed
on-the-job training the most beneficial. Again, however, there is more than adequate response to alternative plans to indicate that other methods are being
attempted and might find greater acceptance if necessary facilities could be provided.

Type of Training	Percentage Response[a]
Internal on-the-job training	33.8
Internal training by visiting instructional staff	22.6
Nonwork night school or junior college format	21.9
Coop training (employees attending a separate training center while on company payroll	21.7

[a]Indicates percent of total response
  favoring selection.

In answering Question 9, of 146 respondents, 86
(58.9 percent) indicated interest in participating
in the development of a management training center
geared to the needs of employees while 60 (41.1 percent) stated that they would not be interested. Additional comments indicated that many employers felt
that general training would not be applicable to
their industries and that this fact would prohibit
their meaningful participation.

The survey, although generally indicating a
favorable management climate for larger employers in
the Philadelphia area, reveals a continuing interest
in management development. There is evidence that
although traditional training and sources are still
preferred consideration is being given to alternatives. Also, considerable interest was indicated by
the sample respondents in participating in an employee management training center.

The Survey of the Small Business Community

To complement the information gained from the
survey of larger corporations, interviews were held
with many of the agencies interested in small business and educational development within the City as
well as with educational research groups, such as
the American Management Association and the Sterling
Institute,* in an attempt to uncover not only needs
but also recent thinking about possible solutions.

The pervasive need for training in basic business skills emerges--with the possible exception of
capital--as the most important problem of the small
business community. This becomes even more apparent
when the needs and problems of minority business
programs are considered. In this area lack of formal
training is often a major roadblock to finding necessary capital for business expansion or for the prospective entrepreneur. In every case in which discussions were conducted, this lack was expressed as the
greatest single problem faced in developing new

---

*See list in Appendix to Chapter 6 (p. 351).

businesses. When it is combined with the interest
indicated by larger companies in participating in a
management training program, it becomes obvious that
there is widespread recognition that the problem
exists and that effective new approaches are necessary and should find widespread acceptance in the
business community.

The problem is being attacked in many ways.
Most development agencies supply at least limited
technical assistance through counseling services and
workshops. The Opportunities Industrialization Center is operating full-scale programs in both management and entrepreneurial training with significant
extremely successful results and participation.
Thirteen training centers now serve more than 1,900
persons, and they have placed more than 9,000 trainees in jobs for a saving to the State of Pennsylvania
alone of over $10 million in public assistance, ac-
cording to the Office of the Mayor of the City of
Philadelphia.

Both Temple University and the University of
Pennsylvania have instituted free or nominal cost
night programs for underprivileged persons to stimulate interest in education and ideally to bring them
into the regular college curriculum. Requirements
for all these courses are simply the desire to attend
and to learn.

These programs include basic orientation courses
in management theory, marketing, finance, and principles of accounting, taught in a manner that is com-
prehensible to the person with limited background.
The optimal goal is to inspire the participant to
enter into a regular full-time or night school university curriculum with whatever scholarship support
is necessary.

Both the Small Business Association and the
Philadelphia Enterprises Development Corporation have
engaged in workshop programs in specific management
areas as an aid to the small businessman. In both
these cases the need for such training was emphasized
in conversation with staff members.

It is obvious that considerable time and effort
are now being expended in providing workable and
meaningful management programs. It was with this in
mind that the following program was outlined.

Application of Modern Management Training Techniques

With the many new breakthroughs in education,
primarily in the field of programmed instructional
techniques--combined with group dynamics, audiovisual
aids, and the revival of psychodramatic techniques--
many effective tools have been placed in the hands
of the educator. Further, methods for business motivation have recently proven experimentally successful
and open new avenues of thought. Also, many educational organizations have become active in producing
educational packages for use by the noncollege-edu-
cated.

The problems of training programs have always
revolved around scope, timing, and interest of the
material being presented. Modern techniques answer
most of these problems. Programmed instruction allows each candidate to work at his own pace, allowing him to expend whatever time he needs to progress
at the rate of the group. Group participation following programmed preparation reinforced with audiovisual and other techniques allows for rapid learning
and maintenance of participant interest. With the
many available programs a trained staff could administer a wide variety of course material, presenting
it as needed to a broad cross section of students.
Also, course material is generally presented in com-
pact units with which intensive application can
present fairly comprehensive material in short periods of time. In addition, temporal variability is
generally possible to suit the needs of the participants. Courses can run on the basis of as many
units a week as can be conveniently arranged, depend-
ing upon the situation of the participants. It is
therefore usually possible to tailor the courses to
meet from a daily to a weekly basis, allowing a freedom of curriculum structure to accommodate full-time
students as well as those who, because of job commitments or other complications, must attend on a less
regular basis.

The large variety of available curriculums is
not the only major benefit that has come from these
new methods. Using group techniques and tested
course outlines a much higher degree of interest can
be maintained among persons who have probably spent
many years away from formal education of any sort.
Further, programmed instructional materials allow
each person to approach the classroom situation prepared to participate fully, thus eliminating in part
the discomfort and hesitance of members who, because
of lack of education or background, are less well
versed in the material. In this way the type of
discouragement resulting from a feeling of inferiority
is lessened while group participation allows for universal benefit from pertinent extracurricular information.

Costs for each course package run in the range
of $150 to $300 per unit per candidate but should be
considerably reduced by greater use of a full-time
staff. Further, the training program would, pre-
dictably, with growing experience, begin to develop
its own courses and methods. Additional savings
would result from cooperation in testing and development with institutions preparing such packages.
These costs have, in some cases, been demonstrably
below the positive benefits of business expansion
and resultant job creation,[3] not to mention resultant
savings from increased tax revenues and decreased
public assistance payments. Physical facilities to
operate such a program need not prove an insurmount-
able problem, for any space that can be arranged into
a conference room format with simple audiovisual
equipment would be quite adequate. Central administrative facilities combined with some classroom space
would probably be valuable, but a large part of the
classroom load could be set up in underutilized
space in public schools, local universities and colleges, and even in conference space available from
local corporations. This would have many advantages
beyond low cost. With satellite centers transportation would be less of a problem for the participants,
and the support of the local community would more
easily be enlisted. Another important benefit would
derive from the greater acceptance that might be

expected from employers for two reasons. The first
would be that an employer would be far more likely
to allow employees to attend an in-shop program or
local program, which minimizes commuting time, and,
further, the program would be more closely identified
by the employee as a benefit supplied by the company.
Second, an in-house program on company time would
promote greater participation while allowing the
employer a feeling of control, which he would lack
under other circumstances. Finally, such geographic
decentralization would allow the candidate to attend
classes under more familiar circumstances and in a
relatively homogeneous group, which would lessen the
tensions inherent in entering the often foreign environment of a centralized facility located away from
home or job.

For the prospective entrepreneur the courses
would open many new opportunities. The training
could be tied into loan programs to allow the candidate to meet minimum educational requirements. By
providing pertinent subject material the training
center would help him to overcome educational deficiencies that might seriously prejudice his chances
for success in business. Further, the program would
supply another backstop to the very important counseling efforts now being made by local agencies, for
it would be possible to refer the client to a program
in which he would receive formal training in areas
in which he was experiencing difficulty. The program
would also be a valuable adjunct to the outside
training program described in the Venture Capital Corporation recommended in this volume.

The business community in general would similarly
benefit in a number of ways. First, it would be
making available local facilities for programs that
already enjoy acceptance in existing management
training programs. Second, it would have the chance
to tap previously unrecognized manpower resources,
in that, properly applied, such programs could be
used to increase the level of aspiration of able persons, perhaps further motivating them to seek additional formal education available from local colleges
and universities. The desirability of this goal is

borne out by the number of employers who are currently
willing to subsidize higher education for their employees. Finally, certainly, since material would
be tailored to the job situation, it would be easier
for an employee to readjust to schooling and make
the goal of self-improvement for advancement through
education a more realistic possibility.

A competent management training center could be
an invaluable asset to economic development in the
Philadelphia area. It would allow large-scale employers to expand their programs while at the same
time making this sophisticated training available to
the entrepreneur and small-scale businessman locally
and at reasonable cost. As management training is a
common problem, the effects of such a facility would
reach all levels of the business community and
equally would have application in the public sector.
The interest and needs are present, and acceptable
materials are available--with the promise of much
more in the near future. All that remains is to organize a program that will draw upon these resources.

Recommendations

It was recommended that two working committees
be set up to establish the needs and desires of the
community. The first would be composed of representatives of groups now providing entrepreneurial and
management training, predominantly for the underprivileged; the second, from industries that have
indicated through the survey that they would have
interest in participating in a management training
center. The activities of both committees would be
coordinated by a staff member of the Economic Development Unit.

The purpose of the committees would be to assess
current programs and to evaluate available material
in the light of how it would fit into a broad and
generally acceptable curriculum for effective management training. This effort would be carried on in
conjunction with suppliers of educational materials,
such as the American Management Association, who have
demonstrated their willingness to cooperate in

establishing such a facility. It would further be
the job of the committees to find ways to integrate
the resultant plan with existing programs to reduce
possible duplication of effort.

After both committees had completed their eval-
uations, the staff of the Economic Development Unit
would structure a plan of training based upon their
recommendations. In this way a comprehensive program
serving the needs of all parties and capable of generating broad community support could be submitted.
Although such committee-based action is often slow
and difficult, it is felt necessary to achieve the
degree of cooperation that would be indispensable in
providing a service to such a broad spectrum of the
community.

**CAPITAL
FORMATION**

VENTURE CAPITAL: WHERE TO GET
IT AND HOW TO PUT IT TO WORK

The Roots of Deficiency

One of the toughest urban challenges facing the
banking industry is the assurance of adequate financing to business enterprises within the inner city.
The continuing growth of urban blight and the growing
demand for economic participation from residents of
ghetto communities attest to the fact that public
effort alone--which is typical of those efforts pre-
dating the period of civil disorders--has not been
able to reverse the deterioration of the ghettos.
Yet private capital, which originally built these
cities, has been drawn into development of the inner
city far less than it should have been.

The Fantasy of Credit Flight

Because in recent years the limited flow of capital to inner cities has become more prominent as
the problems of these areas have become magnified,
financial institutions are often accused of con-
sciously perpetuating inner city deterioration and
the dehumanizing conditions that exist there. This
belief is fiction, not fact.

The underlying factors that, in fact, cause the existence of a "credit deficiency" environment must be recognized and understood. Underemployment, a consequently fluctuating income base, low quality education and educational facilities, inadequate transportation, deteriorated housing, a poor quality of public services, and a host of related market factors are the reasons credit and investment capital have been slow to find their way into the ghetto. There is a direct and indisputable relationship between the economic base of any given area and the allocation of credit and investment capital to it. The simple fact is that the inner city ghetto areas do not have the essential market characteristics necessary to bid effectively for capital in the market as we know it.

Ultimate Solution or Action Now

The ultimate solution to this problem will not be provided by simply infusing substantial amounts of capital into areas that lack the essential socio-economic base to support and sustain growth. To attain real results, the vital fabric of the inner city must be improved. Assured employment, increased income levels, the provision of quality education and training--these factors will help to cure credit and investment capital concerns more quickly than artificial devices of intravenous feeding.

It must be recognized, however, that the realities of urban America today demand action now; that they will not wait for ultimate solutions. Moreover, it would be grossly misleading to suggest that the inner city is totally without a resource base of any substance whatever. There are within the ghetto an undeveloped resource of human talent, energy, and ambition; an underdeveloped but increasingly effective purchasing power; an underutilized capacity for business development; latent market potential; the capacity for leadership; and an untested opportunity for growth. Consequently, affirmative actions are both possible and necessary.

USING TRADITIONAL CAPITAL
SOURCES

Credit Criteria

If one attempts to apply traditional credit analysis techniques to the problem of business development in the ghetto community, the analysis bogs down at a very early stage. Business loans are made on the basis of an established set of criteria, including the competence and character of management; potential for stability or growth of earnings; growth in sales; quality of assets; comparative operating ratios; past performance on loans; the amount of personal equity in initial capitalization; and the amount and quality of market competition. Yet, in the case of the ghetto community's economy, many of the factors required to meet these essential criteria may be lacking.

An individual's past performance on a loan may show a record of some delinquency or, occasionally, a write-off, which makes the lending officer's justification of a new loan extremely difficult. Of the business's fixed assets may be obsolete or in poor working order, which again complicates the lending decision, since the assets cannot be used as security for the loan. The nature of the enterprise may imply extremely volatile sales, which, again, may lead lending institutions to be skeptical about the stability of the venture.

Often the ghetto businessman is attempting to compete with larger and more sophisticated companies in the same market arena. Even though his product or service may be superior in quality, he may lack the skills to market his goods, or his price may be far above that of his competitor because of his small volume and average unit cost of production. Thus, even if one discounts any problems of prejudicial attitude, inherent business risks may be present, and for sound business reasons the lender may determine he cannot justify an extension of credit.

Risk and Rate of Return

From the bank's economic point of view an additional restraining consideration is the adequacy of
rate of return in relation to risk. In many cases
there is simply no interest rate that can be legally
charged for high risk loans that will adequately compensate the lender. While an effective rate of from
25 to 30 percent might be considered commensurate
with risk from the lender's point of view, such rates
are prohibited by law in all states and would also
place an unconscionable and unrealistic repayment
schedule on the borrower's shoulders. Yet every
lender must continuously consider its responsibility
to produce a profit for its investor-sotckholders
and its fiduciary responsibilities to its depositors
and the public. These factors, together with strongly
competing demands for funds in today's tight money
markets, place the ghetto business community in a
highly noncompetitive posture. Moreover, such loans
have been typically small in size and have had dis-
proportionately high servicing costs--still another
factor to dissuade lending officers from "distorting"
their aggregate loan portfolios with any substantial
amount of such high risk paper.

Attitude of Lenders

Finally, there is the issue of attitude on the
part of the lending fraternity. Seasoned lending
officers skilled in analyzing business credit needs
are not normally expected to evaluate the potential
trade-offs between economic and social costs and
benefits. Given an economically sound and bankable
situation, they can easily develop the analysis and
reach a loan decision. In dealing with business applicants from the ghetto community, however, negative
past experiences, failure to apply social benefit
criteria, and, in some cases, prejudice are all factors that influence attempts at objective analysis.

The Social Function of Credit

In theory, banks as multipurpose lenders fulfill
their economic function when funds are channeled into

those sectors where the need is greatest--and need
is traditionally measured by market demand, that is,
price. But such theory does not satisfy those who
today are wrestling with the problems of rebuilding
our inner cities or providing capital to support
minority entrepreneurship. The fact of the matter
is that while making capital available for such efforts may not be justified on the basis of pure economics, it is important for the long run stability
of our communities and our nation that ways be devised to obtain the funds needed to meet our most
pressing social problems.

Recent Approaches

Bankers are developing a deep interest in providing solutions to these problems. Several new ap-
ʔroaches have been designed to help channel funds
into areas where the social need--as opposed to
purely economic demand of the marketplace--is greatest. Such programs are receiving the increasing attention of individual bankers as well as associations
of bankers. They recognize, of course, that frequently credit must be advanced at less than normal
yield and with more than normal risk and effort.

In some instances the lending activity of commercial banks for minority group or ghetto community
business ventures is handled in the normal course of
business with yield as the prime motivating force
and degree of risk on a par with the bank's other
business loans. In a number of other cases in which
banks have provided working capital for minority entrepreneurs, the loans have been made at market
yields. And, although lenders may have had certain
initial reservations concerning the risk involved,
their delinquency and default experience has been
generally as good as the institution's average.

Rationale for Involvement

Many of the institutions now involved in this
field, however, are also concerned with important
but less immediately tangible rewards, some of which
are considered vital enough to justify taking below-

market yields or above-average risks. These include
a long range view by some lenders that minority group
business enterprises and individual accounts constitute a potential market of substantial proportions,
particularly in view of the expectation of substantial rise in income levels among these people. Thus,
penetration of new markets takes on significance,
particularly for those institutions whose market area
is constricted by legal limitation. In some cities,
particularly those in which community tensions have
not yet reached a critical stage, lenders have adopted
a constructive policy toward business loans in the
ghetto communities as a preventive strategy. In
other communities, top executives of lending institutions have taken the even broader view that a metropolitan area cannot remain healthy with a rotting
core. There, lending efforts for business enterprises and housing, together with related programs
to improve employment opportunities, education,
transportation, and the like, are considered foundation stones for the economic revival of the cities.

Action Programs

Numerous investment plans and economic programs
have been suggested to speed the flow of capital to
the ghetto; several have moved past the proposal
stage, been implemented, and produced measurable
benefits. Variations on locus of initiative, per-
ceived rewards, and methodology of operation have
been numerous.

Unilateral Bank Action

One program to effect the flow of capital into
the ghetto involves unilateral action by banks in a
direct action program with the ghetto community and
its business development potential. The bank simply
makes a decision that it is to its own long run advantage to reexamine its credit policy toward "marginal" loans for minority group businessmen. Often
this decision will be prompted by recognition that
the inner city and its minority community is a significant segment of the bank's principal market and
that the bank should begin to meet the needs of the
participants in that market area.

One example of this kind of direct action is the
program of the First Pennsylvania Banking and Trust
Company of Philadelphia initiated in early 1967 when
the bank actively began to seek out potential minority
businessmen and to help them develop a financial
foothold in their businesses. A major factor in the
program's favorable reception was senior management's
aggressive commitment to the program's objective--
to help the inner city regain its status as a viable
economy.

To people long familiar with the syndrome of
welfare, corporate charity, and the like this was a
welcome change, since it offered a segment of the
community a chance to stand on its own and be measured by its economic achievement instead of a social
worker's yardstick. A second and equally important
factor was the selection of a particular group of
bank personnel to administer the program. Instead
of relying on senior management, the bank went to
its younger officers and trainees who, although
schooled in the bank's credit analysis techniques,
could examine such loans with some detachment from
institutional biases. These younger managers also
had the potential to develop more easily a rapport
with the black community and eliminate much of the
distrust the community had long had toward lending
institutions. In addition, loan decisions took into
consideration a combination of economic and noneco-
nomic factors. Often a man's character, sincerity,
and knowledge or his skill would be weighed equally
with his past credit record.

Special Loan Fund

An example of another kind of action program
can be found at the Hyde Park Bank and Trust Company
of Chicago. This bank established an urban affairs
department staffed with bankers, urban economists,
and a sociologist. In this case also the bank actually sought out potential black businessmen and
tried to provide them with financial assistance.
What makes the Hyde Park program so interesting is
that the bank has established a special program to
devote designated time and demand deposits to the
maintenance of a loan fund for investment in inner

city projects, including economic development loans
for minority businessmen. Of course, the bank's primary business is still the servicing of its large
accounts--yet the initiation of this technique is an
unusual departure from conventional banking, and
its initial efforts appear to be highly successful.

Government Guaranties

Obviously the high risk factor may still be
present in such efforts as these. This is particularly true if a significant volume of inner city
loans is being considered. A tool commonly used to
reduce this risk factor for a wide range of small
business ventures has been the guaranty of the federal
government's Small Business Administration (SBA).
While experimental efforts and programs to apply the
guaranty to small-scale minority business loans had
been previously attempted with mixed results, it was
only after the summer of 1968 that it was applied to
larger-scale minority business opportunities in a
concentrated fashion. At that time the banking industry, through the American Bankers Association and
the SBA, under the leadership of Howard Samuels,
joined forces in a concentrated effort to provide increased opportunities for minority business development. Essentially, the program for increased minority
entrepreneurship (dubbed Project OWN by SBA) provided
for a national effort whereby banks would supply the
capital and financial management assistance and SBA
would provide a guaranty of up to 90 percent of the
loan (maximum of $350,000). This arrangement between
the banks and SBA is not unlike other programs in
which the government acts as risk bearer for the private sector in order to achieve desired economic and
social goals. Other primary features of the program
include the provision of expert management assistance
to the new entrepreneur through volunteer efforts of
private industry, revised and liberalized credit
criteria for such loans, utilization of community
groups to identify capably business talent in the
ghetto community, and substantially reduced paperwork.
As for results, while the track record is too short
to evaluate success and failure, at the end of the
first six months after the program was initiated the

program's portfolio consisted of more than 2,100 loans to minority group businessmen valued at more than $50 million, involving participation by a substantial number of the nation's commercial banks. Compared to past years' private and public lending schedules to minority businessmen, this joint effort stands out as an innovative device for "priming the pump" of credit to the depressed ghetto business sector.

Pooling Arrangements

One significant side effect of the increased demand for capital from the ghetto communities as well as the impetus of individual bank initiatives throughout the country has been the formation of special purpose bank pools designed to increase credit flows to inner city communities. Such pooling arrangements have taken various forms: some are loose federations in which the banks agree to share risks for whatever capital needs arise; others are based on very formal arrangements separately administered, staffed and having specific dollar commitments of funds. Under the latter type, each bank may provide a certain amount of money to the pool based on its asset size, while the administration of the program may be centralized in one bank, may rotate from bank to bank, may be handled by the local clearinghouse, or may rest with a newly created administering body. The advantage of a pooling arrangement is that it provides a broad forum for all banks in the community to participate and, as a result, has the potential to generate a greater dollar volume of loan funds while reducing the risk factor any one bank must bear. Variations of such pooling arrangements are currently in existence in Chicago, Houston, Trenton, Richmond, Philadelphia, and other cities.

Continuing Problems

A mere examination of the dollar loan volume generated by these program efforts does not provide a true picture of the benefits and limitations involved. An objective evaluation can only be obtained by examining what transpires after the loans have

been made--business profitability, jobs produced,
dignity inspired--and by analyzing and remedying
problems inherent in program administration. While
results are mixed from community to community, they
do give cause for limited optimism considering the
magnitude of problems that must still be confronted
and, it is to be hoped, resolved.

Management Assistance

Relatively short experience clearly indicates
that the availability and concentrated application
of sound management experience and skilled professional assistance is essential to the viability of
new business ventures in the ghetto community. The
need for such assistance reflects a common need
among the vast majority of new business ventures regardless of race, further aggravated by past exclusions of the black community from the capitalistic
system, which has prevented the full development of
a business tradition in that community. Several
significant steps have been taken to marshal such
assistance, but on a national basis the effort has
been sporadic at best. For example, in many communities CPAs, lawyers, bankers, and others are providing free aid in preparation of loan application
forms and continue to provide follow-up services
after a business becomes operative. Some companies
are providing contracts on a special basis to ensure
product markets, and professional marketing men are
helping the new businessmen learn effective ways to
display, promote, and sell their products and services. The possibilities of business success are
markedly enhanced as a result of such assistance,
but in many communities only a beginning has been
made toward marshaling potential resource inputs of
the private sector.

Identifying Entrepreneurs and Markets

Two problems of identification are also prevalent.
One involves the identification of entrepreneurial
talent in the ghetto communities. Lacking the tradition of business experience and given the prevail-
ing distrust of the business community, solving this

problem could be critical. Several approaches are
being tried with varying degrees of success. Most
attempt to utilize a local screening group from the
community--community action groups or a group of
existing minority businessmen--while in some instances
new organizations have been spawned to fill this role.
The other area of identification involves markets,
competition, and long range growth. Improper identification of market potential could lead quickly to
business disaster, and this problem is compounded by
present lack of operative economies in the ghetto
communities. Accurate identification of both talent
and markets is a major concern of today's committed
businessmen, for they are apprehensive about the
possibility of stimulating failure in the ghettos.

Loan Servicing Costs

The administrative costs associated with such
loans are apt to be high. Once the loan has been
granted, it usually requires fairly close scrutiny
to make sure the borrower uses the proceeds of the
loan according to plan. Often the bank has to be
alert for local business trends that could place the
loan in jeopardy in the future. In many cases the
banks have initially done feasibility studies of the
potential success of the minority group entrepreneur's
venture. All these special services require staff,
time, and money, and they reduce the bank's margin
of profit substantially.

Lack of Equity Capital

Most of the minority group lending programs
attack only one dimension of the problem. In addition to working capital, the majority of ghetto businesses require substantial injections of equity
money. Since many of them have been deficit operations in the past, the owner has had little opportunity to develop an equity base on which to request
additional working capital. Also, it may be difficult
to raise equity money in the ghetto, since the residents often may not understand its nature or, given
the week-to-week existence that is typical for many
ghetto families, may simply have no money to invest
in such business ventures.

Community Understanding of the Financial System

The final problem that must be overcome in communication with the ghetto concerns the impact of
cyclical credit fluctuations. At the very time that
the community becomes aware that conditions are improving and credit is being made available to potential entrepreneurs, credit can become tight during
an inflationary market; what first appeared as a
favorable change then appears highly unfavorable, and
the residents of the community again view the system
as tending to choke off progress whenever the black
man gets too close.

Another problem the bank may face is adverse
community reaction to a foreclosure of a note on a
locally owned business. Residents of the community
may not understand the economics of an individual
situation, and the bank's action may be interpreted
as a racial act, even though the bank's lending record
in the minority community is a good one. It often
makes little difference to certain members of the
community that the business had no chance of success
and that the loan would have been foreclosed regardless of the man's color, race, or name. A misunderstanding of such action can resurrect fears that the
white man's money system holds the black man down
"in his place." Under such pressures bank officers
can easily become hyperdefensive, and a cycle of mis-
trust and animosity can develop, thereby jeopardizing
the success of legitimate efforts.

New Proposals

Recently additional solutions to the problems
of credit flow to the ghetto community have been offered by public officials, major foundations, economic
groups, civil rights organizations, and others. Some
of these proposals are extremely elaborate and would
require significant changes in the economic structure
of the inner cities. Others would make use of existing legislative devices and use large amounts of public funds to lever substantial private capital investment in the ghetto community. Still others would
create new variations of tax incentives to induce

private industry to use its capital and managerial
expertise to develop the ghettos as economic entities.
And, finally, there are those who argue that only
the public sector can marshal the necessary assets
to achieve the face-lifting and that, therefore, the
federal government should oversee the task in its
entirety.

Community Self-Determination Act

Most complex of the new proposals is the Community Self-Determination Act, which proposes to establish a complex system of development companies,
community banks, and entrepreneurial operations within
the confines of a specific geographical sector of the
community. The legislation is based on the premise
that only when the community has direct operating
control over its economic institutions can real economic growth be achieved in accordance with community
desires and that any other arrangement makes the community dependent on outside forces for its development. Though the goal of the Community Self-Determination Act is laudable--economic rebirth of the
ghetto community--many critics have attacked the
proposal on philosophic, economic, and technical
grounds. One primary objection goes to the heart of
the legislation, claiming it is simply an attempt to
establish separate black economic enclaves within
the cities. An economic objection on the same issue
questions the capability of ghetto communities to
function as separate economic units, considering
present diseconomies of such communities and the
interrelated nature of aggregate national, regional,
and local economies.

The banking industry may view with great concern
the proposed creation of a new community banking system, on structural, functional, and competitive
grounds, particularly in light of the proposed incentive features provided to this new banking system.
Others may argue that the methodology of the legislation imposes an unrealistic and inflexible bureau-
cratic framework on communities. Further, the legislation assumes by implication that a vast pool of
talent exists to fill the numerous management and

banking jobs required to operate such a new community
conglomerate structure. Finally, the political complexities of the legislation are massive: It not
only creates a forum for power struggles in the black
community but also implies a potential political con-
frontation between the black community and city hall,
if only on the question of community services. And,
at a time when pressure for tax reform has reached
significant proportions and concern is evident over
concentrations of economic power, this legislation
finds itself in a countervailing position.

Domestic Edge Act Corporations

With regard to the problem of equity capital,
one recent proposal recommends the establishment of
domestic Edge Act corporations, which would provide
a vehicle for commercial banks to assist indirectly
in the equity financing of inner city business development. With only limited exceptions, banks are
presently precluded from direct equity investment in
domestic corporations, while, since 1919, federal
law has provided the opportunity for stock ownership
by banks in specially chartered corporations that
can engage in equity financing of foreign business.
Though the holdings of these corporations are primarily
in stock of financial enterprises, these corporations
have made equity investments in a wide variety of
nonfinancial businesses in foreign countries. Application of this concept domestically would enable
banks to assist indirectly in the equity financing
of those business enterprises necessary to improve
the living conditions and economic development of
inner cities. Because of the high risk nature of
such investments, certain inducements--such as tax
incentives or guaranteed debentures--may be essential
to the effective organization of such corporations.
The obvious and significant advantage of this approach
would be to provide the ghetto with a substantial
equity base.

Other Efforts to Provide Equity Capital

A relatively limited number of programs are now
in effect that address the problem of providing equity

capital. In both New York and Boston pioneering efforts are being tested through the New York Urban
Coalition's Venture Capital Corporation and Boston's
Urban Foundation. Both ventures have raised substantial capital from private sector sources for reinvestment as equity capital in ghetto development enterprises, such capital being provided under liberal
criteria and terms and combined with sophisticated
inputs of management consultation and support. Equity
capital has also been raised successfully by way of
the stock subscription route within the ghetto community itself, the most notable example being The
Reverend Leon Sullivan's remarkable economic development program in Philadelphia, which has provided
required equity for a shopping center, apartment construction, and the establishment of a community-con-
trolled aerospace company. Several other approaches
are also being made through such devices as small
business investment companies specifically designed
to provide equity capital, and at least one mutual
fund has earmarked a limited percentage of its capital gains for high risk ghetto investment.

Leveraging Public Deposits. Another proposal, now
in actual operation in Illinois, is intended to link
the use of public funds deposited in commercial banks
with the achievement of certain social goals. In
Illinois the state treasurer has set aside matching
state funds in those banks that make a commitment to
invest a certain amount in programs for low income
housing or minority group business development. The
Illinois state treasurer feels the program has
achieved a high degree of success, and proposals
have not been made for a similar use of funds deposited in banks by the federal government and other
state and local governments.

Tax Credits to Banks. Numerous additional techniques
have been suggested to compensate commercial banks
and other lending institutions for the extra risk
they assume when lending in ghetto areas; however,
many of these will require legislative changes at
the national, state, or local level. One such technique would be to allow banks and other commercial
lenders an income tax credit against all business

loans made in a ghetto area. Such a credit would be
additional to the normal bad debt allowance granted
to banks. In effect, such a system would increase
the yield for the financial institution without forc-
ing the borrower to assume higher credit costs.

Tax Credits to Industry. A variation in the same
vein would be to provide tax credits to corporations
that maintain deposits in commercial banks for the
single purpose of making loans to ghetto entrepreneurs; for example, a corporation might receive a
credit of 4 percent of its average daily balance, or
it might receive a credit against a portion of the
interest its deposits would earn in time accounts.
The leverage such a program would provide is extremely
large. If, for example, 200 corporations each deposited $100,000 in such accounts, banks could pro-
vide credit to the ghetto in the amount of $20 million.
Assuming such deposits were placed in time accounts
that paid an interest rate of 5 percent, the total
income earned by the corporations would be $1 million.
If the government granted a credit of 20 percent
against such income, the government's revenue loss
would be $200,000, in return for a generated invest-
ment of $20 million. A more limited version of this
proposal, applying to tax credits for direct corporate investment in ghetto programs, is now under way
in Pennsylvania.

Credit Development Corporation. Another possibility
available to banks is the formation of credit development corporations, as was recently done by the
Citizens and Southern National Bank in Georgia. Such
corporations can be formed under present banking
statutes and provide a unique source of funds for
poverty communities. With an initial capitalization
of $1 million, the newly formed Citizens and Southern
Corporation is engaging in special high risk investments that provide long run economic benefits to the
ghetto community and, therefore, to the community at
large. Currently the corporation is providing financing for second mortgages in the ghetto area and
makes long term "equity" loans to new and existing
businesses owned by members of minority groups. Such
corporations seem to provide an excellent opportunity

for creative banking--and this unique approach is
sufficiently promising to warrant consideration by
other banking institutions.

These, then, are some of the alternatives that
could be used to increase the flow of credit to the
ghetto economy. It is only a partial list, and certainly many more avenues need to be considered.

Some Conclusions

There is no doubt that American industry, including the banks, has spent far too little of its
energies and financial resources to correct the inequities of the inner city. That tide is now turning.
Bankers are proud that they have helped build the
cities of America. They have begun to recognize a
responsibility to contribute positively to the revitalization of these same cities. A major goal of
the Bankers Committee on Urban Affairs is to stimulate bank participation in the economic development
of these cities, and their economically depressed
communities in particular. The banking industry is
moving toward positive, responsible action and seeking sustained results.

A SPECIAL RECOMMENDATION
FOR A PHILADELPHIA
VENTURE CAPITAL CORPORATION

As envisioned, a proposed Venture Capital Corporation for Philadelphia would have a threefold
capability in the areas of financing, counseling,
and training. Organized as an investment corporation, its activities would appear primarily financial.
However, the control inherent in equity financing
and its position of having discretion over a highly
attractive capital resource would allow the corporation to be extremely effective in other areas.

The Venture Capital Corporation would be organized as a Pennsylvania nonprofit corporation with
the ability to engage in financial participation in
industrial, manufacturing, financial, commercial,

and retail business in the City of Philadelphia. It would be an aggressive capital supplier for business development within the City, using its ability to supply seed capital to attract new industry to Philadelphia as well as to encourage the efforts of the indigenous entrepreneur.

The Corporation would actively support small business development and employment through a program of entrepreneurial solicitation in combination with referrals from existing agencies. In this context, its ability to provide necessary venture capital and its built-in counseling and training capabilities would ideally provide the needed impetus to make an idea a reality. Further, in cooperation with other business development agencies, it would make available funding and expertise that might prove the decisive factor in attracting new industry to Philadelphia.

The proposal is to create a revolving fund for continuing investment in the City's economy. Initially, this would require making available approximately $1 million for investment in new business ventures each year. Because of the delayed repayment intrinsic in such investment it would be necessary for this investment to be maintained for a projected minimum of five years. However, at the end of this period it would be expected that the fund would become self-sustaining and that further contribution could be curtailed or drastically reduced. At this point a continuing investment fund of $5 million would have been created as an input to the City's economy, and an enduring asset for business development would be available.

In addition to creating a capital resource that would repay its cost many times over, the organization would, through the nature of its equity position, have the ability to ensure the best chances of success for its client enterprises. Because equity investment is secured only by the success of the entity created, the corporation would have a vested interest in the continued well-being of its customers. Therefore, it would be necessary from the outset to establish means to provide management aids and financial safeguards that would ultimately benefit all parties.

The Corporation would, where necessary, require
as a condition of its entering into an agreement, a
controlling interest in the client company. Indeed,
the ability to do so forms the key to the success
of such a program, for it is lack of management
ability and internal control that leads to the demise
of the great number of new businesses. By exercising
control of the new company, the Venture Capital Corporation could provide counsel and, if necessary,
enforce the application of procedures needed to correct shortcomings in the operation of the business.
Such an ability would be particularly useful in lending to minority group owners, since lack of management skills often prevents the most ambitious and
motivated entrepreneur from successful operation.

To utilize such a potential, the Corporation
must have the technical competence to provide the
services necessary, meaning both that a competent
internal staff must be available and that reliable
outside assistance must be organized. Personnel requirements would have to be stringently observed in
order that routine counseling could be effectively
handled within the Corporation. Adjunctively, there
should be an intensive effort to recruit outside assistance in all forms.

Solicitation of investment proposals would be a
multifaceted operation, employing the resources of
all the local industrial and minority business development organizations in the Philadelphia area.
(There is little question that without such cooperation effective investment would be impossible.)
Finding viable investment situations would remain the
first and possibly most difficult hurdle in promoting
business development.

Investment opportunities would be carefully reviewed in relation to commercial feasibility and
needs, as well as for the benefits that would accrue
to the City's economy. If the investment appeared
sound after in-depth study, the Corporation would
consider how best to approach the opportunity and
what conditions would be required as grounds for
making the loan. If all signs were favorable, a
financial package would be assembled that would

allow for the minimal investment to ensure that the
proposal would be acceptable to the designated lending institution, be it private or public.

If additional training appeared necessary for
the entrepreneur to operate effectively, he would be
directed into a private sector training program,
where he would be given on-the-job training experience
in areas relevant to the position and problems he
would encounter when managing his own company. Such
a training program also would have the effect of providing an additional screening of the applicant's
on-the-job interest, and performance would be closely
observed and would serve as a further indication of
the degree of motivation needed.

Other factors that would ensure successful operation would be considered. If possible, guaranteed
markets would be investigated and solicited. In conjunction with this effort would be attempts to involve
private corporations in the venture, through such
methods as subsidiary creation, long term capital
credits for machinery, guaranteed technical assistance,
cooperative business establishment, and any other
aid that might serve to further ensure the viability
of the new enterprise or make its borrowing situation
more attractive.

How a Venture Capital Corporation
Would Operate

The proposed Venture Capital Corporation would
be organized under a board of directors, including
the managing director, drawn from the leaders of the
business community. It would be advisable to have
at least ten directors drawn from industry, retailing, and finance to ensure a measure of community involvement.

Internally, the corporation would be composed of
four or five departments reporting to the managing
director and the assistant director. Under the director would be four department managers who would
variously direct activities in the operational areas
of application review and feasibility, accounting and

finance, business systems, and legal problems--either
by a retainer firm or an internal department, the
decision to be made by the managing director in conjunction with his board of directors. The last department would be an Interview and Applicant Contact
Department, which would be managed by the assistant
director. He also would have responsibility for
overseeing outside training operations.

In addition to his supervisory responsibilities,
the director would have the final approval for all
lending over $25,000 and would review all situations
involving unusual risks. He would also, in conjunction with the Interview and Applicant Contact Department and the Business Systems Department, develop
outside involvement in opportunity solicitation,
counseling assistance, guaranteed orders, and explor-
ation of the possibilities of cooperative business
ventures. Inasmuch as possible, the board of directors, whose contacts would be indispensable, would
be involved.

Departmental Structure

The Interview and Applicant Contact Department,
under the assistant administrator, would have responsibility for initial contact with the applicant seeking funds for business development. Inquiries would
derive from referrals from other agencies, private
application, and outside solicitation in cooperation
with interested agencies, such as the Philadelphia
Industrial Development Corporation, the Greater Philadelphia Chamber of Commerce, and the Southeastern
Pennsylvania Development Corporation. In order to
prevent the dumping of all unqualified applications
on this lender of last resort, stringent standards
of preselection would have to be required so that
referrals would be made only of applicants who had a
legitimate chance of success and needed only second
secured capital to make the venture attractive for
additional lending.

This department would interview candidates and
help to assemble information necessary for referral
to the Review and Feasibility Department for in-depth

study. In addition, through the office of the training coordinator, it would organize and supervise the
private sector training program, recommending the
program and type of training to be employed if training was a condition of affirmative action by the
Review and Feasibility Department.

The training program would be set up in cooperation with interested companies, and the trainee's
salary would be paid by the training corporation,
from the administrative budget of the Venture Capital
Corporation or a combination of the two, the formula
to be determined in each individual case. The training would be individualized in regard to length and
content, including, where applicable, pertinent
classroom instruction from the various available
sources. On-the-job training would be in an area
that would allow the applicant to gain experience
that would allow him to anticipate and overcome more
capably the problems he would encounter in a business
of his own.

The Review and Feasibility Department would
undertake an in-depth study of the viability of the
proposition after the initial interview and affirmative recommendation of the Interview and Applicant
Contact Department. It would conduct credit analysis
and a preliminary market analysis. In cases in
which the candidate did not meet minimal educational
or financial standards or a meaningful financial review was impossible, the Department would participate
in further interviews and recommend training that
would be set up through the outside training department. In cases in which affirmative action was taken
by the Interview and Applicant Contact Department
and training recommended, further action would be
suspended until a satisfactory level of performance
was achieved by the trainee. When training was substantially complete, or in cases in which affirmative action was taken and outside training not required, the application would be forwarded to the
Accounting and Finance Department.

The Accounting and Finance Department would
have both internal and external functions. The former

would be the usual maintenance of payroll and other
internal accounts. The latter function would be the
structuring and placement of an acceptable financial
package. This would include establishing a level of
equity investment that would allow private sources
to be reasonably expected to invest their first
secured monies without the need for the use of guaranteed funds. Failing this, in cases in which interest rates or the required level of equity investment
would prove prohibitive, the proposal would be referred to such agencies as the Small Business Administration or the local Job Loan Corps, where guaranteed funds are available. Again, hopefully, this
would be a composite form of financing whereby only
a part of the loaned funds would have to be guaranteed, thus minimizing the usage of these limited
sources and maximizing the involvement of private
sector funds.

Once financing was completed and the venture
under way, it would be the job of this Department to
complement the other lending institutions in servicing
the investment. It must be emphasized that although
one of the selling points in attracting financing
would be the fact that this additional policing would
be available, it must be agreed that other institutions, public or private, would maintain their normal
account review procedures. In addition to following
review and normal service procedures, this Department
would provide counseling services where required and,
when necessary, establish acceptable internal accounting procedures for the new enterprise. Finally,
it would be the job of the Accounting and Finance
Department to provide tax information and advice and
to recommend, in conjunction with the Business Systems Department, outside counselors and firms when
a need was indicated.

The Legal Department would receive the completed
financial package for review and approval before release. In addition, this Department (or, alternatively, the retainer firm) would set up the equity
agreement and fully explain to the applicant the
conditions upon which financing was granted. This
would be especially important in cases in which con-

trol of the new corporation would be held by the Venture Capital Corporation or when enforced counseling and review formed a part of the agreement. For the applicant must be made to understand fully that his acceptance of counseling is an enforceable part of the contract; careful and complete revelation of this contractual prerogative of the Corporation is undoubtedly necessary to maintain a workable future relationship with the applicant. In the situation in which the guarantee of counseling or assistance from a private corporation is an adjunct to the package, the Corporation must also be completely informed regarding the commitment. Finally, this Department would be responsible for outside legal counseling and recommending or providing access to legal assistance from external sources.

The Business Systems Department would aid the new enterprise where necessary in setting up its procedures and would be the Corporation's general counseling arm. It would advise in such areas as inventory maintenance, sales, purchasing, personnel, and processing. The importance of such a counseling arm cannot be overemphasized, for this Department would have the responsibility, in many cases, for setting up the operation of a new business. Further, it would be the eyes and ears for the Corporation because it would have the closest contact with the client and would be constantly on the alert to find and correct situations that could be detrimental to the direct enterprise or prejudicial to the Corporation's equity investment. In performing these duties, it would have the assistance of all of the other internal departments, as well as external counseling and, when necessary, retention of outside counseling firms.

Because of the breadth of its responsibility, the Business Systems Department would need to develop extensive contact with the private sector, most advantageously in combination with the director and the board of directors. The importance of effective outside support from the business community in matters of management and technical assistance cannot be overemphasized. Assembling a dependable cadre of

individuals who would be lent by their employers on
a prearranged basis would be the first duty of the
Business Systems Department. Recruitment and review
procedures should grant them considerable freedom for
such contact during the start-up period.

Staffing

Personnel in an organization of such complexity,
requiring the depth and variety of technical competence that would be necessary, would present more
than normal problems. The key to this situation
would lie in selecting a director with broad experience in the venture capital market and the stature
in the community that would allow him to function
effectively in the business sector involvement programs necessary to the success of the proposed Corporation. He would probably be drawn from the banking
and financial community and would very likely be an
experienced lending officer with extensive administrative and financial experience. Further, it would
be desirable if he had previous lending experience
with minority groups, as the problems in this area
differ radically from those of the community as a
whole. Failing such additional experience, a demonstrated interest in minority business expansion
would be necessary. Finally, the selection of a locally prominent individual would greatly facilitate
staffing in that it might be assumed that he would
have greater success in recruiting because of his
reputation and his contacts in the community.

The assistant director would need qualifications
of a level similar to those of the director since
he and the director would have extensive outside
duties through the Interview and Applicant Contact
Department. He would also supervise the outside
training program in addition to assuming many of the
duties of the director in his absence. It would
again be necessary to hire a person with extensive
lending experience and very definitely some lending
experience with minorities. Personnel or psycholog-
ical background would also be most valuable. He
would presumably be the second person hired and
would be hand-picked by the director.

From this point, hiring would be up to the director and the assistant director as indicated by the needs of the expanding operation. Under the assistant director would be two counselors, preferably with loan experience and an educational background in business. The outside training program would require a person preferably with experience in minority group contact and a background in education and psychology who would work with the assistant administrator in establishing and managing the external training program.

The manager of the Review and Feasibility Department would ideally be an experienced financial analyst whose staff would be composed of two analysts, graduates holding advanced degrees, respectively, in the fields of finance and marketing. The Accounting and Finance Department would require a qualified financial analyst with experience in lending and, preferably, in equity capital operations. Reporting to him would be an analyst with background in government and financial accounting and a second assistant with a background in finance.

The Business Systems Department would be headed by an individual experienced in the management consulting field aided by assistants with backgrounds in retailing and industrial management. The first job of this Department would be recruiting a number of specialized consultants who could be utilized along with personnel of other departments to achieve the initial degree of management experience to enable effective counseling in the many areas they would be required to service. Additional aid would be received from similar departments in agencies and lending institutions participating in the financing, both as a result of their review and by use of their available counseling services, as in the case of the Small Business Administration's Workshop and Training Programs, SCORE and AIMS.

It must be emphasized that the procedure of staffing the organization would no doubt be difficult, since obtaining persons with the needed abilities will be an exasperating task; but the intrinsic precariousness of venture capital financing precludes the hiring of an inexperienced staff. The director and his assistants would have to be most vigorous in hiring and in securing personnel on loan from local industry to fill in until qualified candidates could be found to fill the positions. Because, however, of the nature of the expanding capital fund, the employment program would probably be spread over a number of years, personnel growth paralleling the increase in the Corporation's activity and consequent client-service requirements.

Funding

Capital Fund. The revolving capital fund would be, of course, the foundation of the Corporation. Envisioned at an eventual level of $5 million, the fund would necessarily be increased yearly for the length of the payback period. Since the nature of equity investment is such that return is delayed, such a continuing funding program would be needed.

Organization and hiring would occupy a major portion of the first year's effort. This, combined with the lead time involved in processing an application and forwarding it through channels, would indicate the need for only partial capital funding in the first year. Therefore, the sum of $250,000 would probably be adequate for the first fiscal year. After that initial year, additional funds for the succeeding four years at the rate of $1 million yearly would be necessary to maintain the level of capital to allow a significant, if conservative, level of investment. The final year would require an investment of $750,000 to complete the capital funding.

The funding would be based on a drawing account. This could conceivably result in funds' being available for certain periods in amounts greater than indicated by the funding program; however, it would serve to limit the temptation to invest in lower grade investments or to contribute equity funds in greater proportion than necessary in order to utilize fully funds that might be lost through the delays

involved in more conservative action. Further, it
would serve to accumulate available funds in the latter years as the expertise of the staff and the cumulative effects of organizing community involvement
made greater levels of investment possible.

Administrative Costs. Administrative costs would
have to be separately funded since the nature of the
Corporation would be such that viable profits, especially in the early years, would be precluded.
Costs would probably range from $150,000 to $170,000
for the first year (incomplete staff and lower associated salary and expense cost) to from $240,000
to $325,000 (at full employment), depending on varia-
bles, such as rent, salary, consulting costs, and
so forth.

Total funding costs as a result would run from
approximately $410,000 in year one to approximately
$1,300,000 at full levels of employment and capital
investment. Actual expenditures might, of course,
vary significantly in response to lending levels for
the year involved.

AN ECONOMIC DEVELOPMENT PROGRAM
FOR THE MODEL CITIES AREA
OF PHILADELPHIA

The Model Cities area of Philadelphia--the
heart of the North Philadelphia ghetto--embodies all
the worst aspects of a stagnant and deteriorating
economy. It represents an enclave of poverty, totally unresponsive to the pull of a vibrant free-
enterprise economy and almost completely alienated
from the upward thrust of national and regional economic growth.

The Economic Development Unit recognized that
only a massive, well-coordinated development program
combining both an implementation vehicle and a meaningful program of research could bring the area back
into the economic mainstream. For this reason the
Economic Development Unit proposed a two-part program
to the Model Cities Administration consisting of

TABLE 26

Optimal Business Development on the Basis of the
Initial Capitalization of a Philadelphia Venture
Capital Corporation

Average Percent Investment	Investment	Average Invest- ment	Number of New Busi- nesses	Capital Investment Created
Year 1				
33.3	250,000	50,000	5	750,000
20.0	250,000	30,000	8-9	1,250,000
10.0	250,000	15,000	16-17	2,500,000
Year 2				
33.3	1,000,000	50,000	20	3,000,000
20.0	1,000,000	30,000	33-34	5,000,000
10.0	1,000,000	15,000	65-66	10,000,000
5 years				
33.3	5,000,000	50,000	100	15,000,000
20.0	5,000,000	30,000	165-170	25,000,000
10.0	5,000,000	15,000	325-330	50,000,000

Note: Figures are not adjusted for losses or
increased capitalization from cash flow or additional credit above initial financing.

Source: Economic Development Unit Staff.

(1) an economic development program embodying a
Model Cities Economic Development Corporation (MCEDC)
as a vehicle to effect the area's economic resurrec-
tion and (2) an in-depth research program to supply
the necessary data inputs by which the Model Cities
Economic Development Corporation could be guided in
structuring specific projects for commercial and
industrial development.

CHART 13

Position of a Philadelphia Venture Capital Corporation
with Regard to the Existing Public and
Private Business Development Community

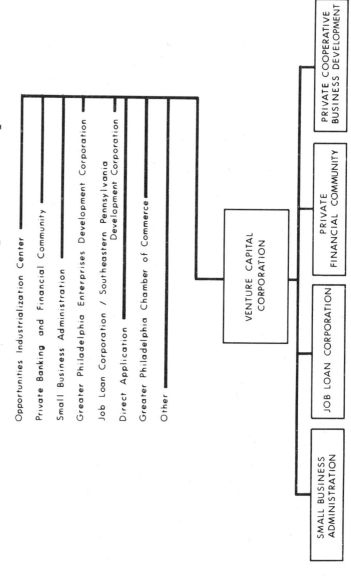

CHART 14

Organization of a Philadelphia Venture
Capital Corporation

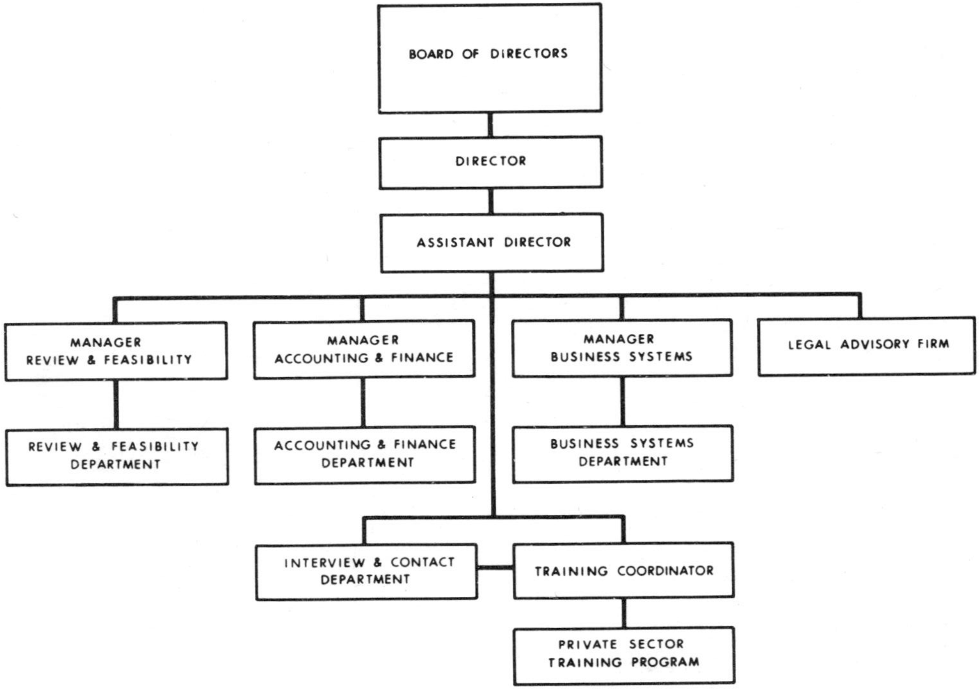

BOARD OF DIRECTORS

DIRECTOR

ASSISTANT DIRECTOR

MANAGER
REVIEW & FEASIBILITY

REVIEW & FEASIBILITY
DEPARTMENT

MANAGER
ACCOUNTING & FINANCE

ACCOUNTING & FINANCE
DEPARTMENT

INTERVIEW & CONTACT
DEPARTMENT

MANAGER
BUSINESS SYSTEMS

BUSINESS SYSTEMS
DEPARTMENT

TRAINING COORDINATOR

PRIVATE SECTOR
TRAINING PROGRAM

LEGAL ADVISORY FIRM

Problems to Be Solved

Failure of the Area to Attract Business and Industry

In proportion to other sections of the Philadelphia area, fewer residents of the area were engaged
in manufacturing occupations and in wholesale and
retail trade, indicative of a tendency of business
to leave rather than enter the area. Because of such
conditions as difficulty in obtaining adequate insurance and security problems, business was actually
repulsed rather than attracted.

Bad Reputation of the Area

Large parts of the area showed signs of physical
decay and dilapidation. Many people from other areas
in Greater Philadelphia felt they were unsafe in the
area. Much of the area was ugly and unclean.

Depressed Condition of Residents of the Area

The area was characterized by low income, low
educational levels, high rates of family instability,
and high unemployment.

Lack of an Economic Catalyst in the Area

Large numbers of black and other minority group
members living in the area had developed a sense of
frustration and hopelessness nurtured by poor education, poor living conditions, unemployment, and a
failure of the area to make economic progress. Most
people in the area were so removed from the mainstream of the commercial, business, and professional
life of Greater Philadelphia and so weighted with
the burden of their immediate problems of day-to-day
survival that they could not be expected to attack
their personal, economic, and social problems spon-
taneously through expansion and revitalization of
the economy of the area. They had neither the motivation nor the skill nor the resources required,
and, to date, there had been no adequate profession-
ally directed attempt closely aligned with the residents of the area to expand industrial and commercial
enterprises in the area.

Poor Use of Existing Inventory of Industrial and Commercial Properties

A program was required that would make the most efficient use of the existing inventory of industrial and commercial properties in the project area by buying them, divesting them of unsightly and unproductive uses, and then selling or leasing the property to attractive, job-creating businesses.

Lack of Venture Capital

There was a need for both short and long term venture capital for financing new business owned and operated by local, as well as outside, businessmen, cooperatives, or local development corporations, for venture capital is not usually available for investment in what is considered a high risk locality, such as the project area.

An Exploitative Area Economy

Profit from goods made, distributed, and sold in the area was going principally to persons who did not reside in the area. There was a need to give the residents of the area a voice and stake in the management and ownership of the means of production, distribution, and sale so that part of the profit from the economy of the area would be retained within the economy for the benefit of its residents.

Purpose and Beneficiaries

The overall purpose of the MCEDC program was to be (1) to rebuild and revitalize the entire economic fabric of the Model Cities area, (2) create substantial new employment, and (3) make possible substantial and meaningful business opportunities for residents of the Model Cities area. This was to be accomplished by bringing into play in the area private economy resources, community peoples, and the assistance of federal, state, and local governments.

These combined resources would be used (1) to provide opportunities for industrial and commercial employment to residents of the area by encouraging

existing businesses to expand in and into the area,
(2) to create new businesses within the area, (3) to
generate entrepreneurial initiative within the area,
and (4) to create local ownership and management in
connection with rebirth of the area's economy.

Specific aims were to be as follows:

1. To plan and execute a coordinated effort to
persuade manufacturing, service, and research and
development industries and substantial wholesale and
retail operations to locate in the project area

2. To acquire land and to construct or rehabili-
tate suitable commercial structures in the area
through the use of private and governmental development funds where available (Such land and structures
would be offered through appropriate arrangements to
business attracted to the area.)

3. To aid businesses attracted to the area or
newly established in the area to acquire necessary
machinery and equipment through marshaling private
financial resources and governmental development resources and programs

4. To persuade and require, where possible,
businesses involved in the project to draw new employees, insofar as practicable, from unemployed
persons in the area (Such a policy would raise the
income levels in the area and should contribute to
greater overall stability of area families.)

5. To plan and execute a coordinated effort to
create conditions in the area that would make it attractive for businesses to come to the area and remain there

6. To make arrangements with the insurance industry and appropriate governmental agencies concerned with the insurance industry for the availability of adequate insurance coverages for businesses
in the area at reasonable rates

7. To develop and disseminate a program to
residents of the area directly and through existing

organizations calculated to instill in such residents
a desire to attract, protect, and foster businesses
in their community because the existence of such
businesses would be a means of improving their own
conditions and maintaining gains made by them

8.   To assist existing small businesses in the
area to expand the scope of their operations so as
to become substantial and meaningful industrial and
commercial entities and so as to employ more persons

9.   To concentrate particular attention on the
establishment and expansion of industries and businesses not highly technical so that unemployed workers with low skill levels might be used in such
businesses

10.   To foster immediate expansion of businesses
primarily controlled by blacks and members of other
minority groups in the proposed project area by making
adequate and useful financing available to them.

The beneficiaries of the program would be primarily the residents of the area and to a lesser extent the Greater Philadelphia community of which the
area is a part. More jobs and consequently increased
income would be made available to area residents who
in turn would be motivated and able to achieve higher
educational levels for their offspring and would
give them the means to achieve and maintain a higher
degree of family stability. A dynamic attitude of
progress with stability would be established that
would convince business and industry that the area
was a good one in which to exist and grow. To the
extent that residents of the area were able to participate in the ownership and management in the economy of the area, they would no longer look upon the
economy of the area as a tool used to exploit them
and would see the economy as a positive instrument
from which they benefit. In the end, the total result
for both residents and nonresidents would be to
change a negative attitude toward the area to a
positive one.

Scope and Content

The purposes and objectives set forth above would be carried out to a large extent through the Model Cities Economic Development Corporation, which would be created under and pursuant to the Non-Profit Corporation Law of the Commonwealth of Pennsylvania of 1933 as amended from time to time. The MCEDC would serve as a device to provide central services in the development work in the Model Cities area, which, because of their expense or the expertise required, cannot be provided easily by smaller units on a noncentralized community basis. Eight central services were planned:

1. A promotional program

2. A manufacturing and industrial incubator

3. A commercial and retail incubator

4. A land exchange program

5. A commercial and retail finance service

6. A manufacturing and industrial finance service

7. A counseling and follow-up service

8. A planning unit.

A Promotional Program

The purpose of the promotional staff would be to serve as a public relations vehicle for the MCEDC--for economic development does not just happen. The residents of the area in which economic development is to occur must be sold on its desirability in the first instance, and, of equal importance, businesses must be sold on the idea of staying in the area, of expanding in the area, and of moving to and locating in the area.

It was recommended, therefore, that the MCEDC employ a director of promotional activities, two assistants, and two secretaries.

Those experienced in economic development and knowledgeable concerning the Model Cities area point out that there are a number of companies in the area that do not increase their business or their employment for the reason that they are in bad or inadequate or outgrown quarters and are not familiar with various government and private programs that could assist them to expand in the area.

It would be the duty of the promotional staff to familiarize such businesses with the tools to assist them if they are desirable businesses from the point of view of the community, which should lead to their creating additional jobs in the community.

One assistant would be in charge of promoting economic development from within the area. He would make a systematic study of all businesses in the area to determine which ones had a potential for expansion. He should then systematically make contact with such businesses to determine, in each instance, any roadblocks to expansion and should consult with the various other component parts of the MCEDC program to achieve means of removing each such roadblock.

Though the economy of the Model Cities area cannot be said to have expanded in recent years, it is an established fact that the economy of the nation has continued to expand and that the economies of Greater Philadelphia and surrounding areas have continued to expand. Much of this expansion in the economy represents a certain amount of new and expanded activities on the part of the companies already in business, some in a local and regional sense and others in a national sense.

It is assumed that at least one member of the promotional staff would keep in contact with and be familiar with the expansion plans and ideas of

national and regional companies and would follow up
all leads that could be developed concerning the development plans of specific companies, with the idea
of selling them on the notion of location in the
Model Cities area. The kind of promotional activity
contemplated is illustrated by the activities of the
promotional staff of the Pennsylvania Department of
Commerce: After Chrysler Company announced in July
1968 that it was looking for a location for a major
assembly plant that would employ from 2,500 to 5,000
people, the staff of the Department of Commerce made
contact with Chrysler Company and gave officers details regarding the possible location in Pennsylvania.
As a result of this promotional activity, it was decided to build the plant in the western part of
Pennsylvania.

The promotional staff would be one of the first
program components staffed after the MCEDC was formed
and funded. At the end of the first project year
the promotional staff would be fully operational and
the first fruits of its endeavors would be apparent.
The economic development promotional staff would report to the executive vice-president of the MCEDC and
would relate to the Model Cities Agency and such
City units as the Department of Commerce and the City
Representative's office through the executive vice-
president of the MCEDC and directly.

The MCEDC would employ at least one additional
person to publicize and recruit for the various
other programs, such as the incubator projects. He
should be from the Model Cities area.

One adverse condition within the Model Cities
area is a lack of orientation by large numbers of
area residents toward business and industrial management, the immediate result of which is a lack of
managers from within the community. The more long
term and far-reaching result is a lack of real economic initiative in the area.

To deal with this condition the development of
an orientation on the part of the residents toward
management and control of business on a large scale

is necessary. Although an increasing number of col-
lege-trained individuals from the community will in
time lead to a heightened awareness and desire for
economic power and control, there are areas of possible development among the present adult population
of the community, even though largely untrained in
management and control of business.

The function of the recruitment portion of the
promotion program would be to publicize the opportunities provided by the MCEDC and other organizations for immediate training in management of industrial, manufacturing, and retail activities. Although
it was hoped that the very existence of operating
training centers, such as those of the incubator
programs, would inspire and create a new orientation
toward management, it was thought that active recruitment should also be undertaken.

Recruiting and publicity would be carried out
throughout the entire community, and all available
media would be employed. Further, the schools in
the community would be approached to provide time
for lectures and workshop sessions to involve the
students in the training programs.

Such annual programs of career planning as
exist in other areas could be developed and employed
to communicate to the students the training opportunity provided through the Model Cities programs.
Such training might even serve as an inducement for
students to remain in school at least through high
school.

The recruitment program would also involve the
use of past and present trainees to meet with members
of the community both at the project sites and at
local meetings and schools to acquaint the community
with the practical aspects of the program. Tours
would be arranged at the incubator sites to stimulate
interest.

Accurate records on the number of contacts
locally, regionally, and nationally would be kept,
and it would be possible to determine how many of

such companies or individuals that were first interested in economic development in the Model Cities
area by the promotional staff carried out projects.
The number of contacts and resulting projects would
be a direct measure of the success of the promotional
staff.

Further, citizen participation in the activities
of the promotional staff would be achieved through
their participation in the board of directors of the
MCEDC. Citizens in the Model Cities area would be
encouraged to refer leads on companies capable of
further development in the area directly to the promotional staff.

A Manufacturing and Industrial Incubator

It was believed that the principal reason that
so few residents of the Model Cities area were involved in industrial and manufacturing management,
notwithstanding possible need for a particular product and the ability to obtain relatively low cost
financing, was lack of skill in the actual day-to-
day management of a business. They evidenced a lack
of orientation to the need for planning incident to
management, compounded by a lack of training in the
methods of realistic planning. The result was a competitively inefficient operation even when the individual was able to enter and remain in business.

It was decided that upon completion and justification of this program, it would be proposed that
the MCEDC acquire a multistory industrial plant for
conversion into and use as a pilot training site for
industrial and manufacturing development and management. The plant would be purchased with Model Cities
program funds and would have to be large enough to
accommodate various unrelated industrial and manufacturing enterprises. The actual site would be within
the Model Cities area and have easy access to public
transportation, a highly visible addition to the
community it would serve. Since one principal aim
of the program as a whole would be to stimulate and
motivate a business-oriented outlook as a way of
life and thought, such a visible example of opportunity should be helpful.

An example of the kind of plant to be acquired is the Strawbridge and Clothier Department Store warehouse, located at Tenth and Poplar streets, in Philadelphia. This facility is located in the heart of one of the major redevelopment areas of the City and would be the necessary size. It offers direct access to the Reading Railroad main line for both commuter and freight operations and to public bus and subway transportation. Such a facility could be acquired for the sum of approximately $1 million.

The plant, once acquired, would be remodeled to permit the training in industrial and manufacturing management of residents of the Model Cities areas, primarily members of the various minority groups. The plant would be supervised by a staff of experts in the various aspects of plant management, and the plant would be divided into areas devoted to various kinds of industrial and manufacturing activity. In this way, it was hoped, sufficient expertise should be developed in practical management to enable an individual to operate his own plant efficiently and competitively.

Within the facility, various manufacturing and industrial "model plants" would be equipped and operated. Although the use of a single plant for more than one manufacturing activity is in itself in-efficient, the plant would not be competing with a given industry. Rather, such a facility would enable a relatively small staff to supervise and instruct the individual trainees on a continuing basis.

Each "plant" would be a separate entity, oper-ating as if it was an individual business. Individ-ual owner-trainees might enter into a lease with the MCEDC for the period of the training program. The trainee would pay a minimum annual rent, together with a percentage rent scaled to cover the overhead and carrying charges of the facility, in conjunction with all other trainees. The rent could be calcu-lated on a square footage basis and could be gradu-ated to reflect the trainee's increasing competence and consequent decreasing need for reliance upon the professional staff during the term of lease. At the

end of the term, the individual would be assisted by
the industrial and manufacturing financing section
in acquiring a plant of its own.

During the term of the training program, perhaps set at a year, the individual owner would operate a manufacturing or other industrial business,
for the purpose of sales to the general public. In
connection with the business, he would be responsible
for maintaining his own books and records. A rental
scheme, such as outlined above, providing incentive
to make as much profit as possible, would provide
the most realistic training.

The heart of the program would be a training
staff to assist the individual on a continuing basis
in all aspects of a going concern. The staff would
have to have a permanent professional core but might
also include area businessmen who would voluntarily
make themselves available to the project for a given
period of time (a week or a month, for instance).
One notable example of such voluntary aid, already
in operation elsewhere, is the use of retired businessmen as instructors and experts. Such a program
provides the businessman with a means of keeping
active and using his invaluable skills and makes
those skills available to persons just starting out
in business.

The permanent staff, which would be compensated
from Model Cities funds, would include trained personnel in each aspect of management. Thus, for an
industrial or manufacturing plant, the staff should
include individuals in at least the following areas:
(1) sales, (2) purchasing, (3) technical operations,
(4) labor relations (personnel), (5) financing and
tax, including bookkeeping, and (6) administration
and public relations.

Temporary volunteer staff members might be assigned directly to individual trainees to assist
them in daily management decisions. As a trainee
became more skilled, the staff volunteer could be
shifted elsewhere within the plant with little or no
dislocation and with the possibility of further

assistance to the trainee when and as necessary.
And an evaluation of the trainee's need could be
easily derived from the statistics acquired as a result of periodic follow-up inquiries of graduates.

A Commercial and Retail Incubator

With the recent development of interest among
businessmen in fostering local ownership of commercial and retail establishments within the Model
Cities area, there has developed a need for training
members of that community in the day-to-day operations and management of retail establishments. This
interest is symbolized by the proposal and development of such centers as Progress Plaza and Poplar
Plaza in the area. Although investment capital is
available for the development and opening of such
businesses, their mortality rate is far greater than
in other areas, because of lack of orientation to
and experience in management.

In order to further foster such interest and
development, it was thought that the MCEDC should
construct and develop a "model" shopping center facility for use as a pilot training facility for commercial and retail establishments.

Approximately from two to three and one half
acres of land would be acquired with Model Cities
Agency funds, and the construction of the center
would be financed initially with such funds. Approximately $1,250,000 should be sufficient to acquire
the ground and construction center. Even though
created as a training facility, the center could be
operated on an economically competitive basis with
other establishments in the community.

Because of the need to publicize the construction and development of the center, it would be
located within the Model Cities area and should provide the kinds of services and businesses that would
be provided as if a private center was being developed. Existing companies, such as chain food and
other stores, might be induced to locate within the
center, especially since management of each of the

establishments would be in a semicontrolled situation, allowing concentrated training.

The individual businesses within the shopping center need not necessarily be owned by the manager-trainee, providing that the business was willing to allow the trainee to be placed in the store by the development company. Other participants in the center might include outlets for franchise chains.

Chains and franchise stores might be willing to work with the program, if only as a training ground for local operators of other stores to be established by them within the Model Cities area, once the training program at the center was completed.

At the inception of each training period, the trainee might be required to draft, with staff personnel, a proposed budget for the "plant," which budget would include all items of expense and income attributable to that business as if run independently, including projected return on "capital." Profits from the business would be the property of the trainee. Each business and each trainee would be assisted by the industrial and manufacturing section in obtaining necessary equipment. As noted above, the rent paid by the trainee to the MCEDC might be tied into production, either through percentage rent or otherwise.

Maintenance charges for each "plant" would be included within the budget, thereby providing the MCEDC with a means of maintaining its operation without continual heavy overhead. Each trainee would hire his own production personnel, with the possibility of the trainee's using such personnel in his own business after the program was completed. Such an arrangement would have the added advantage of providing the novice businessman with employees who themselves had received some "model" training.

At the conclusion of the program the trainee would "graduate" to a business of his own, using private funds and funds obtained through other development agencies. The trainee should have relatively

little difficulty in obtaining such loans inasmuch as
he had received management training while actually
operating a business. In his place, of course, a
new trainee would begin.

The "graduate" might return to the facility to
train others, and he would also be able to aid the
entire program by giving advice about which parts of
the training were insufficient and which needed
specific improvement.

After the initial site acquisition and remodel-
ing costs, the budget of the MCEDC for the program
would include expenditures for salaries of the permanent staff, maintenance of the machinery and equipment, and carrying charges for the plant. In addition, there should be a program director or coordinator, who would act as liaison between this portion
of the project and the development company.

The recapture of the investment of the MCEDC in
the incubator plant might be no more than nominal at
the beginning of the project because of necessary
starting costs. There is no reason, however, that
the industrial plant incubator could not be a reasonably self-sustaining unit in time.

The project could reasonably be expected to be
fully operational at the end of the first year. Its
progress would be measured by the number of successful "graduates" the project could turn out into the
community.

In other instances the trainee might be an individual area resident with no connection with any
chain or franchise, entering into a lease with the
MCEDC for the period of the training program. The
program would probably have a one-year term, and
rent under the lease would include a fixed annual
payment, together with percentage rent scaled to
cover the overhead expenses of the center, in conjunction with all other trainees. The basic annual rent
would be calculated on a square footage basis and
possibly graduated so as to reflect the increasing
competence of the trainee over the period of the

program. The percentage rent portion might be used
as an inducement to the trainee to maximize his sales.
At the end of the training period the individual
would be assisted by the commercial and retail finance
section in acquiring elsewhere in the Model Cities
area the type of business in which he had worked and
provided with funds for equipping and operating the
new venture.

During the term of the training program, the individual would operate his business or service as if
it were really his own. He would be responsible for
the daily management decisions of the business and
for sales to the general public. He would further
be responsible for maintaining his own books and
records, preparing the tax and other statements required, and the hiring and training of employees for
the particular business.

The basis of the training would be a permanent
staff located in the center to assist the individual
on a continuing basis in all aspects of management.
The staff would have a permanent professional core
but might also make use of local area businessmen
willing to make themselves available to the project
for a specific period of time. The core of the staff
would not necessarily have to be a large group,
since the staff would be available to all members of
the center.

The staff would be compensated from the Model
Cities funds and would be trained personnel in various
aspects of management. Thus, for a commercial and
retail center, the staff should include experts in
the following areas: (1) sales, (2) purchasing, (3)
labor relations (personnel), (4) store operation and
inventory control, and (5) financing and tax (including bookkeeping).

The training would involve the initial preparation of a budget for store operations, together with
initial training in inventory control and display of
items to be sold. There would also be training in
proper accounting procedures, so that the trainee
would be kept constantly aware of the profitability
of his daily operation.

As for the manufacturing and industrial incubator, volunteers might be assigned directly to individual trainees, on the basis of the same rationale.

The training program should also include an appropriate format for the members of the center at any given time to meet to evaluate their progress and bring to the attention of the full staff areas requiring additional training or areas not previously covered in the proposal.

At the conclusion of the program, the trainee would have the opportunity to own and operate a commercial retail business of his own, either in a shopping center or in an individual situation--and it might be anticipated that the trainee would donate some of his time at the training center for the aid of future groups.

The same evaluation techniques employed at the manufacturing and industrial incubator would be applied to this project.

A Land Exchange Program

At the present time there are scattered throughout the North Philadelphia area numerous industrial and manufacturing businesses often located in the midst of residential dwellings. This situation tends to downgrade the residential units immediately adjacent to the businesses. Furthermore, plants are often located on small streets through which access to the industry is severely hindered. Truck traffic going to and from the plants adds congestion in the residential areas. The trend with regard to these businesses has been their gradual relocation outside the Model Cities area, resulting in the loss of jobs to the area and the vacating of industrial buildings that often cannot be sold or rented. Their deterioration adds to the general deterioration of the neighborhood.

Ground for either residential or industrial construction is at a premium in the area. Taking present residential ground for industrial use is not popular;

yet many recognize the necessity of developing modern
industrial facilities in the area.

In order to curb further deterioration of business and residential development in the Model Cities
area, a land exchange program would be created. A
survey of all existing businesses within the Model
Cities area would be made to determine the number
and location of present industry. Whenever possible
industries existing in the center of residential development would be encouraged to relocate to other
parts of the Model Cities area more conducive to the
carrying out of their activities. Relocation cost,
including construction or rehabilitation of the new
plant site, would be partially financed with the aid
of private resources, the Small Business Administration, the North Philadelphia Community Foundation,
and the Pennsylvania Industrial Development Authority.
The owners of any residential property to which industry would be relocated would be offered the opportunity of exchanging their property for the property
from which the industry would move; the existing industrial facility in the midst of a residential development would be demolished and new residential
facilities constructed on the property.

The land exchange program, which could be initiated on a limited basis, would have the advantage
of upgrading two areas within the North Philadelphia
community. The residential community where the
business was located would be improved by the construction of new residential housing. And the area
in which the industry would relocate would be improved by the construction of a modern industrial
facility. To the extent that several such projects
could be moved to a given area, it is conceivable
that the creation of an inner city industrial park
could develop with sufficient ground to provide for
open space and attractive landscaping around the
industrial facilities.

A second phase of the land exchange program
would involve the clearing of ground around existing
larger industrial facilities in the Model Cities
area, providing for open space and recreational

facilities adjacent to the industrial location,
rather than the residential development existing
there.   The existing residents would be relocated to
other areas within the Model Cities area, which would
be developed for residential purposes.   Homes would
be rehabilitated, or if their condition would not
permit rehabilitation, demolished and new low cost
housing erected.

The land exchange program would require the
services of one full-time coordinator with secretarial assistance.   The coordinator would work
closely with the planning unit, conduct the initial
surveys, contact the industries involved, and act as
liaison between them and the MCEDC program and with
housing agencies and residents to establish procedures for moving them to the areas vacated by the
relocating of business.   The cost of initiating the
program and providing for the necessary groundwork
and surveys would be approximately $50,000.   A
$500,000 revolving fund for land transactions would
be required.

A Commercial and Retail Finance Service

The purpose of a commercial and retail finance
service would be to provide the expertise to put together necessary applications and financing for
various commercial and retail entities and activities
that would be developed by the incubator projects
discussed above, the efforts of the Urban Venture
Capital Corporation (see page 281), and the MCEDC
promotional staff.

One or more of the following programs that are
now available could be used by the commercial and
retail finance service to assist projects deemed desirable for the Model Cities area:

The Small Business Administration.   Programs including Section 502 of the Small Business Investment Act
of 1958 and various smaller loan programs operated
by Small Business Administration are germane.   Applications are entertained by the SBA on a project-by-
project basis from qualified nonprofit economic

development corporations. (The Section 502 program
is discussed in more detail below.) The small loan
programs can be used to finance real estate, equipment, and working capital. Several Philadelphia
commercial banks are experienced and interested in
participation in these SBA programs.

The Job Loan Corporation. Organized by Philadelphia
commercial banking institutions in conjunction with
the Southeastern Pennsylvania Development Fund and
Greater Philadelphia Enterprises Development Corporation, the Philadelphia Job Loan Corporation has made
and is prepared to make loans to minority group businessmen for purposes of acquiring or starting retail
and other types of businesses. The average loan has
been in the area of from $5,000 to $20,000.

Private Sources. The commercial and retail finance
service would maintain contact with commercial banks
and the Urban Venture Capital Corporation with the
long range goal of shifting much of the financing of
commercial and retail operations in the area to conventional banking channels. Included would be lines
of credit for businessmen for inventory acquisition
purposes, the disposition by area business at fair
rates of installment papers generated by retail sales
to area residents, and financing for area businessmen
of such major inventory items as automobiles and
major appliances.

A further major responsibility of the commercial and retail finance service would be to provide
a mechanism through which area residents desiring to
acquire existing business in the area could be
matched with persons from without the area owning
business in the area that they were interested in
selling. The service would be charged with assuring
fairness and reasonable prices in transactions, as
well as arranging financing.

In order to achieve continuity of efforts and
unity of control the commercial and retail service
would be closely connected with, or be a part of the
MCEDC. However, there is a history of involvement
and expertise in the type of activity contemplated

on the part of the Greater Philadelphia Enterprises
Development Corporation, an existing nonprofit group
with offices in the Model Cities area. This corporation has worked with local banks, with the Job Loan
Corporation, and with the Small Business Administration and has an established staff supported in part
by an Economic Development Administration technical
assistance grant. Greater Philadelphia Enterprises
Development Corporation would be in a position to
undertake the responsibility of the commercial and
retail finance section on a contract basis, provided
there was one person on the staff of the MCEDC who
would provide direct liaison between the Greater
Philadelphia Enterprises Development Corporation and
the executive vice-president and the board of the
MCEDC. An alternative would be to create the same
expertise by including two professional persons and
one secretary directly on the staff of the MCEDC.
However, this alternative would take additional time,
while people were being trained in the complexity
and the processes of the programs involved. The
preferable alternative would be the contractual relationship with the Greater Philadelphia Enterprises
Development Corporation, which would require an additional $80,000 per year.

A Manufacturing and Industrial Finance Service

The purpose of the manufacturing and industrial
finance service would be to provide necessary expertise to put together the applications and financing
for the various manufacturing and industrial projects
and activities that would result from the efforts of
the manufacturing and industrial incubator, the efforts of the Urban Venture Capital Corporation, and
the MCEDC promotion program.

One or more of the following programs would be
used by the manufacturing and industrial finance
service to finance projects deemed desirable in the
MCEDC program.

The Pennsylvania Industrial Development Authority.
Authorized to make second mortgage loans equal to
40 percent of the cost of qualified manufacturing and

industrial projects on a project-by-project applica-
tion-by-application basis at a 2 percent rate of interest for a term of up to twenty five years, the
Pennsylvania Industrial Development Authority (PIDA)
requires a first mortgage lender or the business to
be assisted to put 50 percent of the cost of the
project at market rates of interest. The balance of
10 percent must be raised through the community. In
this instance the Model Cities Community Trust would
be requested to set aside $800,000 per year of its
funds for purposes of investing in PIDA projects in
the Model Cities area totaling $8 million. The pro-
gram is limited to real estate and items that can
be considered real estate.

The Authority is committed to an active role in
the Model Cities area and two smaller development
companies, both of which operate with the same technical team and are associated with the Greater Philadelphia Community Development Corporation, a Pennsylvania nonprofit corporation specializing in the technical aspects of manufacturing and industrial development. The Corporation has expressed a willingness
to work through appropriate arrangements with the
MCEDC upon its formation.

The Small Business Administration. The SBA enter-
tains applications on a project-by-project basis from
qualified nonprofit economic development corporations
to assist in financing projects eligible under Section 502 of the Small Business Investment Act of 1958.
Loans are limited to identifiable small business but
are usually available to finance up to 90 percent of
the total project cost, up to $350,000 per business,
including real estate and equipment but not working
capital. Section 502 can be used in conjunction
with the PIDA program, or it can be used alone.
Again, it was contemplated that the 10 percent local
share required would be made available either by the
Urban Venture Capital Corporation or the Model Cities
Community Foundation and for that reason $350,000 of
the funds of the Model Cities Community Trust were
to be reserved to supply local share requirements
for Section 502 projects. The Greater Philadelphia
Community Development Corporation is already qualified

as an eligible economic development corporation by
the Small Business Administration.

Economic Development Administration. The Economic
Development Administration (EDA) has program monies
for projects eligible under the Public Works and
Economic Development Act. The EDA funds may be used
for long term loans to private business or for public works, such as street relocation and utility systems in connection with major industrial installa-
tions. In addition, the EDA is permitted to guarantee
90 percent of the working capital loans made by private lenders. The Economic Development Administration capabilities are tools that could be used by
the manufacturing and industrial finance section.

Southeastern Pennsylvania Economic Development Fund.
Organized by a group of Philadelphia banks, utility
and insurance companies, and other major enterprises,
the overall interest of the Southeastern Pennsylvania
Economic Development Fund is in promoting economic
growth of companies in southeastern Pennsylvania.
Under certain circumstances it is in a position to
make loans for real estate, equipment, and working
capital. Where necessary the use of the Southeastern
Pennsylvania Economic Development Fund would be encouraged and planned by the manufacturing and industrial finance service.

The Philadelphia Industrial Development Corporation.
By a recent act of the Pennsylvania legislature, the
Philadelphia Industrial Development Corporation or
an affiliate would be permitted to engage in indus-
trial-bond-type financing for economic development
activities in Philadelphia County. And there would
be situations presented in the MCEDC program that
could be appropriately financed through the vehicle
of industrial development bonds.

Private Sources. It was contemplated that the manufacturing and industrial finance service would maintain contact with commercial banks, insurance companies, and such private sources as the Presbyterian
Ministers Fund, which are active in the industrial
mortgage and finance business. The SBA, EDA, and

PIDA programs can be made to operate in the most effective manner when there is private participation either on a first mortgage basis, a substantial cushion being provided by the government source of financing, or on the basis of a guarantee of a part of the risk. For the service to be most effective in structuring the financing for various activities under the program, it would have to be prepared to take full advantage of the opportunity of involving private capital in such activities.

Since the Greater Philadelphia Community Development Corporation is currently engaged in economic development activities in the Model Cities area, establishing a relationship between it and the Model Cities structure would make possible the activation of the manufacturing and industrial finance service immediately upon approval and funding of the program.

The existing expertise now available and the experience of experts in working with some of the agencies involved in industrial development financing, such as PIDA, can be made available to the MCEDC program through a contractual relationship with the MCEDC under which the Greater Philadelphia Enterprises Development Corporation would perform the work of the manufacturing and industrial finance section. The Greater Philadelphia Community Development Corporation may be in a position to undertake such responsibilities on the basis of a contract that would allow it to hire three professional staff persons, several consultants, and one secretary, provided there is one person directly on the staff of the Model Cities Economic Development Corporation to provide a liaison between it and the executive vice-president and board of the MCEDC. It would thus relate to the Model Cities agency and the Model Cities Economic Development Corporation by means of contract and by means of the liaison person. An alternative would be to create the same expertise and experience that exist in the Greater Philadelphia Community Development Corporation as a part of the MCEDC. This would require additional time while people were trained in the complexities and practical aspects of the programs involved.

At the end of the first year the manufacturing and industrial service should have produced sufficient projects to create 700 new jobs in the Model Cities area.

A Counseling and Follow-Up Unit

A basic problem faced by minority group business-men is an absence of business experience, which gives rise to inadequate management capabilities. A counseling and follow-up unit would be formed under the Model Cities program to provide counseling in the areas of business management to the entrepreneurs located in the project area. The program would serve two basic functions. First, it would make available to small businessmen a pool of trained volunteer and paid professional consultants to aid them in formulating and evaluating sound business practices, and, second, it would act as a monitoring agency to correlate information about business experience fed back from the entrepreneurs aided by the various Model Cities programs.

The staff of the counseling unit would categorize all the existing sources of financial and managerial help available and, in addition, would compile lists of available volunteer and paid professional consultants in the areas of law, accounting, business management, insurance, real estate, market analysis, site location, public relations, and advertising, to whom the businessman could be referred for advice and guidance. The staff would also be responsible for establishing guidelines to be used for consultant referral and would organize follow-through procedures that would tie into the various agencies engaged in entrepreneurial capitalization programs.

As a clearinghouse and recipient for financial data supplied by the businesses aided by any of the Model Cities programs, the counseling service would provide a source of information to enable the evaluation of the success of the programs--and it would be able to recognize at an early stage the need for additional assistance by the small businesses. The counseling unit would thus help avoid one of the most common pitfalls of the inexperienced business-man--the inability to recognize his problems until it is too late to solve them.

The staff would develop standardized forms to be used by each business to report basic data per-taining to its operations. The businessman would be instructed in the filling out of the forms and the maintenance of business records. Financial analysts employed in the program would review all fi-nancial data for the businesses receiving aid from various Model Cities programs. Prior to submission of the data to the appropriate lending agencies, a staff member of the unit would consult with the businessman and any other consultants assigned to the business, and the staff member would study trends, examine financial information with reference to dan-ger points, and endeavor to detect problems at the earliest stage.

Since the unit would have access to the broad spectrum of financial information and progress data concerning the business enterprises aided through Model Cities programs, it would be able to act in part as an evaluation team for the success of the various components of the Model Cities program.

The staff would consist of a counseling director, two financial analysts, two accountants, two secre-taries, and a lawyer. Funds for additional consult-ing services should also be provided.

A Planning Unit

A planning unit would be established to develop long range programs to be carried out by the various components of the Model Cities organization. A staff, consisting of a planning coordinator, assis-tant coordinator, and secretary would work with paid architectural and engineering consultants to formu-late progressive programs and locate suitable devel-opment sites within the Model Cities area. The planning coordinator would report directly to the executive vice-president of the MCEDC.

The planning unit would also retain independent
engineers to inspect and evaluate the construction
and design of the industrial and commercial projects
constructed within the Model Cities area to ensure
high standards of construction and site attractiveness.

In addition to the program components outlined
above, which would operate through the MCEDC and
under its executive vice-president and board of directors, the program would require the establishment
of (1) a community trust and (2) a Venture Capital
Corporation to work closely with the MCEDC.

Funding

A Model Cities Community Foundation

A foundation, to be called the Model Cities Community Foundation, would be organized and operated
exclusively for purposes within the meaning of Section 501(c)(3) of the internal revenue code, which
would be supported by a grant from the Model Cities
Agency and gifts, grants, and donations from other
persons, organizations, and corporations. The purpose of the Foundation would be to provide by loan
at below-market interest rates the local share monies
necessary in connection with various commercial, industrial, and manufacturing development projects.
The Foundation would also purchase 100,000 shares of
the Class C common stock of the Urban Venture Capital
Corporation and $4.8 million in bonds or debentures
to be issued by the Corporation.

The Foundation would be most effective if it,
in addition, had available a discretionary fund for
general use and investment in the economy of the
Model Cities area. A fund in the amount of $5 million
would be appropriate. The primary use of the discretionary fund would be investment in business opportunities and services important to the residents
of the Model Cities areas that could not be achieved
through other parts of the MCEDC program.

All gifts, grants, donations and contributions
by the trust would be made exclusively to or for the

use of organizations exempt from taxation under Section 501(a) and within the categories described in Section 501(c)(3) of the internal revenue code. In no event would money or other assets be distributed for purposes or to organizations that would not permit a deduction under Section 170(b)(1)(A) of the internal revenue code. The trustees would distribute funds only to qualified groups, organizations, and associations whose primary charitable function would be performed in the geographical area of the Model Cities program.

The earnings of the Foundation would be reinvested in the Model Cities area economy or used for general charitable purposes in the area. No part of the net earnings of the trust would be distributed to any group, organization, or association whose activities were substantially to carry on propaganda; otherwise attempt to influence legislation; or participate in or intervene in any political campaign on behalf of any candidate for public office, including the publication and distribution of statements.

The Model Cities administrator would appoint all members of the board of trustees of the Model Cities Community Foundation, a majority being residents of the Model Cities area. They would serve for a period of three years.

Upon the dissolution or winding up of the affairs of the Foundation, whether voluntary or involuntary, the assets remaining in the hands of the board of trustees after all debts had been satisfied would be distributed, transferred, conveyed, delivered, or paid over to charitable organizations functioning substantially in the same geographic area as the Model Cities program, which the board of trustees would designate.

Though many of the functions of this trust could be carried out through the MCEDC directly, there would remain sufficient uncertainty regarding the tax status of economic development corporations to justify creation of the Foundation. The Foundation would also permit the channeling of certain nongovernmental private voluntary grant funds into the area.

The administration of the Foundation would require the services of a full-time director, assistant director, and secretary. And it was contemplated that its budget would make allowance for the retention of professional investment advice and financial counseling.

An Urban Venture Capital Corporation

The purpose of the Urban Venture Capital Corporation would be to supply equity funds for the residents of the area who showed a desire to enter manufacturing and industrial ventures or substantial commercial and retail ventures, for most residents of the area who desire to become manufacturers or substantial businessmen have not been able to accumulate sufficient assets to supply their own venture capital. Financing, though it might be available under certain circumstances, is not available in terms of venture capital to area residents in substantial sums. Few lenders will make substantial advances, and few individuals will make investments in the area. A source of venture capital is necessary in order to take full advantage of various loan programs available through both private and public sources.

The Urban Venture Capital Corporation would supply venture capital for businesses developed in the manufacturing and industrial incubator and in the commercial and retail incubator; it would also supply venture capital for other enterprises developed under the MCEDC program. Investments would be made by the Corporation through the following two processes:

1. Identifiable business opportunities involving as operators and entrepreneurs residents of the Model Cities area would be submitted to the Urban Venture Capital Corporation for analysis and review by the program sections of the MCEDC.

2. The Urban Venture Capital Corporation would investigate business opportunities in the Model Cities area that seemed to promise both income production and capital growth. It would then develop a proposal around the particular business opportunity

and work through the MCEDC to recruit a resident of
the area capable of being trained to take advantage
of the business opportunity.

After the identification of a business opportunity and the identification of the individuals who
might operate it, the Urban Venture Capital Corporation would assist in the financial planning to
capitalize and commence the business. Enough venture capital would be injected into the business to
permit it a realistic start-up period.

In each instance the Urban Venture Capital Corporation and the entrepreneur or entrepreneurs would
negotiate a fair arrangement in terms of their re-
spective equity interest in the business. In most
instances the Urban Venture Capital Corporation
would own a majority share of each business initially
but give appropriate options to the individual entrepreneur to acquire a share of the business initially
owned by the Urban Venture Capital Corporation. The
options would be tailored to produce worthwhile capital gains for the Urban Venture Capital Corporation.
And in the event that the business was not operated
satisfactorily by the entrepreneur or entrepreneurs
involved, the arrangements with the Urban Venture
Capital Corporation would permit it to acquire the
interest of the entrepreneurs and to substitute other
entrepreneurs to prevent a loss of the investment
involved.

The Urban Venture Capital Corporation would
analyze each project from the point of view of its
feasibility as a commercial profit-making venture.
In all instances the amount of its investment, and
its decision to make any investment at all would
depend largely on the commercial feasibility of the
business.

Suppose a young resident of the Model Cities
area had invented a process for the rapid molding of
various containers, such as flower pots, which would
allow rapid and low cost production of such items,
but his process had not been tested. The Urban Venture Capital Corporation might advance him $5,000

and agree to advance an additional $50,000 to open a
factory if he could perfect the process to the point
that it could be set up on an assembly line basis.
It might also arrange for him to enter the manufacturing and industrial incubator to work on the further
development of the process. If, within six months,
the process had been perfected to the point at which
large scale production was feasible, the $50,000
start-up and the initial working capital would be
advanced; in return the Urban Venture Capital Corporation would receive a 51 percent interest in a
corporation that owned the process. The young man
would be given an option to acquire the 51 percent
interest at two times the investment of the Urban
Venture Capital Corporation, provided he executed
his option within five years. The Urban Venture
Capital Corporation would participate on the board
of directors of the enterprise and would also continue to render financial advice to the entrepreneur.

The Urban Venture Capital Corporation would be
formed in the first six weeks after approval and
funding of the MCEDC program, and the timetable for
its capitalization would be within the first six
months of the program. The Urban Venture Capital
Corporation should be involved in one or more ventures by the end of the first project year.

The Corporation would be formed as a Pennsylvania
business corporation, and its articles of incorporation would limit it to financial participation in
manufacturing, industrial, financial, commercial,
and retail business in the Model Cities area. It
would derive its initial assets from three sources
as follows:

1. It would sell $4.8 million in debentures
or bonds to the Model Cities Community Foundation,
which debentures would bear a below-market interest
rate, perhaps 2 percent.

2. The corporation would derive further funds
from the creation and issuance of $1 million of pre-
ferred stock in $1,000 denominations, callable at a
premium. The preferred stock would bear a 5 percent

rate and would be cumulative--it being hoped that local banks, insurance companies, and utility companies could be persuaded to buy it as a form of assistance to the Model Cities program.

3. A total of 300,000 shares of $2 par value common stock divided into Classes A, B, and C equal in participation and voting powers would be created. Class A stock would be reserved for sale at par value to residents of the Model Cities area in amounts as small as one share. Class B common stock would be sold at par to interested individuals in the Greater Philadelphia area. And the Class C common stock would be purchased by the Model Cities Community Foundation. To the extent that the Class A stock was not purchased in a three-month period by residents of the Model Cities area, it would be made available in equal amounts to the Class B and C shareholders. To the extent that the option was not exercised during the five-year period by the Class A shareholders, the option would become available to the Class B shareholders, who would acquire it under the same terms and conditions during an additional one-year period.

Appropriate underwriting advice would be sought from the very beginning of the capitalization of the Urban Venture Capital Corporation, and to the degree that registration might be required with the Pennsylvania Securities Commission or the Securities and Exchange Commission, it would be undertaken.

Holders of each class of common stock would be permitted to elect two directors of the Urban Venture Capital Corporation. The preferred shareholders would be permitted to elect one director until such time as all of the preferred stock had been called, at which time the additional director would be elected by the Class A, B, and C shareholders.

To the extent that the Class A stock was not purchased in six months by residents of the Model Cities area, it would be made available for purchase by the Model Cities Community Foundation.

The relation between the Model Cities Agency and the Urban Venture Capital Corporation would be further detailed and outlined in a loan agreement between them, which would be a part of the package for the investment of the $4.8 million. The loan agreement would contain provisions that would set time limits on the investment of its capital by the Urban Venture Capital Corporation.

The Corporation would employ initially one full-time general manager trained in business and financial analysis and a secretary. Its staff would be permitted to grow only to the extent that the investment and business of the Corporation required additional persons to perform additional financial analysis.

It was hoped that the Urban Venture Capital Corporation would develop into a miniconglomerate with interests in different types of businesses, both large and small, located in the Model Cities area. Such businesses could include banking, insurance, services, distribution, retailing, and others.

The Urban Venture Capital Corporation, as a private corporation, would pay its expenses out of its gross income. Other than the $4.8 million loan from the Model Cities Community Foundation and the investment by the Foundation in the Class C common stock, it would require no budget from the Model Cities Agency.

Corporate and Organizational
Structure

It was contemplated that the MCEDC would file its articles of incorporation as soon as the Model Cities program was approved and funded. Steps would be taken to have the charter application heard directly by the Court of Common Pleas of the County of Philadelphia rather than being referred to a master, in order to save time. The charter could be issued within thirty days after the initial application was made. It was contemplated that all program compon-

ents that were the direct responsibility of the MCEDC
would be organized and operational within six months
from the time of approval of the program.

The MCEDC, when organized as a Pennsylvania nonprofit corporation, would have the power, authority,
and ability to enter into a contract with the Model
Cities Agency for Philadelphia to undertake the project components set forth above. It would be authorized and have the power to buy and sell land, machinery, buildings, and equipment; act as a lessor
or lessee of land, buildings, machinery, and equipment; receive and make grants and contributions;
borrow money from public and private lenders; encum-
ber capital by lending or posting its guaranties for
loans made to approved project borrowers by third
parties. It would also have the power to work through
other individuals, nonprofit corporations, and firms
and directly or through community-based organizations,
including cooperatives and other local development
corporations, such as the Greater Philadelphia Enterprises Development Corporation, Greater Philadelphia
Community Development Corporation, and Philadelphia
Industrial Development Corporation.

The Corporation's affairs would be governed by
the board of directors, made up of the duly appointed
representatives of the following organizations and
groups: the Model Cities Agency, the Area Wide Council of the Model Cities Neighborhood, the Greater
Philadelphia Enterprises Development Corporation,
the Greater Philadelphia Community Development Corporation, the North City Congress, the Philadelphia
Industrial Development Corporation, the Urban Coalition, the Office of the City Economist, the major
utility companies in the area, the commercial banks
and federal and state savings and loan institutions
in the area, the Philadelphia Chamber of Commerce,
the Model Cities Community Foundation, and the Urban
Venture Capital Corporation. Though it was intended
that each of the organizations and groups should have
one representative, it was contemplated that the North
City Area Wide Council of the Model Cities Neighborhood and the Office of the Model Cities Administrator
would have three representatives each, making a total

of six, which number would be sufficient to ensure an appropriate voice of the Model Cities neighborhood and the Model Cities Agency in the decisions of the board.

The composition of the board would thus be such as to achieve the broadest possible participation and support from the private business sectors, the community, and the government.

The Model Cities Economic Development Corporation would have an executive vice-president who would devote full time to directing the activities of the Corporation. He would have a high level assistant executive vice-president, and each of the component parts of the Model City Economic Development Corporation's program would have a director for the particular activity who would report directly to the Corporation's executive vice-president or his assistant. (The balance of the staff of the MCEDC is set forth in the outlines of the individual program components.)

The Corporation would relate to the Model Cities Agency by virtue of an appropriate delegate agency contract that would define its function and duties. On a day-to-day basis it would relate to the Model Cities Agency, the City departments, the Urban Venture Capital Corporation, the Model Cities Community Foundation, and the Area Wide Council of the Model Cities Neighborhood through a Model Cities economic development coordinator and a coordinating committee.

The coordinating committee would be staffed by the MCEDC coordinator, who would be chosen by the Model Cities administrator from a list of recommendations numbering no less than five names from the Model Cities Economic Development Corporation board of directors. He would be paid directly from the Model Cities Agency. His sole function would be to keep himself apprised of the activities, progress, needs, and demands of the various component parts of the MCEDC program and to evaluate the work of each component part. The coordinator would work with the advice and counsel of a Model Cities economic development coordinating committee composed of representatives of the Model Cities Community Foundation, the Model Cities Economic Development Corporation, the Urban Venture Capital Corporation, the Greater Philadelphia Enterprises Development Corporation, the Greater Philadelphia Community Development Corporation, and such other entities or persons as would be designated by the Model Cities Agency.

In no respect would the coordinator be, or considered to be, an operating officer of any of these agencies. His primary role would be one of coordination and evaluation of the programs and activities undertaken by each, and his primary responsibility would be to keep in such direct contact with the individual programs that he would be cognizant when they were not moving ahead at the appropriate rate or with the degree of coordination and cooperation required. He would be responsible for bringing about the desired rate of progress and coordination whenever it might be lacking in the operations of the independent units.

The MCEDC coordinating committee would be given the power to make recommendations to each of the component agencies on the committee, and the failure of any agency to accept the recommendations would be grounds for canceling the various contractual relationships each would have with other members of the committee, including the Model Cities Agency.

The person selected as coordinator should have capabilities in the planning, financial, technical, executive, and operational phases of the economic development projects. He should be a strong personality capable of having a leadership impact on all the programs.

Evaluative Control

It would be possible to measure and determine whether or not each individual component part of the program of the MCEDC was achieving its specific objectives, recognizing, however, that they each interact. If the idea of economic development in the area was not successfully promoted, then neither the manufacturing and industrial section nor the commercial and retail development section could be successful. The same is true of every other component.

In the end the degree to which all the programs were working together to produce a more viable economy for the Model Cities area would be determined by two important measures. One measure would be the unemployment rate in the area, or, stated another way, how many jobs were preserved in the area and how many new jobs were created. A respectable goal for the first project year would be to create a net increase of 3,500 jobs. The rate of new job creation should be greater in subsequent years.

Another measure of the success of the program would be the degree to which area residents became participants at the management and ownership levels of the economic development activities undertaken. Careful statistics would be kept with respect to every enterprise being assisted under the program, and an accurate report of these statistics would provide a tool for evaluation of the program. One of the chief roles of the coordinator and coordinating committee would be to keep a careful watch in terms of jobs perserved and new jobs created in the area and the degree of participation by area residents in terms of management and ownership.

The quality of development is an item more difficult to measure, though efforts along these lines should be made on a continuing basis by the MCEDC coordinator. In the second year of the operation of the program an outside independent consultant would be hired (budgeted for in the first year) to provide a study and evaluation not only of the quantity but also of the quality of the development activities.

Citizen Participation

Citizen participation is provided by representation of the Area Wide Council of the Model Cities Neighborhood on the board of directors of the MCEDC. Representation is also provided for the community with respect to the Urban Venture Capital Corporation and the Model Cities Community Foundation. The composition of the board of directors of the MCEDC would include other groups, such as the North City Congress, which is a broad-based community organization that speaks with a high degree of relevance to the residents of the Model Cities area. Appropriate representation of the Model Cities Agency and Area Wide Council of the Model Cities Neighborhood would be sought on the boards of the Greater Philadelphia Enterprises Development Corporation and the Greater Philadelphia Community Development Corporation as a prerequisite to their becoming consultants to the Model Cities Economic Development Corporation, and the same such requirement would be attempted, where appropriate, with respect to other community groups and development organizations having contractual relationships with any component part of the Model Cities Economic Development program.

8

THE ART
OF THE POSSIBLE:
WHAT SOME
CITIES ARE DOING

Few people, including even the public administrators involved, realize the dimensions of the role
of local government in the functioning of the U.S.
economy. City hall and county courthouse make a wide
range of decisions that deal directly with the work-
ings of the economic system. The fact is that the
strategic application of economics to public policy
is rapidly shifting from a national to a local arena.
Or, to put it more accurately, the local leverages
of economics are now assuming an importance equal
to those at the national level. An increasing number
of the critical decisions of local government call
for an economic input. From the standpoint of the
city or county the viability of the local government
itself is at stake in these decisions. Strengthening
the local economic base and making maximum use of
local economic resources are matters of sheer survival.

Few cities, large or small, are not caught in
the vise between hard costs and a softness in their
economic vitality. Few suburban jurisdictions, despite their rapid growth, are generating an economic
base that matches the rising demands for services.

These forces also work in the other direction.
The effectiveness of local government in dealing
with urban development problems is a critical element
in the health of the national economy. Local trans-

portation, utilities, public services, resource use,
taxes, public interest controls--these are decisive
factors in the functioning of the nation's free enterprise economy. If the delivery systems of local
governments break down, the efficiency of the private
economy will be sharply impaired.

There is already stark evidence of a deterioration in both areas--in the viability of local government and in the efficiency of the private economy.
Municipalities are finding it increasingly difficult
to make ends meet. Urban business and industry are
facing growing diseconomies in increased tax loads,
mounting congestion, and rising cost of service
imputs.

In dealing with these problems, local governments around the country are increasingly using the
tools of applied economics. They are trying to get
at the bottlenecks that are slowing down new investment; taking a hard-headed look at their economic
development potentials; using public works as effective pump primers; and giving economic development a
high rank in the setting of action priorities.

In short, local governments are playing a much
larger--and strategically a new--role in economic
development. It is likely to become an even larger
role when current reorganization proposals (including
revenue sharing) become operative and more discretionary funds become available. Moreover, only a bare
beginning has been made in dealing with the problems
of air, water, and soil pollution; mass transportation; decentralized housing for low income and moderate income groups; and inner city redevelopment.
Action taken in regard to these problems will have
profound implications for the private economy and
for the economic well-being of cities.

Most of the economic leverage applied by local
governments relates to the efficiency and profitability of private economic activity at specific locations. The federal government deals with the
economy primarily through fiscal and monetary devices
and the application of national standards and incen-

tives. City hall and the courthouse deal with the
nitty gritty of the locational and operational decisions of the entrepreneur and investor at the local
level.

Until now many cities--and indeed many counties
--have been fighting a losing battle. The incentives
to new investment, new job creation, and new entrepreneurship have been overwhelmingly linked to a
horizontal dispersal of economic activities. The
economies of central cities have been in the back-
water of development, fighting the forces of decay.
Negative factors affecting most central city economies
have had a double-barreled impact. The direction of
new investment and reinvestment has veered sharply
away from the central city. At the same time, the
tax-paying capacities of the city's economic base
have been static and in a relative sense declining.

It has been, and still is, a tough row to hoe.
Obsolescence, vacancies, congestion, crime, difficulties of land assembly--added to the dispersal of
markets and the forces of disinvestment--pose a formidable set of problems. But some cities are rising
to the challenge. Their approach has been pragmatic
and in most cases effective--to capitalize on the
assets at hand, to use the leverage of public action
to spark private investment, to knock out as many
negative factors as possible, and to hold on. A few
of the ways in which local governments have used
their muscle in numerous areas of economic activity
are these:

1. Setting development targets toward which
both public and private resources can be mobilized

2. Maximizing the direct leverage of public
expenditures upon private investments

3. Taking public positions on the importance
of economic development

4. Exploring new areas of "creative economics"
and making innovative approaches to the use of land

5.   Engaging directly in redevelopment programs to produce new private investments and enterprises

6.   Working out new interjurisdictional arrangements to cut costs and provide better services

7.   Utilizing vacant land or surplus land to generate new economic activities

8.   Protecting and capitalizing on the city's most important economic assets

9.   Creating conditions to meet the specialized needs of industries that can profit by central city locations

10.   Taking the "total" approach to economic development, giving it high priority in the allocation of resources.

Examples of local government actions in these fields are legion. A few are mentioned below.   In all cases the cities are aware of the leverage they exercise in economic development. In the "new federalism," the ball game so far as local governments are concerned has just begun.

DEVELOPMENT TARGETS

Through economic base studies and other types of hard-headed inquiry, cities can get a clear picture of their competitive economic functions and capitalize on them.

Atlanta is a case in point. In the early 1960s the city set out on a deliberate course to exploit fully its position as a work center in a rapidly changing region. It geared most of its public and private actions in pursuance of that goal. It made heavy investments in its airport, expressway connections, and downtown urban renewal.

Top leadership also agreed that the solution of social problems (housing, race relations, neighbor-

hood redevelopment) and the provision of amenities
were as important to its special kind of economic
role as physical improvements. It mobilized its efforts in those directions. Private business put millions of dollars in a "Forward Atlanta" campaign,
advertising Atlanta as a "new kind of city." The
efforts paid off; the annual increase in employment
more than doubled within three years.

When local hotel operators protested against a
new 600-unit motel in the central urban renewal area,
the city had an economic study made. The study supported the contention that the addition would hurt
existing hotel occupancies; instead it recommended
at least 2,000 new hotel units to put Atlanta in a
new competitive position in the hotel business. The
2,000 were built, then doubled, and today hotel occupancy in the city is at an all-time high.

The same hard-headed approach to development
potentials focused attention in South Bend, Indiana,
upon the city's unique assets for the skilled labor
force of the area. Greenville, South Carolina,
geared most of its efforts to its potentials for attracting new kinds of manufacturing plants in the
industrial Piedmont, once dominated by the textile
industry. Memphis, Tennessee, is capitalizing not
only on its mid-South location but also on its unique
complex of "mid-city amenities," all identified by
economic analysis.

LEVERAGE OF EXPENDITURES

Virtually every dollar spent by local government
on capital improvements holds some potential for
generating new private investments, directly or indirectly. And administrators are increasingly taking
this multiplier effect into account.

Fort Wayne, Indiana, in rejecting an outlying
location for its new city hall in favor of a more
expensive central site, sparked the development of
new downtown office buildings and helped stabilize
the district for other retail and service operations.

Greensboro, North Carolina, put its new public library close to the 100 percent block of the central business district.

Dozens of cities, guided by an analysis of long run rather than short run arithmetic, have made similar decisions that recognize the linkages between civic convention centers and hotels, stores, service facilities, and places of entertainment. Cases in point are Tulsa, Oklahoma; Tampa, Florida; Mobile, Alabama; and Springfield, Massachusetts. Others, however, have succumbed to the attractions of low cost land away from the centers of activity. Not only have they lost leverage; many have impaired the operating efficiencies of their auditoriums, arenas, and other civic centers.

DEVELOPMENT POLICIES

An understanding of the forces affecting all segments of the existing city economy is important in setting public policies relating to development.

In Ann Arbor, Michigan, the issue was whether or not the city council should oppose a large regional shopping center on the grounds that it might adversely affect the central business district. The city had a study made of the market and competitive factors involved. This appraisal showed that different economic functions would be played by the new center and existing downtown stores and that the overall economy would benefit from construction of the new facility.

Such a rationalization is not always indicated, of course. Public policies frequently create adverse conditions for existing businesses and industries. But all such situations are amenable to hard-headed economic analysis that can provide insight into the implications of different policy options.

CREATIVE ECONOMICS

New approaches must be taken in most cities
to set the conditions under which new private enterprises will be generated. The cards are stacked
against the city in most cases; there are too many
barriers in the way of profitable and secure close-
in investments.

Cities are removing these barriers in innovative
ways. Arlington, Virginia, employed the techniques
of high incentive zoning to create its spectacular
new Rosslyn and Crystal City complexes of office
buildings, motels, apartment houses, and entertainment facilities. Rochester, New York, broke new
ground in facilitating the development of Midtown
Plaza, a multiuse complex in the heart of the city.
Greenville, South Carolina, hampered by the absence
of urban renewal powers, devised a scheme for utilizing the air rights over municipal parking areas to
generate plans for new office and retail investments.

The surface of such innovative possibilities
has been hardly scratched. The process is likely to
be difficult, involving changes in zoning and building regulations, public fund outlays, and new state
legislation in many cases, but the potential payoff
is great. Much attention is now being given to the
joint use and multidevelopment possibilities of
highway right-of-way.

REDEVELOPMENT PROGRAMS

Many cities have substantial programs of redevelopment. The more spectacular successes are those
of the big cities--Pittsburgh, Philadelphia, and
Hartford, for example--where massive new investments
and job-creating activities have been generated.

Smaller cities have also applied the same economic leverage through redevelopment. Norfolk,

Virginia, has virtually rebuilt its downtown and
waterfront areas with impressive results in terms of
new commercial, residential, and industrial investments. Examples of this kind are testimony of the
potential viability of most city interjurisdictional
arrangements; short of metropolitan government, cities
and counties are finding numerous ways to cooperate
in the joint provision of services and facilities.
The economic implications are far-reaching, not only
in cost savings but also in creating more favorable
conditions for economic development.

The progressive cooperation between Indianapolis
and Marion County (including the early development
of a city-county office building) laid the groundwork
for the UNIGOV consolidation plan. In Dayton, Ohio,
the agreement of local governments in the region to
share in the responsibility for low and moderate income housing will help rationalize the regional availability of labor and relieve the central city of
heavy economic pressures. The proposal in the Min-
neapolis-St. Paul area to redistribute a portion of
the annual increments to the property tax base can
have a direct bearing upon the economic viability of
the constituent governments.

VACANT SURPLUS LANDS

In most cities land is a scarce resource. Its
unavailability for profitable private development is
a major factor in limiting the city's development
potential. There are immense development possibilities on land that is no longer in use, however, and
local governments are beginning to take advantage of
them.

In Portsmouth, Virginia, an effort is now under
way (based on a comprehensive analysis of local economic needs) to convert surplus federal land into
industrial parks relating to water transportation.
Greenville County, South Carolina, was highly successful in transforming a phased-out air base to large-
scale industrial uses. DeKalb County, Georgia,
created a profitable general aviation field on the
site of an old naval air station.

In Charlotte, North Carolina, the city's redevelopment efforts persuaded a major railroad to put
its surplus lands to new commercial and industrial
uses. Shelby County, Tennessee, is planning a new
town on the site of its former old folks' home.

SPECIAL LOCAL ASSETS

Cities must maximize the development potentials
inherent in their strongest assets. And often the
importance of these features is overlooked in the
search for new ways to beef up the economy in face
of competition.

The support of state government functions in
Nashville, Tennessee, resulted in the Capitol Hill
redevelopment program that has brought in new industries, office buildings, and apartment houses. In
New Orleans studies of the importance of the Vieux
Carré district have resulted in major new investments
within the framework of a tight policy of protecting
the French Quarter environment. Charleston, South
Carolina, and Savannah, Georgia, have likewise taken
steps to protect their historical areas, which are
major assets in the attraction of tourists.

A large number of university towns--Ann Arbor,
Michigan; State College, Pennsylvania; Middletown,
Connecticut; and others--have made economic studies
to determine how the economic as well as the educational and cultural value of their institutions can
be protected and expanded.

INDUSTRIAL DEVELOPMENT

Faced with the general trend of industrial location in outlying areas, cities have taken steps to
protect their existing industries and to provide
land and facilities for new industries seeking
close-in locations.

Many New England towns have been successful in
converting buildings formerly occupied by the textile
industry into "industrial park buildings" for small

firms.   Other cities have focused on using vacated
buildings for incubator industries, assisting them
through rehabilitation and improvements in traffic
and parking facilities.   In Binghamton, New York,
and Kansas City, Kansas, among many other cities,
clearance for close-in industries was given top
priority in urban renewal programs.

TOTAL DEVELOPMENT

The importance of taking a total approach to
the problem of economic development in the city is
becoming increasingly recognized.   Isolated steps,
although significant in generating new economic activities or stabilizing particular situations, do
not fully realize the city's development potential.
In many cities (Newark, for example) even major projects can have relatively little impact--and indeed
can fail as projects--unless accompanied by an across-
the-board attack on a range of negative forces.

In Cincinnati the city's redevelopment efforts
have been broad enough to affect all areas of economic
development critically--efforts related to large-
scale industrial districts, massive downtown redevelopment, close-in housing projects, waterfront redevelopment, and neighborhood rehabilitation.   And
other cities have taken similar steps to coordinate
their efforts to reach all sectors of the local economy.   The costs in both time and money are high, but
the payoff is great.   The basic fact is that virtually every city has a potential economic vitality,
but in most cities the full potential will not be
realized unless a range of economic leverages is employed to support it.

In the immediate future the city's muscle in
economic development will be immeasurably strengthened
by proposed changes in the methods of administering
federal aid funds.   HUD has proposed the consolidation of 701 community renewal programs into a community planning and management assistance program.
There are plans also for integrating existing urban
renewal, Model Cities, water and sewer, and rehabili-

tation assistance programs under a community development program umbrella.

The apparent thrust is to help improve the management capabilities of cities--to encourage them to
apply PPB techniques in the allocation of their resources and in the evaluation of program effectiveness. Running parallel to these proposed new directions in administration is the trend toward revenue
sharing, promising to make new funds available to
localities.

The city administrator will be the key decision
maker in such programs at the local level. His
leverage on overall economic development and on the
economic viability of his government will be greatly
expanded in the process. He will, in short, be up
to his ears in economics--and not one moment too soon.

9

A PROGRAM
FOR THE FUTURE

The national trend toward urbanization has initiated among policy planners a continuous dialogue
about what the posture of the federal government
should be. The thesis has been offered that the
scale of cities is already unmanageable, that people
are too densely crowded together, and that the consequence is necessarily social disorganization. Ad-
vocates of this position argue that if job creation
leads to population shifts, policy should encourage
decentralization of mass metropolitan functions
through a more even geographic distribution of jobs.
This line of thinking leads to the conclusion that
it is appropriate to induce manufacturers and industry generally away from the very large cities to
medium size cities or rural areas--that, given a
highly mobile population, the distribution of people
throughout the states can be shifted into less dense
population centers with the result that the problems
experienced by the nation's very large cities will
be mitigated.

This line of reasoning is, on the whole, very
attractive. Perhaps it suggests a model of policy
that may serve as an ideotype for action. But it is
an approach that requires reconstituting the whole
fabric of American life and thus poses many dangers--
some of which could seriously harm the nation. The
most serious of these dangers is that such a policy

could lead to even greater problems of economic and
racial segregation. So far, attempts to provide
low cost housing in the suburban rings surrounding
central cities have been ineffectual. Consequently,
migration of jobs outward to the suburbs has left
the inner city with major and continuous unemployment
problems. The suggestion that policy can gently
stimulate the creation of "new towns" or medium size
cities without a major public commitment, and concomi-
tant appropriations, must be very carefully examined.
Before the general thesis about the benefits of decentralization can be considered to be meaningful,
it must be demonstrated that adequate economic integration can be achieved in the ex-urban metropolis
to which jobs have moved in tens of thousands.

To attempt to implement this hypothesis without
such a commitment would aggravate the problems of the
inner city substantially. It would further alienate
and isolate the inner city population from the rest
of society and eliminate the opportunity for economic
improvement that would permit real change in the
quality and character of the inner city community.
In this light, the only viable solution to urban
economic problems remains the concurrent restructuring
of the inner city economy and the pursuit of housing
opportunities within suburbia, while transportation
links between places of work and places of residence
are improved.

In the same vein, arguments have been made that
the connection should be finally severed between the
"right to income" and the source(jobs). The theorists
who espouse these arguments claim that the engine of
the economy produces enough to support the whole of
the populace without requiring its work in traditional kinds of jobs--that the nation can afford to
guarantee an adequate level of annual income to all
families, whether or not they work. Again, there is
a real question about whether such separation is
desirable. Perhaps more relevant is the question
whether such a public commitment is likely or possible.

Over the short term future the answer to this
latter question probably has to be "No." The economy

of this country is likely to continue to be "mixed,"
but with heavy reliance on the private sector.

The conclusions to be drawn from these considerations for urban planning are straightforward.
First, a program must continue to be based on generating a stable and growing economy strong enough to
provide significant economic opportunity to inner
city residents. Second, the tenets of such a program
must be directed toward reinforcing the strengths of
the private sector in inner city communities and
joining these forces with constructive planning and
programming by citizens themselves. If the city is
to continue to provide economic sustenance for its
citizens, it must deal with various major issues,
which are closely interrelated.

Competition for scarce land and resources requires that economic activity be conducted with respect to the limited amount of land available in a
city, with a real awareness of the effects of economic processes on the total environment. And it is
only necessary to examine the inner city superficially
to perceive quickly a paramount economic issue of
the coming decade. The inner city, above all else,
is a place. As such it comprises a fixed amount of
land, and vacant space is a relatively scarce com-
modity. As the core of the city, the inner city is
the oldest and most densely developed sector. This
scarcity-density factor gives rise to strong pressures from competing users of the existing and available land. Residents call for additional housing
units. Companies want room for plant expansion. Developers search for vacant or underutilized parcels
that can be assembled for new housing complexes or
inner city industrial parks. Comprehensive planners
evaluate the continuing need for educational facilities, recreation areas, new roadway systems, and
other public services designed for the use of all
the people. In the face of such competitive pressures a basic issue for the 1970s is finding the best
ways to utilize this scarce and desirable land fully
and wisely. It must be allocated to maximize its
benefits to all and to improve as much as possible
the quality of life for those who live and work in
the inner city.

The implications of pressures for industrial development are profound. While older areas of economic activity sustain employment densities of nearly a hundred jobs per acre, new developments sustain only between thirty and fifty jobs per acre. Even at the upper end of this range these densities are not sufficient to warrant new industrial development in near-in city locations, and a tack must be developed that will permit more intensive utilization of land even at middle-distance sites.

The companion issue to that of land scarcity and density of development is the issue of physical redesign. The physical and economic infrastructure of the inner city is a creature of another age. Most of its physical features were determined prior to the turn of the century and were the products of a radically different technology. The building stock is relatively old and often functionally obsolete. Today a significant percentage of the inner city's companies are housed in structures built before the Great Depression. In few instances are such structures suitable, without modification, to accommodating the needs of current industrial technology-production techniques, packaging methods, and the like.

Obsolescence does not end at the factory door. The inner city streets were not designed or constructed to meet modern trucking requirements. In most cases alleys, bridges, and parking facilities were all designed to meet the needs of another time, another way of life. While impressive strides have been made to improve the existing public services and facilities and to create new ones, much still remains to be done. The primary emphasis of a successful program of physical redesign is modernization.

The inner city in the 1970s must be redesigned so that it can, through the application of modern planning concepts and technology, achieve a level of functionality for today's residents and businesses comparable to what it achieved in its successful past. But redesign of the support system of industrial functions must deal not only with economic efficiency; it must also convert industrial capacities to be functional with respect to the whole environment.

Effectuating significant programs of conservation and development that will modernize the inner city's economic base will, without question, require a new breadth and depth of resources. There is little dispute that the creation of an adequate supply of appropriate resources constitutes a third issue to be addressed in the 1970s. As the decade begins the state of the national economy and the fiscal posture of the national administration give no cause for optimism that the early years of the 1970s will be characterized by bold new programs of relief to cities. Once again it may be necessary to mobilize the resources of the private sector to an unusual degree in order to attract federal interest and attention.

To ensure the future of economic potential for the city and its central core requires a quantum leap in the discovery of a variety of new technologies.

Economic development activity has been built on the base of physical structure, both public and private, necessitating the use of a grid system of streets to service internal transportation needs and the maintenance of the same unit of blocks. Economic advantage in the inner city originated from a complex of central transportation advantages and accessability to labor. Intensive redevelopment will depend on recreating central place advantages out of the requirements for future movement of goods and materials.

Containerization for shipping permits intermodal changes between types of transportation--and this development may yield innovative schemes for industrial parks built around central places (nodes). Such schemes might even eliminate in new industrial areas the need for traditional streets by replacing them with conveyor communication of goods to and from the transportation nodes. Such plans would permit production materials to be handled fully on one floor of a company, which is itself part of a multi-story condominium of industries, and thus establish the potential for intensive industrial development.

The technology of economic development, however, must extend even beyond new physical treatment. It must develop programming models that expose fully the goals of programs and the assumptions on which such programs are based, that include measures of output permitting validation of performance. Even such measures must improve substantially upon traditional measures of economic output (GNP) to account for the social costs accrued through negative by-products of economic processes--such as water and air pollution, the generation of nondisposable solid wastes, and so forth. These by-products must at the same time be controlled, measured, and eliminated at the earliest possible date.

Perhaps most fundamental to long run viability not only of the economy but also of the quality of life in the inner city and the city at large is quality of education. Empirical economic studies have thoroughly validated the thesis that among a variety of types of investments, investments in human development have the highest returns. Basic public education must equip its students with the fundamental tools to permit continuing adaptation to a changing job market. Substantial evidence indicates that where such fundamentals are lacking, the attempt at training and retraining of adults suffers markedly.

The issues that have been identified here certainly do not embrace all the pressing socioeconomic problems of the inner city. An enormous task remains with respect to matching men to jobs. The whole field of manpower training and placement requires unceasing attention and innovation. New efforts must be made to link the place of work with the place of residence for members of the inner city's labor force. In fact, the whole problem of the efficient movement of men, goods, and services, both in areas and in buildings, will claim increased consideration in the next few years. The very broad issue of uneven income distribution will continue to move up as an issue requiring priority in programming. The need to develop new middle income, white-collar, managerial, and entrepreneurial opportunities for the residents of the inner city will continue to have profound social and economic implications.

APPENDIXES

SOURCES FOR WAGE RATE DATA

All data are from the area wage surveys conducted
by the Bureau of Labor Statistics, U.S. Department
of Labor. Data for July 1962-June 1965 are from BLS
Bulletins No. 1430-83 (Part I), No. 1385-82 (Part I),
and No. 1345-83 (Part I), and data for July 1965-
June 1967 are from individual metropolitan area
bulletins.

Metropolitan areas are surveyed in different
months of the year; but each area except Seattle was
surveyed in the same month in every year covered.
The following list notes coverage by month:

    August: Seattle (1962)
    September: Cleveland, Seattle (1963, 1964)
    October: Boston, Washington, St. Louis,
      Seattle (1965)
    November: Philadelphia, Baltimore, Dallas
    December: Buffalo
    January: Detroit, San Francisco, Pitts-
      burgh, Minneapolis-St. Paul
    February: Newark
    March: Los Angeles, Cincinnati
    April: New York, Chicago, Milwaukee
    May: Paterson-Clifton-Passaic, Atlanta
    June: Houston.

Data for each metropolitan area are obtained by BLS field representatives either through personal visits or by mail. Included in the sample are representative establishments, drawn from the entire area, within six broad industry divisions: manufacturing; transportation, communication, and other public utilities; wholesale trade; retail trade; finance, insurance, and real estate; and services. Major industry groups excluded from these studies are government operations and the construction and extractive industries. A greater proportion of large than of small establishments is studied, but all establishments are given their appropriate weights in combining the data.

Earnings data are for regularly scheduled work of full-time workers and include cost-of-living bonuses and incentive earnings but do not include overtime pay and nonproduction bonuses.

Areas studied are Standard Metropolitan Statistical Areas as defined by the Bureau of the Budget. Several areas underwent definition changes between 1962 and 1967, but those changes probably had little effect on average earnings data. The only major change in area coverage during the period was for Los Angeles; the 1966 Los Angeles study covered the Anaheim-Santa Ana-Garden Grove SMSA in addition to the Los Angeles-Long Beach SMSA.

The Bureau of Labor Statistics defines each occupation so that earnings data will relate to the same job description for all industries and areas covered. Several occupational definitions changed after 1962, but, although the data are not strictly comparable with prior years, they provide a useful indicator of relative wage levels. Job descriptions may be found in any individual area bulletin or in the summary bulletins.

CONSTRUCTION OF PHILADELPHIA
UNEMPLOYMENT SERIES

The major sources used in estimating the Philadelphia unemployment series were the estimates of

total civilian labor force, total employment, and
total unemployment for the Philadelphia SMSA compiled
by the Pennsylvania Bureau of Employment Security.
These statistics are published monthly (<u>Labor Market
Letter: Philadelphia Area</u>).

The following adjustments were made in the data
to arrive at estimated Philadelphia unemployment as
a percentage of the available Philadelphia force:

1.   March bench-mark data on the total Philadelphia covered work force was obtained from the Bureau
of Employment Security (<u>Employment and Wages of Workers Covered by the Pennsylvania Unemployment Compensation Law</u>). The annual ratio was interpolated over
the intervening months. This ratio times total SMSA
employment yielded monthly estimates of the Philadelphia work force covered.

2.   Monthly data on Philadelphia noncovered employment in government manufacturing industries was
obtained from the local Bureau of Employment Security.

3.   Yearly data on total self-employment for
Philadelphia were derived from data prepared by the
Office of the Development Coordinator, and bench-mark
data were also provided by the local Bureau of Employment Security. Philadelphia self-employment was
expressed as a percentage of total SMSA self-employment. This ratio was interpolated over the intervening months to obtain Philadelphia self-employment
from the SMSA totals.

4.   Annual data on noncovered service employees
and federal-local government employees, except those
engaged in government manufacturing, were obtained
from data prepared by the Development Coordinator's
office and the local Bureau of Employment Security.
Because of the extreme regularity of this series,
the actual numbers were straight-line interpolated
over the intervening months.

5.   The sum of (1) through (4) yielded total
monthly employment for Philadelphia.

Philadelphia Unemployment Rate, 1956-68

1956		1959		1962		1965		1968	
Jan.	6.31	Jan.	8.43	Jan.	6.89	Jan.	5.61	Jan.	3.55
Feb.	6.04	Feb.	8.47	Feb.	6.69	Feb.	5.30	Feb.	3.42
Mar.	6.70	Mar.	8.16	Mar.	6.78	Mar.	5.14	Mar.	3.34
Apr.	6.11	Apr.	8.17	Apr.	6.59	Apr.	4.89	Apr.	3.27
May	6.15	May	7.98	May	6.41	May	4.80	May	3.30
Jun.	6.61	Jun.	8.12	Jun.	6.54	Jun.	4.69	Jun.	3.36
Jul.	6.24	Jul.	7.60	Jul.	6.43	Jul.	4.62	Jul.	3.35
Aug.	6.19	Aug.	7.50	Aug.	6.59	Aug.	4.53	Aug.	3.44
Sep.	6.03	Sep.	7.64	Sep.	6.53	Sep.	4.15	Sep.	3.49
Oct.	6.12	Oct.	7.92	Oct.	6.40	Oct.	4.14	Oct.	3.28
Nov.	6.37	Nov.	7.68	Nov.	6.82	Nov.	3.52	Nov.	3.48
Dec.	6.48	Dec.	7.01	Dec.	7.04	Dec.	4.06	Dec.	3.25

1957		1960		1963		1966	
Jan.	6.30	Jan.	7.10	Jan.	6.79	Jan.	4.09
Feb.	6.39	Feb.	6.52	Feb.	7.06	Feb.	4.24
Mar.	6.10	Mar.	6.81	Mar.	6.78	Mar.	4.10
Apr.	6.64	Apr.	6.44	Apr.	6.97	Apr.	3.78
May	6.42	May	6.55	May	6.85	May	3.47
Jun.	6.21	Jun.	6.46	Jun.	6.94	Jun.	3.56
Jul.	6.33	Jul.	6.17	Jul.	6.57	Jul.	3.74
Aug.	6.47	Aug.	6.40	Aug.	6.64	Aug.	3.59
Sep.	6.86	Sep.	6.77	Sep.	6.81	Sep.	3.59
Oct.	7.31	Oct.	6.97	Oct.	6.84	Oct.	3.49
Nov.	7.47	Nov.	6.70	Nov.	6.84	Nov.	3.49
Dec.	7.73	Dec.	7.53	Dec.	6.90	Dec.	3.75

1958		1961		1964		1967	
Jan.	8.11	Jan.	7.19	Jan.	6.57	Jan.	3.49
Feb.	8.31	Feb.	7.77	Feb.	6.67	Feb.	3.32
Mar.	8.62	Mar.	7.51	Mar.	6.62	Mar.	3.58
Apr.	9.10	Apr.	7.43	Apr.	6.82	Apr.	4.01
May	9.11	May	8.02	May	6.58	May	4.40
Jun.	9.48	Jun.	7.57	Jun.	6.12	Jun.	4.49
Jul.	8.76	Jul.	7.95	Jul.	5.86	Jul.	4.31
Aug.	9.10	Aug.	7.36	Aug.	5.96	Aug.	4.08
Sep.	9.25	Sep.	7.38	Sep.	5.88	Sep.	3.99
Oct.	9.49	Oct.	7.45	Oct.	5.70	Oct.	4.67
Nov.	9.31	Nov.	7.09	Nov.	5.72	Nov.	4.29
Dec.	8.78	Dec.	6.92	Dec.	4.82	Dec.	3.67

Source: Prepared by the Philadelphia Economic Development Unit.

Leading Index, January 1956–July 1969

1956		1959		1962		1965		1968	
Jan.	100.00	Jan.	103.20	Jan.	113.91	Jan.	123.96	Jan.	133.35
Feb.	101.70	Feb.	104.40	Feb.	113.23	Feb.	123.99	Feb.	136.00
Mar.	101.51	Mar.	105.43	Mar.	112.73	Mar.	125.95	Mar.	133.05
Apr.	103.35	Apr.	106.59	Apr.	114.33	Apr.	126.15	Apr.	131.88
May	101.80	May	107.07	May	114.64	May	127.20	May	134.85
Jun.	100.99	Jun.	108.07	Jun.	115.72	Jun.	128.11	Jun.	135.65
Jul.	99.85	Jul.	108.17	Jul.	114.25	Jul.	128.77	Jul.	136.91
Aug.	99.76	Aug.	107.56	Aug.	113.89	Aug.	128.81	Aug.	140.87
Sep.	99.91	Sep.	109.07	Sep.	112.99	Sep.	130.03	Sep.	140.68
Oct.	101.03	Oct.	108.65	Oct.	113.62	Oct.	129.83	Oct.	140.86
Nov.	100.96	Nov.	107.17	Nov.	115.53	Nov.	131.43	Nov.	138.07
Dec.	100.88	Dec.	108.48	Dec.	115.42	Dec.	131.46	Dec.	138.73

1957		1960		1963		1966		1969	
Jan.	102.03	Jan.	108.04	Jan.	116.74	Jan.	130.61	Jan.	141.53
Feb.	102.52	Feb.	109.70	Feb.	116.07	Feb.	131.16	Feb.	142.47
Mar.	102.22	Mar.	109.25	Mar.	115.12	Mar.	133.23	Mar.	137.38
Apr.	101.20	Apr.	106.60	Apr.	115.36	Apr.	133.37	Apr.	135.22
May	102.70	May	108.36	May	115.55	May	133.27	May	141.37
Jun.	101.44	Jun.	107.86	Jun.	114.69	Jun.	135.04	Jun.	142.49
Jul.	100.75	Jul.	106.49	Jul.	115.40	Jul.	137.25	Jul.	141.06
Aug.	99.90	Aug.	106.99	Aug.	116.02	Aug.	135.54		
Sep.	98.45	Sep.	105.37	Sep.	115.13	Sep.	134.84		
Oct.	97.14	Oct.	104.77	Oct.	115.33	Oct.	134.35		
Nov.	97.42	Nov.	106.02	Nov.	115.10	Nov.	134.73		
Dec.	97.19	Dec.	100.04	Dec.	115.21	Dec.	131.47		

1958		1961		1964		1967	
Jan.	97.23	Jan.	104.52	Jan.	112.17	Jan.	133.01
Feb.	94.47	Feb.	105.12	Feb.	115.04	Feb.	125.51
Mar.	93.57	Mar.	106.73	Mar.	116.29	Mar.	132.17
Apr.	94.35	Apr.	106.80	Apr.	117.77	Apr.	133.89
May	95.12	May	107.84	May	118.28	May	131.93
Jun.	96.08	Jun.	108.61	Jun.	118.68	Jun.	131.71
Jul.	97.73	Jul.	109.12	Jul.	120.42	Jul.	132.16
Aug.	98.68	Aug.	110.40	Aug.	120.56	Aug.	132.86
Sep.	98.42	Sep.	111.04	Sep.	120.73	Sep.	131.90
Oct.	99.72	Oct.	112.44	Oct.	120.57	Oct.	132.53
Nov.	99.67	Nov.	113.15	Nov.	119.50	Nov.	133.62
Dec.	102.60	Dec.	112.35	Dec.	122.96	Dec.	134.43

Source: Prepared by the Philadelphia Economic Development Unit.

6. A total for unemployment for the three New Jersey counties of the SMSA--Burlington, Camden, and Gloucester--was obtained from the New Jersey Department of Labor and Industry (Area Trends in Employment: Camden Labor Area). This total was subtracted from the unemployment total for the Philadelphia SMSA.

7. The remaining unemployment total was allocated to Philadelphia on the basis of Philadelphia's percentage of the five SMSA Pennsylvania counties' total of unemployment claims filed with the Bureau of Employment Security (Monthly Activity Report of Pennsylvania Employment Offices).

8. The sum of (5) and (7) yielded monthly estimates of the total available labor force in Philadelphia.

9. The division of (7) by (8) yielded Philadelphia unemployment as a percentage of the available labor force.

WHAT THE FED SAYS ABOUT
PLUGGING THE GAP

Even assuming growth in tax revenues and rapid
expansion of nonlocal aid, new measures must be implemented to head off fiscal chaos in the 1970s.
One alternative, President Nixon's revenue-sharing
proposal, holds promise of easing the burden on local
governments. But higher tax rates and some new
taxes very likely will have to be added to the existing package of local collections. Also, public pressure will continue to mount for budget cutting.

New Dough: Revenue Sharing

By 1975 federal revenue sharing could help relieve Philadelphia's financial headaches. The current Presidential proposal would give $5 billion of
"new money" to the states and cities of the nation.
Under the proposed formula of distribution, the City
would receive $44 million and the school district
would garner the more modest sum of $10 million.*
Of course, passage of the measure is far from assured.

————————————————

*This estimate derived from U.S. Department of
the Treasury, "Federal Revenue Sharing with State and
Local Governments," July 1970.

And some of the principal bills that may supplant
revenue sharing would provide little direct help to
Philadelphia. A federal take-over of responsibility
for supporting monthly welfare payments, for example,
would ease the Commonwealth's problems. However,
since Philadelphia's welfare responsibility does not
extend to financial aid to the needy, the proposal
would be of little direct aid to the City.

Upping the Local Ante

On the local front, pushing up tax levies is
often the first tack taken when deficits appear.
One strategy for the future would be to jack up rates
at a pace similar to recent trends. How much would
this strategy produce? A one-point jump in the wage
tax to 4 percent, for example, would account for
$92 million of new revenue; a 5 percent increase in
the real estate tax would yield $7 million; and a
one-point increase in the unincorporated business
net profits tax to 4 percent would produce $7 million.
If revenue-sharing funds were forthcoming and the
City of Philadelphia instituted these tax increases,
its deficit would still be $180 million.

For the school district, tax increases would be
less fruitful. None of the large taxes that make up
its local revenue--the real estate tax and corporate
net income tax, for example--keeps up with the economic growth of the City as does the wage tax. Consequently, even substantial increases in tax rates
would not generate enough revenue to plug the deficit.
Increases consistent with past jumps in the school
district's two big taxes would generate only $30
million in new funds. This amount, combined with
$10 million in revenue-sharing funds, would still
leave the school district with a $140 million deficit
in 1975.

New Nuisances.

Possibly, sharp-eyed officials can find new
local sources of funds. The principal sources of
revenue-personal income, real property, and business
receipts are already being tapped. Thus, new taxes

must be on narrower bases, and collections would be
smaller. A further problem with new taxes is that
unless they are planned ahead local officials may be
forced, as they have been in the past, to push the
measures through with little time allowed for attention to details.

Two recent taxes of the school district illus-
trate this point. One, a tax on sale of liquor at
bars and restaurants, was declared illegal a few
months after enactment--after the school district
had begun to count on it. The other, a tax on payments by business for rented space, is being collected,
but the proceeds are expected to be small,and collection costs may be high.

With $140 million in outstanding bills to be
met in 1975, school leaders may be tempted to invent
four or five new small taxes. An early start on
these taxes may help. But the pay-off is bound to
be small, expensive, and uncertain.

Trimming the Fat

Cost-cutting is the other side of the fiscal
coin, and beleaguered taxpayers have been outspoken
in their demands for budget cutbacks. Unfortunately,
savings from budget trimming may be less lucrative
than many critics expect.

Budget trimming may be done in two ways: improving the efficiency of government or cutting the
services provided by government. Undoubtedly, some
inefficiency is present in Philadelphia schools, and
government inefficiency can be found in almost all
agencies and firms. However, the amount that could
practicably be eliminated is probably small and would
go only a short way toward plugging the gap.

The other line of budget trimming is by way of
reducing the services performed by City and school
government. Certainly a large part of the impending
deficit could be eliminated in this way. Voters
constantly divide on what they want government to
provide, and they may cut back their demands as new,

higher prices for government services are established. However, the appeal of service cutting, strong in the abstract, is less appealing when translated into specific cuts, such as fewer police, less hospital care, or fewer teachers--each of which provides an important service in the eyes of some segment of the community.

No Panaceas

Philadelphia's financial crisis will continue into the 1970s. Spiraling costs of labor, a sagging local tax base, and highly uncertain assistance from other levels of government will complicate the yearly task of balancing the City and school district's budgets.

Several alternatives are available for closing the prospective gap in the public budget--new or higher local taxes, greater aid from the Commonwealth and federal governments, and reductions in the local public budget. Also, a number of new measures that would directly or indirectly aid the ailing public sector are waiting in the wings: revenue sharing by the federal government, provision for crediting local taxes against amounts due state or federal governments, and transfer of responsibility for some services to state government, for example. But none of the solutions will be easy or costless. Moreover, if they are to be effective, they must be planned and appropriately timed to meet deficits as they arise.

The deficit projected for the 1975 fiscal year is large, but not nearly so large as the cumulative total of deficits that could occur between now and 1975. Budgets for the coming year probably will have a moderate amount of red ink, with the shade deepening for later years. Next year's problems allow little time for planning. But, hopefully, an early start on the fiscal problems of later years will help head off increasing deficits.

METHOD USED TO ESTIMATE
PHILADELPHIA INCOME TAXES
PAID BY INCOME GROUPS

The primary source of data on income in Philadelphia, as defined by the federal government, was a project of the Internal Revenue Service Statistics Division. The publication was entitled "Selected Income, Exemption, and Tax Items from Federal Individual Income Tax Returns with Philadelphia, Pennsylvania Addresses." Data on adjusted gross income by income class for returns with Philadelphia addresses were obtained from this publication.

From these data a distribution of the Philadelphia income tax base by income class was computed. Since the Philadelphia income tax applies to wages and salaries and profits of unincorporated businesses, it was necessary to compute the distribution of wages and salaries of Philadelphia residents. To make this estimate the percentage of total U.S. adjusted gross income that is composed of wages and salaries by income class was calculated. Thetotal of the computed wages and salaries in the various income classes was compared with total wages and salaries reported on tax returns with Philadelphia addresses. The total of computed wages and salaries was $3,563,433,900, whereas the actual total was $3,545,582,000.[1] The total of the computed wages and salaries was within 0.5 percent of the actual, which indicates that the method of computing the distribution of wages and salaries for residents of Philadelphia was probably correct. However, the individual entries in the distribution of wages and salaries were adjusted downward by 0.5 percent in order that the total of computed distribution would not be overstated, and it thus conforms to the actual total of wages and salaries reported for Philadelphia residents.

Since the Philadelphia income tax applies to the net profits of unincorporated businesses, a dis-

tribution by income class of profits of unincorporated
businesses was computed. The same method used to compute the distribution of wages and salaries by income
class was used to compute the distribution of business
or professional profits and partnership profits for
residents of Philadelphia. The percentage of adjusted
gross income composed of business or professional
profits and partnership net profits for the United
States by income class was multiplied by the adjusted
gross income by income class for residents of Philadelphia.

Data were available on the composite total of
business net profit and loss for residents of Philadelphia. But, since the Philadelphia income tax did
not allow the carrying forward or back losses for income tax purposes, the total of profit and loss has
to be adjusted for losses that are not offset by positive income on individual income tax returns. The
ratio of total net profit added to the sum of total
net profit minus total net loss for the United States
was multiplied by the business net profit and loss
for Philadelphia residents.

$$\frac{\text{U.S. Total Net Profit}^{a}}{\text{U.S. Total Net Profit} - \text{U.S. Total Net Loss}^{b}} \times \frac{\text{Philadelphia Net Profit and Loss}^{c}}{} = \frac{\text{Estimated Net Business Profit for Philadelphia Residents}}{}$$

$$\frac{\$24,801,637}{22,992,275} \times 206,947 = \$223,233.7289$$

[a]Internal Revenue Service, U.S. Treasury Department, Statistics of Income 1964: Individual Income Tax Returns (Washington, D.C.:
Government Printing Office, 1964), Table 2.

[b]Ibid.

[c]Statistics Division, Internal Revenue Ser-
vice, U.S. Treasury Department, Statistics
of Income-Selected Income, Exemption, and
Tax Items from Federal Individual Income
Tax Returns with Philadelphia, Pennsylvania
Addresses, Project 65-31 (Washington, D.C.:
Government Printing Office, July 1966),
Table 1.

The data available for partnership profits of Philadelphia residents was the total of net profit and
loss. Therefore, the net partnership profit of Philadelphia residents also had to be estimated. The
same procedure was used that was used to estimate
partnership profit of Philadelphia residents.

$$\frac{\text{U.S. Total Net Partnership Profit}^a}{\text{U.S. Total Net Partnership Profit} - \text{U.S. Total Net Partnership Loss}^b} \times \begin{array}{c}\text{Philadelphia}\\\text{Partnership}\\\text{Net Profit}\\\text{and Loss}^c\end{array} = \begin{array}{c}\text{Estimated}\\\text{Net Part-}\\\text{nership}\\\text{Profit for}\\\text{Philadel-}\\\text{phia}\\\text{Residents}\end{array}$$

[a]Internal Revenue Service, U.S. Treasury Department, Statistics of Income 1964: Individual Income Tax Returns (Washington, D.C.:
Government Printing Office, 1964), Table 2.

[b]Ibid.

[c]Statistics Division, Internal Revenue Ser-
vice, U.S. Treasury Department, Statistics
of Income-Selected Income, Exemption, and
Tax Items from Federal Individual Income
Tax Returns with Philadelphia, Pennsylvania
Addresses, Project 65-31 (Washington, D.C.:
Government Printing Office, July 1966),
Table 1.

     Since the Philadelphia income tax applies to
net profits of unincorporated business and wages and
salaries, data on the distribution of these sources
of income by income group for Philadelphia residents
made it possible to compute the wage tax paid by
residents of Philadelphia in various income groups.
The total wage tax paid by each income group was
divided by the total adjusted gross income of each
income group to obtain the rate of taxation in relation to total adjusted gross income by each income
group.

The income tax paid to Philadelphia is deductible
on federal income tax returns, and the value of the
deduction depends on the marginal rate of the federal
income tax paid. For example, if an individual pays
a 20 percent marginal rate of federal income tax and
has a deduction of $100, the value of this deduction
will be $20. If the value of the deduction as a re-
sult of a municipal income tax is subtracted, the
actual cost of the municipal income tax will be $80.
The actual cost of the Philadelphia income tax will
be:

$$
\begin{array}{c}
\text{Philadelphia} \\
\text{Income Tax} \\
\text{Paid}
\end{array}
\times
\begin{array}{c}
1 - \text{Marginal} \\
\text{Rate of Fed-} \\
\text{eral Income} \\
\text{Tax Paid}
\end{array}
=
\begin{array}{c}
\text{Cost of} \\
\text{Philadelphia} \\
\text{Income Tax} \\
\text{after Its} \\
\text{Deduction on} \\
\text{Federal In-} \\
\text{come Tax} \\
\text{Returns}
\end{array}
$$

The median marginal rate of federal income taxation in each income group was chosen because this
particular measure of central tendency depicts the
most common situation of the taxpayers; if the mean
marginal rate of federal taxation had been chosen,
an extreme grouping at either end of a distribution
within an income class might have given a distorted
picture of the actual situation most often facing
the taxpayer. Moreover, since the Philadelphia income tax was currently set at 2 percent and income
classifications for federal income tax purposes were
large, it was not likely that the deduction of the
Philadelphia income tax would substantially affect
the marginal rate of taxation paid within an income
class. Also, if the marginal tax rate is affected
for particular taxpayers within an income class, only
a portion of the deduction will be in the lower marginal tax bracket.

The total Philadelphia income tax payments by
income class after allowing for deduction for federal
income tax purposes was divided by the total adjusted
gross income for each income class to obtain the
rate of tax paid by Philadelphia residents on total

adjusted gross income in various income classes.
(The results of these calculations are shown in Table
20.)

The definition of interest and dividends used
was that of the Internal Revenue Service for federal
income tax purposes. The tax was computed assuming
that the excluded items and deductions pertaining to
interest and dividends for the federal income tax
were duplicated in the Philadelphia income tax.

It was necessary to compute a distribution of
interest and dividends for residents of Philadelphia.
The method used was to multiply the percentage of
adjusted gross income in various income classes that
is composed of dividends and interest for the country
as a whole by the distribution of adjusted gross income by income class for Philadelphia residents.

The total of the computed interest distribution
for Philadelphia residents was $106,618,000, and the
total of the computed distribution of dividends was
$114,692,000. The actual interest received by Phila-
delphia residents in 1964 was $102,469,000.[2] The
computed total was 4.049 percent greater than the
actual. The actual dividends in adjusted gross income were $191,974,000.[3] The computed dividends re-
ceived by Philadelphia residents using national percentages were considerably lower than the actual
amount reported. The understatement of dividend income was probably caused by the fact that national
data include large low income rural areas in which
investment in stocks is relatively unpopular.

The computed interest and dividend distribution
was proportionally adjusted so that the total of
these distributions equaled the actual amount reported.
This adjustment is correct in relation to dividend
income if added knowledge of stock investment is
greater in all income classes in an urban environment and the greater knowledge increases proportionally with income. However, it must be pointed out
that the adjusted computed distribution of individual
income is not as reliable as the other distributions
computed.

The income tax payable with interest and dividends and included in the tax base was divided by
the adjusted gross income for each income class to
determine the tax rate that would have been paid as
a percentage of adjusted gross income if those items
had been included in the income tax base. And it
was found that the inclusion of dividends and both
dividends and interest tends to make the rate of
taxation that would be paid as a percentage of adjusted gross income almost proportional. With dividends included, the rate of taxation would vary from
1.97 percent to 1.60; and with dividends and interest
included, the range would vary from 2.00 percent to
1.63 percent for Philadelphia residents. (The results of these calculations are shown in Table 25.)

PARTICIPANTS IN THE SUBPROGRAM
COMMITTEE ON ECONOMIC DEVELOPMENT

Industrial, Commercial,
and Institutional
Development

Redevelopment Authority
Philadelphia Industrial
  Development Corporation
Development Coordinator
City Planning Commission
Economic Development Unit
Business Service Director
  of Commerce

Convention and Tourism
Service

Philadelphia Convention
  and Tourist Bureau
Director of Commerce
  Office
Philadelphia Civic Center
Economic Development Unit

Manpower

Philadelphia Anti-Poverty
  Action Committee
Manpower Utilization Com-
  mission
Department of Public
  Welfare-Neighborhod
  Youth Corps
Philadelphia Employment
  Development Corporation
Opportunities Industrial-
  ization Center
Economic Development Unit

Airport and Port

Port Liaison Officer,
  City Representative's
  Office
Philadelphia Interna-
  tional Airport
Philadelphia Port Corpor-
  ation
Economic Development Unit

REPORT ON PROBLEM STATEMENTS AND GOALS
BY THE SUBPROGRAM COMMITTEE ON
ECONOMIC DEVELOPMENT FOR THE
OPERATING BUDGET, FISCAL 1971

Subcommittee on Industrial, Commercial,
and Institutional Development

Caucus on Economic Development Planning

I. Problems

   A. The need to analyze the economic resources
       of the City in order to provide a basis for
       the formulation of an overall economic devel-
       opment program and to provide government and
       business with inputs for decision making;
       specifically, the need for the following:

       1. An analysis of the existing structure
           of the City's economy in relation to the
           region and the nation and how it responds
           to both internal and external changes in
           economic trends

       2. A study of the best allocation of lim-
           ited resources

       3. Development of statistical data, fore-
           casts, analyses, planning, and consulta-
           tive services

       4. Support of planning efforts of economic
           development activities

   B. The need to coordinate the planning and im-
       plementation of economic development programs
       of the various agencies involved in these
       activities

II. Goals and Objectives

   A. Development of an overall economic develop-
       ment program for the City to guide specific

program formulations by governmental agencies and decision making by the City's administration and private business

   1. Analysis of the structure of the City's
       economy

   2. Development of policies and programs to
       achieve the best allocation of resources

   3. Coordination of the planning and selec-
       tive implementations of activities that
       will directly improve the City's income,
       employment level, and tax base

Caucus on Industrial, Commercial, and Institutional Development

 I. Problems

   A. The scattering of industry in predominantly
       residential areas

      1. Conflict between different activities
          and needs--the needs of industry versus
          the needs and preferred character of a
          residential environment

      2. The desirability of having job opportu-
          nities and places of employment near
          and easily accessible to places of
          residence

   B. Blighted areas: the problem of industry as
       areas become increasingly blighted (as
       blight increases, deterioration of industrial
       plants increases)

   C. Loft-type buildings

      1. Inefficiency of this type of building
          for many industries; for example, ele-
          vators present problems (too slow, in-
          sufficient in number)

   2. The increasing age of these buildings
      increases difficulties and inefficiency

D. Congested streets

   1. Lack of rapid access to specific build-
      ings

   2. Inadequate parking

E. Inadequate truck-loading facilities

   1. Congested streets causing problems of
      truck access

   2. A high percentage of land coverage,
      providing only a minimal area for truck
      loading

F. Employee and management fear of dangerous
   environmental conditions

   1. Personal injury and threat of gangs,
      individual attacks, and so forth

   2. Damage to autos, company equipment, and
      property from area residents, and so
      forth

   3. Robbery and threat of other crime and
      violence

G. Aging industrial buildings

   1. Inefficiency of aging and deteriorating
      buildings

   2. Cost of rehabilitation or reconstruction
      on site

H. Need for acreage in City: unavailability
   of usable acreage or space for many industries desiring location, relocation, or expansion in City areas

I. Changing complex of industry in general

    1. Increase in service-type industry

    2. Increase in clerical and managerial skills

    3. Automation

    4. Regional pattern change; for example, relocation of textile industry out of Philadelphia

J. Financial problems

    1. High cost of borrowing money because of market conditions

    2. Limited availability of money to borrow because of market conditions

    3. Credit rating of company (if rating is questionable, financing may not be obtained)

    4. High cost of land in developed areas

K. Relocation of businesses

    1. Firms moving out of the City or being forced out of business as a result of redevelopment action, highway construction, need for more functional facility, expansion, or consolidation

    2. The need to supply suitable locations for businesses to either expand or consolidate or acquire more functional facilities

II. Goals and Objectives

A. Provision of more effective utilization of land for the expansion, relocation, and

attraction of business and institutions
in/into the City

1. Minimization of the hardship to business
   and institutions displaced by governmental action

2. Replanning of streets and lots to provide efficient circulation, off-street
   loading and parking, and building layout
   to meet the needs of technologically
   and economically efficient industry and
   commerce

3. Removal or effecting of rehabilitation
   of substandard, inefficient, and obsolete industrial, commercial, and institutional structures and land uses in
   blighted areas

4. Assistance to individual businesses and
   institutions in assembling blighted land

B. Removal or mitigation of detrimental environmental factors in blighted areas of all
   types by coordinating activities of governmental agencies so as to provide a favorable
   climate for holding and attracting industry
   and commerce

C. Increase in the tax base of the City directly
   through urban renewal activities of all
   types and indirectly by providing a positive
   image of a progressive and attractive city

D. Provision of adequate financing to assist
   industry, as necessary, in location or relocation, development, or expansion in Philadelphia

Caucus on New Business Development

I. Problems

A. Hampering of new business development, which
   is an important contribution to the economic

growth of the City, by one or a combination
of the following:

1. Lack of entrepreneurial-managerial skills

2. Inability to recruit skilled managers
    from a financially secure position to a
    high-risk position

3. Lack of liberal and flexible financial
    support

4. Limited commitment by the business com-
    munity to provide aid and counseling
    services

II. Goals and Objectives

A. Encouragement and assistance in the forma-
    tion of new business

1. Provision of financial and management
    counseling

2. Encouragement of liberal and flexible
    financial support

3. Encouragement of commitment on the part
    of the private sector

Caucus on Services to Business

I. Problems

A. The need for an improved working relation-
    ship between the City government and the
    business community and the retention, expan-
    sion, and attraction of business in/into
    Philadelphia, which can help the City to
    maintain and expand the economic base; spe-
    cifically, the need for the following:

1. One-stop service to direct business to
    sources of financial, technical, and
    administrative assistance

   2. Rapid analysis of proposed renewal proj-
       ects in terms of tax and job losses and
       gains

   3. Continuing intelligence on individual
       business development plans, including
       a mechanism capable of anticipating
       problems

   4. An effective business relocation service

II. Goals and Objectives

   A. Provision of effective business services to
       encourage the retention, expansion, and at-
       traction of industry and commerce and to
       effectuate a strong liaison between the
       City government and the business community

       1. Development of one-stop business ser-
           vices for advice, counsel, and City aid

       2. Creation of a mechanism to analyze
           economic and job costs of renewal activ-
           ities and development of an effective
           industrial and commercial relocation
           service

       3. Development of a business liaison device
           to respond to immediate problems and to
           anticipate future business problems

       4. Development of an effective industrial
           and commercial relocation service

           Subcommittee on Convention
             and Tourism Service

 I. Problems

   A. The need to bring more visitors to Philadel-
       phia and to keep visitors in the City for a
       longer period of time; specifically, the
       need for the following:

1. Research to determine which tourist market poses the greatest potential for the City

2. Repeal of legislative restrictions prohibiting liquor sales on Sunday, laws prohibiting the operation of private clubs, and other laws that create hardships for private enterprises in Philadelphia

3. An adequate number of hotel and motel accommodations

4. Planning and coordination among various tourist attractions and convention facilities

5. Adequate transportation and directional signs to convention facilities and tourist attractions

6. An advertising and promotional budget to attract tourists and recruitment to attract conventions

7. Adequate convention facilities

    a. Modern exhibition, convention, and auditorium facilities for trade shows, conventions, commercial exhibitions, athletic events, and cultural and entertainment programs

    b. Space for nonprofit groups and public agencies

II. Goals and Objectives

A. Increase of City income by attracting more visitors and encouraging them to remain in the City for a longer period of time

    1. Conduct of research to define the best possible market for the City

2. Generation of proper marketing to increase conventions and tourism

3. Promotion of an adequate number of hotel/motel accommodations, transportation facilities, and coordinated tourist activities

4. Change or removal of legislative restrictions

5. Provision of adequate convention and exhibition facilities

Subcommittee on Manpower

I. Problems

A. The existence of a large number--probably more than 50,000--of unskilled adults with no salable skill or training, a great majority of whom are disadvantaged in terms of being members of a racial minority and in terms of their total deficiency, educationally and environmentally

B. Grossly inadequate training facilities to deliver skill training to out-of-school youths and adults who are unemployed or unemployable

C. Inadequate educational services and facilities to prepare unskilled youngsters for employment, including both vocational skill training and comprehensive vocational guidance programs

D. Lack of an overall continued job bank system to provide information on job availability and also lack of an effective system to utilize openings in terms of the overall placement of persons seeking employment

E. Lack of adequate and effective communication and interaction with the target population to be served

F. Lack of valid information about the target
    population to be served

G. Inadequate involvement and commitments on
    the part of business, industry, and the com-
    mercial community in efforts to deal with
    the problems of hard-core unemployment

H. The confusion of programs and services being
    offered in this area and the absence of over-
    all coordination of same

I. Lack of public transportation facilities to
    the areas of principal employment from the
    concentrations of unemployed persons

II. Goals and Objectives

A. The reduction of the number of unemployed
    and underemployed persons in the City, es-
    pecially those who constitute the disadvan-
    taged of the community

    1. Obtainment of complete and comprehensive
        information about the target population
        to be served

    2. Achievement of effective and continual
        communication and interaction with the
        target population to be served

    3. Provision of improved and enlarged edu-
        cational services and/or facilities to
        prepare unskilled youths for employment,
        including basic education skills, com-
        prehensive vocational guidance, and
        vocational skill training

    4. Provision of improved and enlarged
        training facilities offering skill
        training for out-of-school youths and
        adults who are unemployed and unemploy-
        able and who have difficulty in obtain-
        ing and keeping employment

5. Improvement of overall coordination of manpower programs and services, thereby mitigating the confusion and overlapping present in these programs

6. Improvement of involvement and commitment from the business, industrial, and commercial communities in their efforts in dealing with the hard-core unemployed

7. Implementation of an overall job-bank system to provide information on the availability of jobs as well as an effective system to utilize openings in the placement of persons seeking employment

8. Improvement of transportation facilities to the areas of principal employment from those in which unemployed persons are concentrated

9. Elimination of all barriers of discrimination to employment and job advancement

Subcommittee on Airport and Port

Caucus on Airport

I. Problems

A. Land; specifically, the need for the following:

1. Land acquisition for expanded passenger requirements

2. Land development for air freight facilities

3. Land development in connection with parallel instrument runway

4. Land development for additional hangar and fuel requirements on the south side of the airport

    B. Physical facilities; specifically, the need
        for the following:

        1. Maintenance and operation of cargo and
            passenger facilities

        2. Construction of new passenger and cargo
            facilities to meet the increasing demand

        3. Demolition of obsolete facilities

    C. City, state, federal, and airline coordina-
        tion of ground transportation; specifically,
        the need for the following:

        1. Improvement of current access roads

        2. Development of additional access routes

        3. Development of mass transit routes

        4. Rescheduling of departures and arrivals
            of aircraft to minimize peak hour re-
            quirements

        5. Development of a service road system
            within the airport area

    D. Airport-community relations; specifically,
        the need for the following:

        1. Abatement of the acute noise problem for
            communities surrounding the airport

        2. Elimination of safety hazards for sur-
            rounding communities generated by air
            and ground facilities

        3. Public support of the airport capital
            expansion program

        4. A public information program on airport
            physical development plans and progress
            toward noise abatement and safety im-
            provements

E. Marketing: inadequate marketing of airport facilities to stimulate more cargo and passenger traffic to expand the economic base of the City

F. Research and planning: the need for study of the advances in air technology for possible utilization by the City

II. Goals and Objectives

A. Development of a modern system of facilities to meet the needs of expanded air commerce in the Greater Philadelphia area

B. Ensuring of rapid and convenient ground transportation and highway access routes to service the airport

C. Support of the City's effort to expand its economic base by stimulating cargo and passenger traffic

D. Promotion of efforts to eliminate safety hazards and air and noise pollution

E. Development of an airport community relations program

Caucus on Port

I. Problems

A. Research and planning; specifically, the need for research and planning for the proper development of the Port of Philadelphia

B. Coordination, particularly in relation to the duplication and conflict in the development of the Port of Philadelphia among the various port agencies serving Pennsylvania, Delaware, and New Jersey

C. Physical development in light of the continuous change in the market and in technology; specifically, the need for the following:

1. Land acquisition for adequate waterfront
    development

2. Channel maintenance and pier dredging

3. Demolition of obsolete piers

4. Modernization of usable piers

5. Upgrading of bulk facilities

6. Modern container facilities

7. Sufficient ancillary facilities to ser-
    vice the port

8. Recreational areas in waterfront areas
    not developed as marine terminals

D. Labor mediation, particularly the creation
    of an independent agency to keep in contact
    with and help solve the developing problems
    between labor and management

E. Marketing and public relations to stimulate
    more cargo, passenger and local commuter
    traffic

II. Goals and Objectives

A. Provision of a modern system of port facili-
    ties to meet the needs of commerce and in-
    dustry

B. Promotion of the full utilization of the
    port

C. Creation of a strong central port agency
    that will eliminate duplication and con-
    flicts and provide for the coordination of
    planning activities

D. Provision of parks and recreational areas
    on the waterfront in the areas not suited
    for terminals

E. Maintenance of a good relationship between labor and management

SURVEY OF MANAGEMENT DEMAND

Special Survey of the Economic Development Unit
of the
City of Philadelphia
Tel. (215) MU 6-5635

Name of Firm:

Address of Firm:

Name of Person Answering This Questionnaire:

Title:

Date:

For clarification of any part of this questionnaire
please consult the "Instructions for Answering Management Demand Survey" enclosed.

Analysis of Present Sources

1. Comparing the present with conditions of two
    years ago, would you estimate that your manage-
    ment personnel situation has:

_____Improved

_____Remained static

_____Deteriorated

a. Please explain further the nature of the
    changes you have experienced.

_____

_____

_____

2. What are your present sources of lower and middle
    management personnel? Please indicate order of
    importance by assigning numbers beginning with
    No. 1 as most important and ending with No. 7 as
    least important. Categories not used by your
    Corporation should be indicated by entering an X
    before that selection.

    _____Internal   _____Direct Advertising

    _____Personnel   _____Pennsylvania State
                                       Employment Agencies
    _____Private Employ-
          ment Agencies   _____Employee Referral

    _____Other (Explain)_____

    _____

    _____

3. In selecting sites for new facilities or relo-
    cating older facilities, in what general order
    might you consider the importance of the follow-
    ing manpower assets. Please indicate order of
    importance by assigning numbers beginning with
    No. 1 as most important and ending with No. 5 as
    least important.

_____Executive   _____Clerical
     Management
                                  _____Production
_____Middle & Lower
     Management   _____Unskilled

Future Demand

4. In Column a. below please indicate the number of
    persons currently employed in the listed areas
    of responsibility. In Column b. please estimate
    your anticipated needs two years from now. In
    Column c. please estimate your anticipated needs
    five years from now. In the marked lines (d)
    "Required" please enter the optimum number needed
    if different from the line above.

	Mid-March 1969 a.	Mid-March 1971 b.	Mid-March 1974 c.
Executive Management			
(d) Required			
Lower and Middle Management			
(d) Required			
Management Training			
(d) Required			
Total Employment (other than management)			
(d) Required			

Possible Sources

5. Current estimates indicate a need for an addi-
    tional 200,000 managers in the next five years.
    With this in mind, what, in your opinion, would
    be the most productive source of recruitment for
    management training programs with regard to your
    organization's employment needs? Please check
    one.

    _____Current high school graduates

    _____Employees in lower skilled jobs selected
          for their interest and ability

    _____A combination of the above

    _____Other (Explain)_____

    _____

    _____

    _____

Program Approaches

6. In what order would you rank the following ap-
    proaches to up-grading the skills of clerical and
    production personnel for entry level management
    positions? Important considerations may be re-
    cruiting and retention. Please indicate order
    of acceptability by assigning numbers beginning
    with No. 1 to indicate the most acceptable and
    ending with No. 4 to indicate the least acceptable.

    _____Internal training by visiting instructional
          staff

    _____Internal on-the-job training

    _____Co-op training, i.e., employees attending a
          separate training center while on company
          payroll

_____A non-work night school or junior college format

7. Optional - Would you further explain your views in answering the above, adding any thought you may have concerning alternative methods.

_____

_____

_____

8. Are you currently using programmed instruction techniques available from sources such as the American Management Association?   Yes___   No___

    a. Please identify program_____

    _____

    _____

    _____

    b. If you are currently employing such techniques have your results generally been: (Please check one.)

    _____Successful

    _____Satisfactory

    _____Unsatisfactory

    _____Unascertainable

9. Would your organization have interest in participating in a Management Training Center devoted to management science and development designed specifically for the needs of the employee?

                                        Yes_____   No_____

Instructions for Answering
Management Demand Survey

For the purpose of this survey the term management shall be functionally defined to mean not only
those persons now employed as "managers" but also
those in areas which are commonly used for management
training or from which future management talent is
commonly selected. In other words, those persons
who were recruited as, or have achieved recognition
as, management potential. This definition is specifically intended to include management trainees.
Present employment is to be defined as the level of
full time equivalent employment as of mid-March 1969.
Projected employment is to be defined as the level
of full time equivalent employment anticipated as of
mid-March 1961 and mid-March 1974 respectively. All
figures are to be for the Delaware Valley Region exclusively. The site of employment being the pertinent criteria.

Question 1 requests a comparison of present and
past management employment position. Please indicate
your organization's experience by checking one of the
three alternatives.

Part (a) allows space for further in-depth explanation. Additional space, if desired, is available
on the reverse side of Page 1.

Question 2 presents seven sources of personnel,
six are specific and the seventh is "other" which is
to encompass any means not included above. Degree
of importance should be indicated by assigning the
numbers 1 through 7. Use an X before any selection
which is not used by your organization.

Question 3 presents five general employment
classes and asks that they be evaluated in terms of
site location decision making. They should be ranked
in order of importance, using the numbers 1 through
5 to indicate their relative importance.

Definitions:

Executive management shall indicate management personnel as herein defined with policy-making status.

Lower and middle management shall indicate management personnel as herein defined with little or no policy-making status. This would encompass supervisory personnel if they would be definitionally included.

Clerical and production shall indicate all other skilled personnel.

Unskilled shall indicate all employees categorized as unskilled personnel.

Question 4 presents four two-part categories, the first part of each category (e.g., Executive Management) is intended to elicit the current (mid-March 1969) employment or actual projected employment for mid-March 1971 and mid-March 1974 respectively. The second or "Required" component is to be answered with optimum or necessary employment if different from the current or actual projected employment.

Question 5 asks for selection of one of four alternative choices of sources of management training candidates. Please check the one of the four which would be the most advantageous in your situation. If "Other" is the indicated choice, please enter such alternates in the space provided. Additional space is provided on the reverse side of Page 3.

Question 6 asks for a numerical rating of suggested alternatives for employee education formats. Degree of acceptability should be indicated by assigning numbers 1 through 4.

Question 7 is optional. Space is supplied for an in-depth answer to Question 6. Commentary based on your knowledge and experience is invited. Additional space is provided on the reverse side of Page 3.

Question 8 requires a simple yes or no answer.
If the response to Question 8 is positive please
answer Parts (a) and (b). Part (a) asks for identification of any such programs utilized. Please indicate the names and sources of materials used. Additional space, if required, is provided on the reverse
side of Page 4. Part (b) asks for an evaluation of
your experience with programmed instruction. Please
answer by checking one of the four alternatives.

Question 9 requires a simple yes or no answer.
You may expand upon that answer in the space provided
below if you so desire.

*   *   *   *   *   *

When you have completed the Management Demand
Survey questionnaire please put it in the enclosed
postage paid return envelope for return to this office.

PARTIAL LIST OF INTERVIEWED
AGENCIES AND INSTITUTIONS

American Management Association

Behavioral Science Center, Harvard University

Gratz Vocational High School

Greater Philadelphia Enterprises Development Corporation

Job Loan Corporation

Opportunities Industrialization Center

Philadelphia Industrial Development Corporation

Southeastern Pennsylvania Development Corporation

Small Business Administration

Stirling Institute

University of Pennsylvania Community Wharton School

REFERENCES AND DATA SOURCES

Employment Data were developed from monthly "Labor Market Letters" of the Bureau of Employment Security, Commonwealth of Pennsylvania; and from monthly tables A-9 and A-10 of the "Monthly Labor Review," Bureau of Labor Statistics, U.S. Department of Labor.

Labor Force Data were developed from interviews and unpublished data from individual building trades unions; the Building and Construction Trades Council of Philadelphia; AFL-CIO; Bureau of Apprenticeship and Training, U.S. Department of Labor; and from the Office of Federal Contract Compliance, U.S. Department of Labor.

Building Construction Data were obtained from "The State of the Economy--1967," Philadelphia Economic Development Unit; Series C-40 and Series C-42 "Construction Reports," Philadelphia Department of Licenses and Inspections; and "Building Operations in Pennsylvania Municipalities," Department of Labor and Industry, Commonwealth of Pennsylvania.

Population and Household Data were obtained from various series P-25, "Current Population Reports," U.S. Bureau of the Census.

Planned Expanded Programs were defined in the housing field by the Office of the Deputy Managing Director for Housing and for schools by the School Board's proposed "Capital Program--1969-1974."

Other specific sources include the following:

Bancroft, Gertrude, and Stuart Garfinkle. "Job Mobility in 1961," Monthly Labor Review, LXXXVI, 8 (August 1963).

CRP. "Philadelphia Housing Analysis," Technical Report No. 14, Robert Gladstone Association, February 1965.

Gallaway, Lowell E. "Inter-industry Labor Mobility in the U.S., 1957-1960," Research Report No. 18, U.S. Department of Health, Education, and Welfare (Washington, D.C.).

Hamel, Harvey R. "Job Tenure of American Workers," Monthly Labor Review, LXXXVI, 10 (October 1963).

Hamel, Harvey R. "Moonlighting--An Economic Phenomenon," Monthly Labor Review, XC, 10 (October 1967).

Mills, Daniel Quinn. Manpower in Construction: New Methods and Measures. Cambridge, Mass.: Harvard University Press.

Myers, Robert J., and Sol Swerdoff. "Seasonality and Construction," Monthly Labor Review, XC, 9 (September 1967).

NOTES TO CHAPTER 2

1. "Philadelphia's Position in the Regional and National Economy," prepared by National Analysts for the Philadelphia Community Renewal Program, April 1964.

2. See Julius Shiskin and Geoffrey Moore, "Composite Indexes of Leading, Coincident, and Lagging Indicators," Supplement to National Bureau of Economic Research Report No. 1, January 1968.

NOTES TO CHAPTER 3

1. Ahmad Al-Samarrie, "Outlook for the American Economy in the 1970's," Looking Ahead, XVII, 4, p. 2.

2. Pennsylvania Economy League, Trend of Employment, Philadelphia, PEL Reports Nos. 282, 318, and 345. Data for 1968 were interpolated on the basis of October payrolls from the Bulletin Almanac.

3. Ibid.

4. See the Philadelphia Inquirer, August 14, 1969.

5. Ibid.

6. The Committee for Economic Development also relies on a more theoretical argument, that is, that in principle funds should be raised and disposed of by the same responsible body--that to do otherwise is to invite irresponsible squandering of the money granted from above. See the Committee's press release of testimony before the House Banking and Currency Committee, June 10, 1971, pp. 103; and "Statement on Revenue Sharing," issued by the American Friends Service Committee, August 1971.

7. Richard A. Musgrave and Darwin W. Darcoss, "Who Pays Michigan Taxes?" in Harvey E. Brozer, ed., Michigan's Tax Crises (Ann Arbor: Bureau of Government, Institute of Public Administration, University of Michigan, 1958).

8. Juan de Torres, Financing Local Government, National Industrial Conference Board Studies in Business Economics, No. 96 (New York), p. 80.

9. Robert Murray Haig, "The Concept of Income--Economic and Legal Aspects," Reading in the Economics of Taxation (Homewood, Ill.: Richard D. Irwin, 1959), p. 59.

10. Fortune magazine published a long survey article on the value-added tax subsequent to the preparation of this paper, and a number of other business publications have given it considerable publicity. The present national administration allegedly also views it with favor, but it has not made a formal proposal to institute the tax.

11. Dan Throup Smith, The New York Times, November 3, 1970.

12. Margaret Reid, Housing and Income (Chicago: University of Chicago Press, 1962), p. 348.

13. Ibid.

14. George Sternlieb, The Tenement Landlord (New Brunswick, N.J.: William Byrd Press, 1966), p. 220.

15. Dick Netzer, The Economics of the Property Tax (Washington, D.C.: The Brookings Institute, 1966).

16. Dick Netzer, "Some Alternatives in Property Tax Reform," The Property Tax: Problems and Potentials (Princeton, N.J.: Tax Institute of America, 1966), p. 394.

NOTES TO CHAPTER 6

1. Bureau of Labor Statistics, U.S. Department of Labor, The National Industry-Occupational Matrix and Other Manpower Data, Bulletin No. 1606, Tomorrow's Manpower Needs, Vol. 4 (Washington, D.C.: Government Printing Office, 1968).

2. Ezekiel, Methods of Correlation Analysis (2d. ed.), p. 66.

3. Bureau of Labor Statistics, U.S. Department of Labor, The National Industry-Occupational Matrix and Other Manpower Data, Tomorrow's Manpower Needs.

4. Business Leadership Training Project, 1967-68, prepared for the Economic Development Administration, U.S. Department of Commerce (Boston: Behavioral Science Center, Stirling Institute, October 1968).

NOTES TO APPENDIX TO CHAPTER 3

1. Statistics Division, Internal Revenue Service, U.S. Treasury Department, Statistics of Income-Selected Income, Exemption, and Tax Items from Federal Individual Income Tax Returns with Philadelphia, Pennsylvania Addresses, Project 65-31 (Washington, D.C.: Government Printing Office, July 1966), Table 1.

2. Statistics of Income-Selected Income, Exemption, and Tax Items, Table 16.

3. Ibid.

JOSEPH OBERMAN is Executive Director of the Council for Urban Economic Development. For the past eighteen years he has concentrated largely on the problem of local economic and community development. Prior to his present position he was associated with a United Nations mission to the Ministry of Finance of the government of Jamaica directing a study and training program entitled "Cost Analysis for Proposed Regional Development Plans." Before that he was City Economist for the City of Philadelphia, involved in the formulation of an economic plan for the City to develop a multimillion dollar program for the Model Neighborhood of Philadelphia.

Mr. Oberman was graduated from Temple University in Philadelphia and received an M.S. in Economics from the University of California at Berkeley. He is a member of the American Institute of Planners, the National Planning Association, the Committee for Economic Development, the American Society of Planning Officials, the American Economic Association, and The Urban Land Institute. He has written numerous documents in his field of competence, which have been distributed to the public.